Napoleon once famously remarked 'If I had had two Marshals like Suchet I should not only have conquered Spain, but have kept it'. Louis-Gabriel Suchet was one of the few French commanders to leave the Peninsular War with his reputation enhanced, and the only one to win his marshal's baton in that war. When Suchet was first appointed to take command of French forces in Aragon in 1809 as a *général de division*, the French were on the verge of losing control over that province. Through a string of brilliant battlefield victories and sieges against Spanish regular forces as well as an initially successful counter-guerrilla campaign, Suchet managed to not only secure French control of Aragon, but moved on to conquer Lower Catalonia and Valencia as well. Like all French commanders in the Peninsular War, Suchet was faced with the challenges of Spanish popular resistance, but stood out above his colleagues for his notable success in pacifying Aragon. Yet despite initial triumphs in 1809-1811 against the 'traditional guerrilla', Suchet's counter-guerrilla policies were less successful than is often popularly perceived. As the war went on, French resources became thinly stretched, while conversely, the guerrilla war was increasingly spearheaded by Spanish regular forces to great efficiency, which contributed to the eventual collapse of French control in Eastern Spain.

Despite being universally accepted as among the best of Napoleon's marshals, the pivotal role Suchet played in the Peninsular War has largely been overlooked thus far. Through analysing a variety of sources from both French and Allied perspectives, ranging from modern viewpoints to those who saw the war themselves, Yuhan Kim examines both Suchet's successes and failures in his sieges, battles, counter-guerrilla operations, and administration. Each of Suchet's major actions, as well as those fought independently by his subordinates, is explained in extensive detail with maps and orders of battle. This first volume addresses the opening battles between Suchet and the Spanish commander Joaquin Blake, showing how Suchet recovered from an initial defeat to decisively crush his opponent, before considering the string of successful sieges that ended with the fall of Tarragona and a Marshal's baton.

Yuhan Kim is currently an undergraduate student at Yale University. He resides in Hudson, Ohio.

To Conquer and to Keep

Suchet and the War for Eastern Spain, 1809-1814

Volume 1: 1809-1811

Yuhan Kim

Helion & Company

To Mom, Dad, and my sister

**And to the hope that someday wars will only be in
books and in histories and never in our lives.**

Helion & Company Limited
Unit 8 Amherst Business Centre
Budbrooke Road
Warwick
CV34 5WE
England
Tel. 01926 499619
Email: info@helion.co.uk
Website: www.helion.co.uk
Twitter: @helionbooks
Visit our blog at http://blog.helion.co.uk/

Published by Helion & Company 2023
Designed and typeset by Mach 3 Solutions (www.mach3solutions.co.uk)
Cover designed by Paul Hewitt, Battlefield Design (www.battlefield-design.co.uk)

Text © Yuhan Kim 2023
Illustrations © as individually credited
Maps by George Anderson © Helion and Company 2023

Cover: Marshal Suchet. Original artwork by Patrice Courcelle © Helion and Company 2023

ISBN 978-1-915070-47-0

British Library Cataloguing-in-Publication Data.
A catalogue record for this book is available from the British Library.

For details of other military history titles published by Helion & Company Limited, contact the above address, or visit our website: http://www.helion.co.uk

We always welcome receiving book proposals from prospective authors.

Contents

List of Plates

List of Maps

Introduction

Despite being considered by many historians as amongst the best of Napoleon's famed marshals, Louis-Gabriel Suchet is too often only mentioned in passing, or simply acknowledged as a 'good general' without the context of a thorough study of his operations. Suchet's campaigns are some of the most fascinating of the Peninsular War, but at the same time amongst the least studied, especially in the Anglosphere. This is largely due to circumstance: while other French commanders in the Peninsula were rotated out of Spain to fight directly under Napoleon in the memorable campaigns in Germany, Austria, and Russia, Suchet only saw service in Spain until the end of the Peninsular War. That he remained to be promoted within that theatre of war is a testament to Suchet's successes. Additionally, British forces were only minimally involved in this theatre prior to 1813, and even after that, their campaigns were not met with any particular distinction or success, compared to the brilliant victories of Wellington.

This volume covers Suchet's appointment as commander of III Corps up to the Siege of Tarragona and Suchet's promotion to *Maréchal d'Empire* in 1811. Volume 2 will cover Suchet's invasion of Valencia up to the end of the Peninsular War in 1814.

There are several points to be made about the scope of coverage of this book. With the focus of this book being on the operations of Suchet and the men under his command, I left out French operations in Catalonia unless there was a significant connection to what Suchet and his army were doing. As closely linked as the two are, the war in Catalonia is another theatre of the Peninsular War worthy of its own book to cover it in its detailed entirety. Similarly, the war in Eastern Spain prior to Suchet's arrival, particularly the Siege of Zaragoza, is only covered briefly, as these events were prior to Suchet's tenure as commander in Aragon.

Some minor points on terminology. The force commanded by Suchet is alternatively referred to by historians as III Corps and the Armée d'Aragon (Army of Aragon). I refer to Suchet's force as III Corps until the 1811 Tarragona campaign, when it became greatly augmented by the addition of units from the French Armée de Catalogne (Army of Catalonia); it was only then that it becomes truly an army in size. I also use the word 'guerrilla' to ubiquitously refer to Spanish irregular insurgents, organized guerrilla bands (*partidas*) and the *Divisiónes Volantes*, the latter of which were regular army units that engaged in rapid strike operations and had their origins in guerrilla units. Most places use their modern Spanish names except for certain places of key importance, which are referred to by their commonly known historical names, such as Lérida (today Lleida) or Sagunto (today Murviedro).

It is my hope that this book can shed some light on not only *Maréchal* Louis-Gabriel Suchet, but his subordinates, from the *généreux de division* to the junior officers and common infantrymen, and the soldiers of Spain, whose names are so little known or have been unjustly tarnished by history.

Acknowledgements

As with any large undertaking, this project could not have been completed without many people who kindly lent me their time, expertise, and encouragement. Thank you to Juan José Penadés Olaso for sharing with me his wonderful maps and going beyond what I asked to further my research. I would also like to thank Professor Rafael Zurita Aldeguer of the University of Alicante, Toby Groom of EpicHistoryTV, historian and author José Luis Arcón Domínguez, and Adam Quigley, the author of *Antes morir que rendirse*, for their kind answers to my inquiries related to their respective areas of expertise. I also give my sincere thanks to Colonel Nicolas Lipscombe, the author of *The Peninsular War Atlas* and *Wellington's Eastern Front*, who has been a wonderful source of advice and direction in the research process by sharing his resources and knowledge with me.

The accounts of soldiers and officers provide a refreshing empirical look on the war that remind us that conflict is grounded in humanity, and the consequences of war are not only geopolitical but personal. Many of the invaluable primary sources which I used in my research were brought to my attention by the work of my friend Jonas de Neef whose meticulous and energetic work on rediscovering the countless letters and memoirs written by the soldiers of the Napoleonic era has been a key contribution to the historiography of this era. Throughout the course of my research, I would get an email from Jonas every now and then informing me about some long-forgotten memoir that held vital snippets of information pertaining to my book.

Featuring the portraits of generals and wonderful selection of colour plates depicting the variety of uniforms worn by Suchet's men in this book was made feasible due to the contributions of multiple people. Thank you to Peter Harrington, curator of the Anne S. K. Brown Military Collection for sharing with me his wonderful uniform colour plates. Colonel Nicolas Lipscombe and José Luis Arcón Domínguez continued their contributions to this book by kindly providing me with engravings from their collections. The uniform plates depicting French cavalry and Spanish troops that add so much to this book were due to the hard work of Eunice Kiang, Yinuo Liu, to whom I am grateful for sharing their artistic talents with me.

Thank you too to Patrice Courcelle for the many hours spent painting what I can only describe as the perfect cover. I was excited when I heard that M. Courcelle would be doing the cover art for my book, and it is his masterful command of the brush that has allowed for my vision of the cover to manifest beautifully. The maps in this book are all due to the talent and skill of George Anderson, who patiently responded my ever-intricate requests to create the invaluable maps that add so much more detail and depth to this book.

As a first-time author, I initially expected the process of publishing a book to be difficult, complicated, and layered with fine print. Thank you to my editor Andrew Bamford for proving me wrong in all those aspects, for guiding me through the process of writing and publishing, for his steadfast support, and above all, for believing in this book.

The completion of this book would certainly have taken much longer were it not for countless friends who offered their support and encouragement throughout the writing and research of this book. I sincerely appreciate the contributions of my Yale University friends Cole Snedeker, Julian Daniel, Louie Lu, Henry Carroll, and Clay Skaggs; and my sister Yeji Kim, in reading over my drafts and editing them. Knowing that I had an audience I could not let down motivated me to work harder to provide the very best I could.

Finally, I would like to thank my parents, Minho Kim and Jinhee Hur, and my sister Yeji Kim. I am forever grateful to my family for giving me their encouragement and unwavering support in my endeavours.

1

The Peninsular War

A Marshal is Born

On 2 March 1770, in the French city of Lyon, a Marshal of France was born. Louis-Gabriel Suchet was born the eldest son of Jean-Pierre Suchet (1736-1789) and Marie-Anne Jacquier (1742-1773). Sadly for the young Suchet, his mother passed away in 1774. Suchet's father Jean-Pierre was a prominent silk manufacturer in Lyon's renowned silk industry, who had 'acquired a certain eminence by his discoveries in his profession.'[1] Suchet planned to carry on the family business alongside his brothers, and to that end, he enrolled in the College of Ilse Barbe to study economics. In 1787, he entered his father's business as an apprentice, however, Jean-Pierre Suchet passed away two years later. The early death of his father meant that 19-year-old Suchet and his brother Gabriel-Catherine inherited the family business. The duo rebranded their silk enterprise as 'Maison Suchet Frères,' and devoted all their efforts into expanding their father's legacy. However, fate was to have an altogether different course for Louis-Gabriel Suchet, for like many of his future colleagues, the young Suchet became swept up in the Revolutionary fervour and whirlwind of events shaking French society at the time. Suchet evidently found the ideals of *liberté*, *égalité*, and *fraternité* to far outweigh the economic damage the Revolution was having on his business, and enlisted as a common soldier in the *Garde Nationale* in 1791. Bestowed with good common sense and the inheritor of his father's organizational and innovative skills, Suchet proved himself to be an excellent soldier and a staunch republican, and made a rapid ascent up the ranks of the Revolutionary army, where one's charisma and talents mattered more than lineage. By 1793 he had been elected *Chef de Bataillon* of the 4e Bataillon d'Ardèche, assigned to the army besieging the city of Toulon, which was held by royalist and coalition forces. There he made the acquaintance of a talented young artillery officer by the name of Napoleon Bonaparte, and during one incident in the siege, had the distinction of capturing the British Major General Charles O'Hara who thereby obtained the dubious honour of being the only person to personally surrender to both George Washington and Napoleon Bonaparte.

Suchet got his first taste of counter-insurgency warfare not long after the taking of Toulon when he and 250 of his men were ordered to embark on a punitive expedition to the

---

1   R.P. Dunn-Pattinson, *Napoleon's Marshals* (London: Methuen & Co., 1909), p.219.

commune of Bedouin where a liberty tree had been cut down.[2] Houses were burnt, and some 63 people were executed. To what extent Suchet was involved in the brutal suppression of counterrevolutionaries is uncertain, but in any case, it is known that he was fervently loyal to the Revolution. In 1795, Suchet's battalion was incorporated into the 18e Demi-Brigade, which was attached to the Armée d'Italie under his old friend Napoleon Bonaparte. Suchet participated with distinction in many major battles of the campaign including Lodi and Castiglione. During the long marches and rests between battles, Suchet observed first-hand how a lack of proper supplies degenerated the hard-fighting and courageous Republican warriors of the Armée d'Italie into ill-disciplined thugs and looters.

Suchet was wounded in action in September of 1796 and continued to serve valiantly, though he was often frustrated at his lack of recognition. Despite having served with Napoleon at Toulon, Suchet was not part of Napoleon's inner circle of generals and aides, a major factor in promotions and awards. In December of 1796, Suchet joined Massena's division as commander of the 1/18e Demi-Brigade and fought at Arcola and Rivoli in 1797. Suchet was wounded at Tarvis, and again at Neumarkt. This time, his courage did not go unnoticed, for in October of 1797 he was promoted to *chef de brigade*. In 1798, Suchet enjoyed a brief stint as chief of staff to *Général de Division* Guillaume Brune, who commanded the French army in Switzerland. Suchet was given the honour of bringing 19 captured enemy flags back to Paris, and on 23 March finally received a promotion to *général de brigade*. Suchet remained outside of Napoleon's inner circle, having missed an opportunity to join the Egyptian Expedition, but he at least enjoyed the patronage of another general, Barthélemy Catherine Joubert. Dashing, brilliant, and courageous, Joubert was one of the rising stars of the French army and was marked out for great success. When Suchet was assigned back to the Armée d'Italie, Joubert, who had replaced Brune, immediately placed a request for Suchet to remain with him in Switzerland, recognizing Suchet's skill as an organizer and administrator.[3] In December Suchet was accused of intrigue, corruption, and a number of other politically charged claims, odd given that Suchet had little dabbled in the confusing world of Revolutionary French politics. Forced to either be exiled or face charges, Suchet was left in a difficult spot until Joubert stepped in and threatened his own resignation as well. Nevertheless, despite Joubert's support, Suchet was sacked on 27 December.

However, talent did not go unnoticed, and right after Suchet was fired he was picked up by *Général de Division* André Masséna. Masséna's faith in Suchet was justified, for in a desperate action against the Austrians, Suchet managed to extricate his surrounded brigade by leading it over a frozen lake. Later, Suchet was appointed Masséna's chief-of-staff. Not long after, Suchet's old friend and mentor Joubert arrived to take command of the Armée d'Italie. Joubert immediately appointed Suchet as his own chief of staff, with the rank of *général de division*, and together they led their army to battle – and disaster. In spite of Suchet's wishes to retreat and wait for reinforcements, Joubert was drawn into battle against the brilliant Russian general Alexander Suvorov at Novi. Joubert's 35,000 hungry and exhausted troops were no match for the 50,000-strong Russo-Austrian army, and were defeated with losses of

---

2   Jean-Phillipe Rollet, 'Conqueror and Administrator: Civil and Military Actions of Marshal Louis-Gabriel Suchet in the Spanish Province of Aragon 1808-1813' (Master's Thesis, United States Marine Corps Command and Staff College 2008), pp.29-30.

3   David Chandler (ed.), *Napoleon's Marshals* (London: Weidenfeld and Nicolson Ltd, 1987), p.483.

Portrait of Marshal Louis-Gabriel Suchet, 1815, by Louis François Aubry. (Anne S.K. Brown Military Collection, Brown University Library)

6,600 men.[4] Worst of all, Joubert was shot through the heart while leading a counterattack in the early stages of the battle and died in Suchet's arms.

After a miserable retreat and the loss of a valuable patron and close friend, Suchet decided to return to France, only to be persuaded back into the army by his old friend, Masséna. The ensuing campaign of 1800 was Suchet's shining moment, for he held his first-ever independent command of a group of two divisions. Against superior Austrian forces, Suchet ably held his own and defended the route into southern France, even going on the attack and decisively defeating the Austrians to set the stage for Napoleon's famed march over the Alps to victory at Marengo.[5] Though Lazare Carnot heaped praises on Suchet for his brilliant performance, Suchet was passed over at his chance for glory and the next few years were dull and frustrating. After getting into an argument with Masséna in the aftermath of the Marengo campaign, Suchet found himself without powerful friends or patrons. Suchet enjoyed a brief stint as governor of Padua, where he honed his administrative skills, before returning to France in May of 1801. There he threw himself into high society, attempting to ingrain himself with First Consul Napoleon Bonaparte. Suchet's attempts to win friends amidst the powerful bore little fruit, for his own talents and dependability were outshined by other more flamboyant or characterful, but equally successful and talented, generals.[6] Suchet was also not in Napoleon's inner circle, due to his own strong republican views and as such, found himself again passed over for any of the major promotions that came in the wake of the formation of the First French Empire and the Grande Armée, though 1804 saw his appointment to a Grand Officer of the Légion d'Honneur. Despite having proven himself to be more than capable of leading an army corps during the Marengo campaign, Suchet was assigned a division in *Maréchal* Nicolas Jean-de-Dieu Soult's IV Corps at the Camp of Boulogne in preparation for the invasion of England. But the plans for conquering Britannia were shelved when France came under threat from the east by the Third Coalition. Suchet was transferred to command the 3e Division in *Maréchal* Jean Lannes' V Corps for the upcoming campaign against the Austrians and Russians. He led his division with distinction in all the major campaigns of the ascending French Empire in its glory years, fighting in numerous battles: 1805 (Austerlitz), 1806 (Saalfeld, Jena, Pultusk), and 1807 (Ostrolenka), and gained experience in administration by commanding occupation troops in Silesia in 1806.[7] In February of 1806, Suchet was awarded the Grand Eagle of the Légion d'Honneur with a yearly salary of 10,000 francs.[8] On 10 March of 1808, Napoleon rewarded Suchet for his service by upgrading his yearly salary to 24,000 francs and bequeathing two requisitioned Prussian estates. Later that month, Suchet was named Chevalier of the Iron Crown and a Count of the Empire, bringing him into the folds of Napoleon's new nobility and at last receiving the recognition he deserved, though it still could not be said that he was close with the Emperor.[9] In September of that year, Suchet and V Corps were ordered to Spain.

---

4   Chandler (ed.), *Napoleon's Marshals*, p.484.
5   Dunn-Pattinson, *Napoleon's Marshals*, p.221.
6   Chandler (ed.), *Napoleon's Marshals*, p.486.
7   Jaime Latas Fuertes, *La ocupación francesa de Zaragoza (1809-1813)* (Zaragoza: Asociación Cultural "Los Sitios de Zaragoza", 2012), p.28.
8   Chandler (ed.), *Napoleon's Marshals*, p.487.
9   Chandler (ed.), *Napoleon's Marshals*, p.488.

Before heading off to his next campaign, the 38-year old Suchet decided that it was time he got married. He was, after all, one of the more eligible bachelors in France at the time. Decades devoted to military service had left little time to spend with his family, something Suchet realized the importance of. But Suchet stayed out of the picture while his brother Gabriel-Catherine worked out the marriage arrangements with the Antoine de Saint-Joseph family for Suchet to marry Honorine Antoine de Saint-Joseph. It was an arranged marriage in the most traditional sense, for the Suchets had much to gain from the wealthy and powerful Antoine de Saint-Josephs, who were part of both the *ancien regime* nobility and the new imperial nobility. Honorine was the niece of two of France's most powerful and influential women at the time: Julie Clary, the wife of Joseph Bonaparte, and Desirée Clary, the wife of *Maréchal* Jean-Baptiste Bernadotte.

The marriage, being one of arrangement for political, economic, and social advancement, had rocky beginnings. The 18-year old Honorine was concerned that she was to marry someone she first thought was 45-years old, but was persuaded by her mother and Julie to enter the marriage. They would not be wrong. Suchet too, balked at marrying someone 20-years his junior, and feared that the present match would be a loveless one.[10]

On 16 November, 1808, Louis-Gabriel Suchet and Honorine Antoine de Saint-Joseph were married at Joseph and Julie's home, the Luxembourg Palace.[11] The newlyweds enjoyed their honeymoon at Suchet's country estate, and as Julie Clary had predicted, the marriage seemed to be a happy one. Honorine would come to play a valuable role in not just Suchet's personal life but his military life as well. Though she lived in a time when most generals' wives remained at home (even Julie Clary, the queen of Spain, lived in Paris throughout King Joseph's reign), Honorine became an active part of Suchet's military and administration in Spain.[12] Despite the dangers of coming under fire and kidnappings by guerrillas, she visited Suchet frequently in his campaigns (always with a heavy escort), was beloved by his troops and the local inhabitants Suchet governed, and even kept privy to confidential campaign operational details, the latter to Napoleon's chagrin.[13] Honorine's brother Anthonie would serve in the privileged position of Suchet's aide-de-camp. But such was the life of a soldier that on 1 December, Suchet left his wife to re-join V Corps as it marched into Spain. Suchet would have little guessed that Spain would be his home for the next five years and the place where he would find his desired glory.

The Peninsular War

With Austria crushed, Prussia humiliated, and Russia forced into an alliance, the restless Napoleon had next set his sights west to the Iberian Peninsula. In order for his 'Continental System' to work, Napoleon needed to defeat Portugal, Britain's last remaining ally on the continent. It was without a doubt that Portugal's timid ruler, Prince-Regent João (later João

10   Chandler (ed.), *Napoleon's Marshals*, p.490.
11   Chandler (ed.), *Napoleon's Marshals*, p.490.
12   Fuertes, *La ocupación francesa de Zaragoza*, p.103.
13   Letter 18305, from Napoléon Bonaparte, *Correspondence de Napoléon 1er* (Paris: Imprimerie Impériale, 1867), Vol. XXIII, p.57-58.

VI), would have conceded to most of Napoleon's demands if enough pressure was applied. João had already agreed to join the Continental System in a desperate bid to save his throne and nation. But Napoleon wanted much more. On 27 October of 1807, Napoleon drew up an agreement with Spain, dubbed the Treaty of Fontainebleau, to partition Portugal between themselves. Already on 18 October, an invasion force of 25,000 men under *Général de Division* Jean-Andoche Junot was on its way from Bayonne and across Iberia. Three Spanish divisions were mobilized to support the French operation. Junot bungled his way to triumph. Despite tremendous logistical failures and the breakdown of discipline, Junot and his men faced little opposition in their march into Portugal. As Junot's bedraggled army streamed into Lisbon, two more French corps, 25,000 men under *Général de Division* Pierre Dupont de l'Etang and 30,000 men under *Maréchal* Bon-Adrien Jeannot de Moncey, crossed over the Pyrenees into Spain, slowly marching to the Portuguese border. But the following month, another French corps of 14,000 under *Général de Division* Guillaume Philibert Duhesme entered Spain, heading not towards Portugal, but into Catalonia. By February of 1808, Napoleon's troops were in position to initiate the complete takeover of not just Portugal but all of Spain as well.

The Franco-Spanish alliance had been one of convenience by two historic enemies against another historic enemy, marked with mutual dislike and distrust. From the start, Napoleon never trusted Spain, for how could this unholy marriage between the Spanish Bourbons and the upstart Bonaparte dynasty last when Napoleon had only risen to power by overthrowing the French Bourbons? Napoleon viewed Spain as a country with massive potential, especially given its empire, but deemed its current government impotent and weak. One of the main motivating factors for the Franco-Spanish alliance had been the Spanish *Real Armada*, the last vestige of Spain's bygone era of glory. France's navy alone was not strong enough to challenge the Royal Navy, but with Spain's navy at his side, Napoleon imagined he could change that. This came to an end in 1805 at the Battle of Trafalgar, where the core of both the French and Spanish navies were destroyed, crushing Napoleon's hopes of invading England and depriving Spain of its main leverageable asset as an ally. But for Napoleon, it was better to keep Spain as a useless friend than turn it into an enemy.[14]

At the same time, the unpopular reformist Spanish Prime Minister Manuel Godoy was plotting to escape the increasingly one-sided alliance with France. Spain had gained little from the wars France had dragged her into, which had damaged Spain's economy and frayed her colonial relations. The opportunity to end the alliance arose when Napoleon went to war with Prussia, which had the promised support of Russia. Godoy hardly expected Napoleon to win against this coalition; Austerlitz was one thing, but this time, Napoleon would be fighting against the famed Prussian army, which had held off all of Europe in the Seven Years War. As Napoleon geared up for war against Prussia, Godoy issued a vague proclamation on 5 October calling for the Spanish people to rise up and aid their government in a war against an unnamed enemy – while not directly stated, all clues in his message hinted that the proclaimed enemy was Napoleon.[15] All of Europe, but most especially Spain, was stunned then, when France not only defeated, but wholly annihilated the Prussian

14   Charles Oman, *A History of the Peninsular War* (Oxford: Clarendon Press, 1914), Vol.I, p.3.
15   Oman, *Peninsular War*, Vol.I, p.4.

Army at the Battles of Jena-Auerstadt and then mounted a pursuit which saw Frederick the Great's legacy scattered to the four winds. If there was ever worse timing, then this was it. Godoy went on full damage control, blabbering apologies, retracting the proclamation, and explaining that there was no way that France could have been the target. The excuse may have worked, had the proclamation not been so focused on Spain's ground forces, which ruled out England as the target. When Napoleon got wind of Godoy's machinations, he flew into a rage. Had Godoy carried out his ill-conceived threat, the Spanish army could have walked right into an unguarded Southern France. There was nothing Napoleon could do at the moment but accept Godoy's excuses, for the French army was still far off in Prussia and about to face the Russians.[16] Spain managed to placate Napoleon's wrath by sending a division of 14,000 men under La Romana to aid the French campaign in Eastern Europe.

Rather than an interstate incident, it was an attempted coup within the Spanish court that triggered the French invasion. Seeking to protect Spain's interests and regain their eroding power, aristocratic supporters of the crown prince Fernando sought to overthrow the current King Carlos IV and marry the prince into the Bonaparte family. The plot was discovered, and its perpetrators exiled (Fernando was not found to have been deeply involved, so was pardoned).[17] With Spain's government in chaos and believing that Spain's armed forces were hardly capable of putting up a fight, Napoleon decided to make a gamble for the Spanish throne, and moved French troops to the Spanish border. Historian Charles Esdaile believes that Napoleon harbored greater plans to become the dominant Mediterranean power and sought to use a subjugated Spain as a base of operations to conquer North Africa, eventually the Ottoman Empire and Egypt.[18]

It was by that long and convoluted road that the Peninsular War began. The invasion of Portugal now served as a pretence for Napoleon to get his troops in position to conquer Spain. As Napoleon's divisions marched through Spain, the Spanish government was in a panic, for the wiser heads there knew what was to come, but the real figures of authority, Godoy and King Carlos IV, had been lulled into a stupid complacency by Napoleon's flattery. Thus, no real opposition was mounted when French troops suddenly seized Spanish fortresses from their confused garrisons, who had thought only a moment before that the French were their allies! The vital fortresses of Pamplona, Figueras, San Sebastian, and Barcelona were all taken by force or various forms of trickery and treachery. With the road into Spain now wide open, the invasion could begin. On 10 March, *Maréchal* Joachim Murat crossed the Biadossa to assume command of the French army in Spain, followed by a corps of 30,000 men under *Maréchal* Jean-Baptiste Bessières. The French invasion threw Madrid into political and social chaos, which in short, resulted in Carlos IV and Godoy being deposed and the crown prince Fernando ascending to the throne. If the new King Fernando VII hoped that the regime change would placate the French invaders and that Murat would support him, he was to be sorely disappointed. Fernando VII was lured to Bayonne, where Napoleon coerced his abdication by nothing less than threatening him with death before imprisoning him at Valençay. To Napoleon, a Spain under the Bourbons was

---

16   Oman, *Peninsular War*, Vol.I, p.4-5.
17   Charles J. Esdaile, *Napoleon's Wars: An International History 1803-1815* (New York: Viking Penguin, 2008), p.328.
18   Esdaile, *Napoleon's Wars*, p.334-335.

a Spain that could always stab him in the back. Replacing Fernando VII as King of Spain was Joseph Bonaparte, Napoleon's brother, who Napoleon easily kept under his own thumb.

The Spanish people were taken aback by this coup and were even more outraged when Murat attempted to cart away the rest of the Spanish Royal family to Bayonne. On 2 May, French troops attempted to take Fernando's brother Francisco, when they were assailed by a mob. The angry, but unarmed, mob destroyed the carriage set to take Francisco, to which Murat reacted by ordering his troops to open fire. Thus began what is famously known as the 'Dos de Mayo', as, all over Madrid, Spanish civilians rose up in revolt and were brutally suppressed by the French garrison.

Dos de Mayo changed everything. News of the uprising in Madrid spread all over Spain, and, in the absence of centralized leadership, regional Juntas were formed to organize militant efforts against the French. In response, French forces were dispatched to all corners of Spain to quash the rebellion. In eastern Spain, *Général de Division* Charles Lefebvre-Desnouettes advanced with a small corps against Zaragoza, where *Capitán General* José de Palafox y Melzi had taken command. Despite the lack of regular Spanish army units in Aragon, Palafox managed to raise an army of armed civilians to defend Zaragoza. The French intensified their efforts to take the city with the arrival of more troops and a siege train, but even this failed to break the spirit of the defenders. Brutal house-to-house fighting ensued, yet Palafox's civilian army stood its ground and made the attackers pay for every yard. Other French forces assigned to eastern Spain fared little better. Duhesme was pinned down in Barcelona by a massive Catalonian uprising, while Moncey had marched on Valencia, only to be forced to retreat due to determined resistance by the Valencian citizenry and tenuous supply lines.

French attempts to conquer Spain came to a total collapse at the Battle of Bailen in late July. Dupont's corps, which had been sent to subjugate Andalusia, was defeated, trapped, and forced to surrender with 18,000 men to Francisco Javier Castaños' Army of Andalusia. The Battle of Bailen marked a decisive point in the Napoleonic Wars. The myth of invincibility cultivated by the Grande Armée was shattered, Rocroi had been avenged, and all over Europe new hope was given to those opposed to Napoleon: Spain had shown that France could be beaten. Even worse for Napoleon, Britain had entered the war in the Peninsular as an active combatant with its small but highly professional field army, for if Portugal and Spain were lost, Britain would be all alone. In Portugal, Junot was defeated by a British expeditionary force under Sir Arthur Wellesley, the future Duke of Wellington, and Portugal was liberated. In the wake of these successes, the Spanish armies launched an offensive to retake Madrid, and the French did the unimaginable – they retreated, north behind the Ebro River in Old Castile and Navarre, even abandoning their siege guns at Zaragoza.

However, the Spanish were wrong to think that this was a final victory. The army Napoleon had sent into Spain was not made up of his victorious veterans, but of second-rate troops: conscripts, foreign auxiliaries, and provisional regiments. Spain would learn this the hard way. Infuriated at the failure of his initial invasion, Napoleon now directed the bulk of his Grande Armée against the Peninsular. This next invasion would not be led by second-rate generals as had the first; this time Napoleon was there in person, and with him were his A-list commanders – Lannes, Ney, Soult, and Lasalle, to name a few. The enthusiastic, but inexperienced, Spanish armies stood little chance against Imperial vengeance and suffered defeat after defeat. Napoleon drove his army on to take Madrid, sweeping all opposition before him, and forced Sir John Moore's British expeditionary force into a harrowing retreat all the way off the Peninsula. As Napoleon's field army pressed on further into Spain, a number of units were left behind to snuff out the flames of resistance remaining in conquered territory. It was to one of these units that Suchet was attached to, commanding the 1st Division of Mortier's V Corps, assigned to besiege Zaragoza alongside Moncey's III Corps. The Second Siege of Zaragoza would become one of the most famous sieges in all of history, and can be rightfully called the 'Stalingrad of the Napoleonic Wars.'[19] By the time of the second French invasion, Palafox's army had ballooned to 36,000 regulars and 10,000 civilian volunteers, all of whom he kept within Zaragoza to conduct a fanatical and desperate defence of the city.[20]

Beginning on 20 December, the French began the long and gruelling process of grinding down Zaragoza's defences.[21] Fortunately for Suchet, he and his division were assigned from 2 January to guard the lines of communication at Calatayud and were thus spared much of the horrors of the siege. From Calatayud, Suchet gained a steady understanding of the situation in the Peninsular War, from the emerging role of guerrillas to the adverse effects of infighting between French generals. Command of the siege effort switched over from Moncey, to Junot and Mortier, and then to Lannes. By late January the French had managed to breach the walls and gain a foothold in the city, but that was not to be the end. Palafox and his defenders had turned Zaragoza's winding streets into a labyrinth of barricades, artillery batteries, and fortified houses. Brutal house-to-house fighting ensued, and the French inched their way into the city at a crawl, moving block by block. Taking each fortified church became a siege of its own, for these the French were forced to attack by sap and mine. The Aragonese fought back just as hard, launching counterattacks at every turn and continuing their tenacious defence without rest. Both sides were suffering heavily from attrition – it was clear that the Spanish were in a fight to the death, and Lannes was taking on more casualties than he could afford. So heavy were his losses that he slowed his siege efforts to a snail's pace to preserve his men: there were to be no more stormings; French troops would advance onto a house or barricade only after the defenders had been cleared out by explosives. A typhoid epidemic triggered by overcrowding, poor sanitation, and the general privations of war began in the city, weakening and demoralizing the defenders more than the French ever did. Lannes redoubled his efforts, maintaining a relentless bombardment, and as the French cordon tightened, Zaragoza became ever-more crowded and typhoid raged like wildfire. At last, the resolve of the defenders broke and, on 20 February, Zaragoza finally capitulated. The horror of the siege was indescribable. Some 54,000 of the Spanish garrison and Zaragoza inhabitants had died, of whom only 6,000 had perished in combat – the rest from illness. French casualties stood at 10,000, of whom 4,000 had died in battle. The horrific Siege of Zaragoza set the tone for the rest of the war, and the 'last-stand' resistance of its defenders propelled it into Spanish military mythos. It became a high standard by which all Spanish garrisons under siege would be judged.

Nonetheless, a defeat is a defeat, and the fall of Zaragoza was a major blow to the Spanish cause. In committing his entire army to defending Zaragoza from within, Palafox had gambled all or nothing and lost it all. Aragon was now virtually defenceless, save

---

19   David Gates, *The Spanish Ulcer* (London: George Allen & Unwin, 1986), p.127.
20   Nick Lipscombe, *The Peninsular War Atlas* (Oxford: Osprey Publishing, 2010), p.104.
21   See Oman, *Peninsular War*, Vol.II, pp.90-142 for a full account of the Siege of Zaragoza.

for some guerrillas and a division of 4,000 men under *Teniente General* Luis Rebolledo de Palafox y Melzi, Marqués de Lazán and older brother of José Palafox.[22] The French were swift to capitalize on their triumph and launched an offensive to conquer the rest of Aragon: Mortier's V Corps took the left (northern) bank of the Ebro River, while Junot's III Corps took the right (southern) bank. Stunned at the magnitude of the defeat at Zaragoza, the Aragonese put up little opposition – Jaca's 500-man garrison surrendered to Mortier without a fight, and the strategically vital fort would remain in French hands for the rest of the war. As for Junot, he advanced *Général de Division* Anne-Gilbert de Laval's 1st Division all the way to Morella in Valencia, while *Général de Division* Louis François Félix Musnier de La Converserie's 2nd Division went south to Daroca and Molina. Laval's division had been until recently commanded by Charles Grandjean, who was recalled to France in April to fight in the Austrian campaign. Laval was promoted to *Général de Division* to assume command of the division, but the official promotion only occurred in September. Junot's 3rd Division – formerly commanded by Antoine Morlot, who had passed away in March from a fever sustained during the Siege of Zaragoza, and now without a commander – was occupied with escorting the prisoners from Zaragoza to France. But the French situation would be wholly reversed at the snap of a finger. Another war with Austria was looming on the horizon, and on 5 April, Napoleon ordered Mortier's V Corps to Old Castile so that it would be more readily available should it be needed in France. In an instant, French forces in Aragon were deprived of half their strength and reduced to just the 15,000 exhausted men of III Corps. A number of higher-ups, namely *Maréchal* Lannes and Grand Marshal of the Palace Géraud Duroc, but especially Suchet's uncle-in-law King Joseph, vouched for Suchet as a replacement for Junot, who was sick and wanted out of Spain.[23] Napoleon accepted their advice, considering that Suchet was technically part of his extended family by marriage and that the general had thus far had an excellent combat record.[24] However, a mishap in timing and communication led to Suchet's appointment reaching Zaragoza long after Suchet had left with Mortier's corps and moved to Valladolid. As such, it took over a month for the appointment to reach Valladolid and for Suchet to travel back to Zaragoza.

Mortier's departure left III Corps far too overstretched to maintain control over its newly conquered territories in Aragon. Worse for the French, the Spanish were quick to regroup and exploit this sudden weakness. From their bases in Catalonia, thousands of guerrillas under the leadership of officers such as *Coronel* Felipe Perena and *Brigadier* Mariano Renovales equipped themselves to launch raids against French outposts and convoys. It is estimated that in May of 1809 there were 8,000 active guerrillas in Upper Aragon (the elevated regions around the Pyrenees north of the Ebro) alone. All that opposed them was *Général de Brigade* Pierre Joseph Habert's single brigade of 3,000 infantry and two squadrons of the 13e Cuirassiers, which replaced the three brigades Mortier had needed to patrol the same area. Mortier's sudden departure had cost the French all the progress they had made along the Cinca, and Habert was forced to start from scratch. Perena had since seized and abandoned Monzón; though evidently, he did a poor job at sabotaging

22   Gates, *The Spanish Ulcer*, p.168.
23   Fuertes, *La ocupación francesa de Zaragoza*, p.58.
24   Chandler (ed.), *Napoleon's Marshals*, p.491.

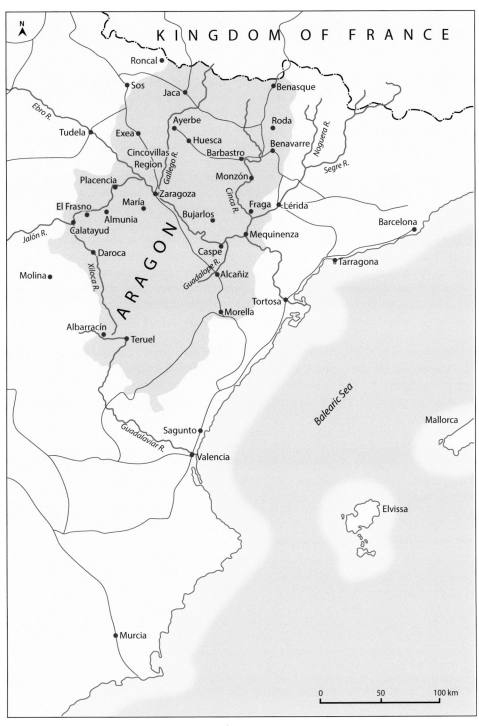

Aragon.

the fortress, for the cannons and ammunition were still intact and some of the powder Perena had dumped into the wells was still salvageable, all of which the new French garrison made good use of. Habert set up headquarters in the city of Barbastro, from where the situation along the Cinca River only deteriorated for the French. Habert came under real danger when Perena led a large partisan band out of Lérida and ambushed a French tax collection unit of 700 men headed to the town of Albalda, which had refused to pay its taxes, forcing the French to retreat to Barbastro.[25] Perena then moved on to besiege Monzón. The tiny French garrison managed to hold off the guerrillas with their artillery, but the situation was untenable. The citizenry of Monzón was festering with revolt, and on 6 May, Governor Solnicki ordered the garrison to evacuate to Barbastro before he and his men were caught between Perena's encirclement and a full rebellion from within the city.[26] The French column was harassed by guerrillas throughout its retreat out of the town and to the Cinca, but managed to reach the boats with their sick and wounded and escaped to Barbastro.

Mismanagement of oversight over outposts led to the frequent murder or harassment of French sentries in the night.[27] Habert took to this violently, unleashing his potent anger on both his own soldiers and the Spanish civilians, ordering a suspected guerrilla publicly executed on flimsy evidence. Their commander's visible frustration certainly damaged the spirits of his troops. After days of idleness and attrition of morale, Habert received orders from Junot to reoccupy the Cinca valley and Monzón. Habert quickly organized a force consisting of two squadrons of the 13e Cuirassiers and six battalions of infantry and set out to retake Monzón on 12 May.[28] The violent spring storms and muddy roads made marching conditions terrible for the column. On the 15th the column reached Alcolea where Habert had been hoping to cross the Cinca River, but Perena had stationed a significant force on the other bank to contest any such attempt. The French moved south in hopes of finding another suitable crossing point, and on the 16th found one at Pomar, several miles downstream from Monzón. Light artillery was set up to cover the crossing, and two barges were commandeered, each one large enough to carry nearly an entire company. *Lieutenant* Heinrich von Brandt, law-school-dropout turned voltigeur officer of the 2e Légion de la Vistule, was part of this operation, and writes of how the Spanish boatmen attempted to warn the French of a coming danger:

> …the eldest of the bargemen kept looking up at the sky and showed distinct signs of unease. The sky was clear overhead, but menacingly dark over the mountains. He attempted to share his fears with the general and inform him that this river was prone to sudden and violent storms in the Sierra and that he would be wise to postpone the crossing.[29]

---

25   Robert Southey, *History of the Peninsular War* (London: John Murray, 1827), Vol.II, p.368.
26   Oman, *Peninsular War*, Vol.II, p.412.
27   Heinrich von Brandt, *In the Legions of Napoleon: The Memoirs of a Polish Officer in Spain and Russia 1808-1813* (Barnsley: Frontline Books, 2017), p.72.
28   Oman, *Peninsular War*, Vol.II, p.412.
29   Brandt, *In the Legions of Napoleon*, p.73. Such risings of the Cinca were frequent due to the flow of water and melting snow from the Pyrenees.

With a brusque response that typified French ignorance and arrogance to the Spanish throughout the Peninsular War, Habert kicked the boatman while insulting him, and ordered the crossing to continue without hesitation. The French and Polish elite companies were the first to be ferried, establishing a vanguard on the far bank of the Cinca. Suddenly, a violent wave swept down the river, throwing rocks, logs, and debris into the barges, and the ropes spanning the river broke. Soldiers on the banks scrambled away for their lives as the storm flooded the area rapidly, and the unfortunate soldiers who had been cast adrift on the barges just barely managed to get back to land. Of the 80-strong cuirassier company that had been ordered to ford the river, only 37 made it across. The storms of the Cinca had hampered the legions of Caesar centuries ago, and now the very same river struck against the regiments of Napoleon.[30]

Worse, this sudden storm left the vanguard of 800 men stranded on the other side of the river.[31] Habert bellowed across the river to try and re-establish communication, but not even his booming voice could be heard amidst the crashing and thunder of the waves. In desperation, the general asked for the best swimmers among his troops to volunteer to reach the other side. All who tried were either forced back or drowned before even reaching the half-way point. To make matters worse another heavy storm struck while the French were deliberating on what to do, and the dense rain made visibility across the river impossible. From the other side of the river, voltigeur *Lieutenant* Frédéric Billon of the 14e Ligne recounted 'our wounded were suffering; we lacked food; cartridges were becoming rare and precious, and we could not perceive, on the other side of the water, any of the brigade which we had left there.'[32] The rest of Habert's column marched north to Monzón and attempted to force a crossing there to allow his beleaguered vanguard to retreat. But the bridge was heavily defended, as were the town and the castle. The French spent the entire day probing the Spanish positions, but could not take Monzón nor coordinate an attack with their lost men. Brandt later found the depressed Habert sitting alone under a bridge, 'and this otherwise energetic and cold-hearted man was crying and wringing his hands repeating "My poor grenadiers, my brave voltigeurs!" He could think of nothing better to do than to march back to Barbastro on the 18th, from where we had set out six days previously on this unfortunate expedition.'[33]

Two days later, French sentries at Barbastro were surprised by the arrival of several dozen weary, soggy, and bedraggled cavalrymen. At their head was *Capitaine* Robichon, who had commanded the cuirassier company that had been stranded on the other side of the Cinca. Habert and the rest of his army had been sick with worry for news of their comrades and

---

30   Aymar-Olivier Le Harivel de Gonneville, *Recollections of Colonel de Gonneville* (London: Hurst and Blackett, 1875), Vol.I, p.326.

31   Charles-Laurent Dupré, *Les Fastes du 14e Ligne* (Paris: Anselin, 1836), p.205. This force was made up of four voltigeur companies from the 14e Ligne, two voltigeur companies from the 2e Vistule, two grenadier companies and 20 voltigeurs of the 121e Ligne, and 37 cuirassiers. Brandt, *In the Legions of Napoleon*, p.74, lists the vanguard as: two voltigeur companies from the 2e Vistule, three voltigeur companies of the 14th line, one grenadier and two voltigeur companies of the 116e Ligne, and one company of the 13e Cuirassiers.

32   Jonas De Neef, *Devils, Daggers, and Death: Eyewitness accounts of French soldiers and officers during the Peninsular War (1807-14)* (Lulu, 2022), p.91,

33   Brandt, *In the Legions of Napoleon*, p.74.

eagerly pressed the cuirassiers for news. Unfortunately, Robichon's men were the only ones to have escaped the debacle.

Command of the stranded vanguard had fallen upon the shoulders of a *Capitaine* Richard, for the *chef de bataillon* designated to take command had been left on the other bank. The vanguard attempted to reach the bridge at Fraga, but learned that a strong Spanish force had occupied it. The situation was dire, for the French were without maps, supplies, and their guides were untrustworthy. In desperation, Richard decided to continue upriver in hopes of finding a ford, against the advice of the junior officers who advocated following the high ground.[34] The Spanish were quickly alerted to the presence of an isolated band of French troops, and swarms of guerrillas converged on them while a unit of regular infantry was dispatched

Pierre-Joseph Habert, by Ambroise Tardieu Direxit, From Ch.Th Beauvais, V. Parisot, *Victoires, conquêtes, revers et guerres civiles des Français, depuis les Gaulois jusqu'en 1792*, Vol XXXIII (1817). (Public Domain)

from Lérida. For three days the French column trudged northwards, harried by guerrillas but always repelling their attacks, until they found their path blocked by the Spanish regulars. To be trapped and forced to surrender, especially to irregular forces, was every French commander's nightmare – one did not have to look back many years to see the full extent of imperial wrath brought down on Dupont and Vedel after the disaster at Bailen. But with little hope of reinforcement, surrounded by foes, and out of ammunition, it seemed for the French that Bailen would repeat itself on a minor scale. The officers gathered to discuss their options, and finally it was agreed that surrender was the only choice. Robichon alone dissented, eagerly backed by his troopers, for their honour and prestige as *élite* cuirassiers went against giving up so easily, and so they departed before the surrender was completed on 19 May.[35] The Spanish captured a total of 25 officers and 717 men. These men were sent to Tarragona, then deported to starve at the island prison of Cabrera where Dupont's men were interred, and later suffered in British hulks–most were not released until 1814.[36]

---

34 De Neef, *Devils, Daggers, and Death*, pp.91-92.

35 Billon describes the surrender as more of a chaotic last stand rather than an organized capitulation, and notes that a hundred or so men managed to swim across the river, where most of them were cut down or captured, including Billon himself. See De Neef, *Devils, Daggers, and Death*, p.93.

36 Brandt, *In the Legions of Napoleon*, p.74. Brandt learned of this when he met one of the Polish voltigeurs after the war. The tragic fates of these men is distorted by Southey, *History*, Vol.II, p.369,

Robichon and his men had ridden to where Habert's brigade had been a few days ago, but by then Habert was long gone and the other bank was occupied by armed peasants. By now the Cinca had settled down and the cuirassiers were able to swim their horses across the river. Inaccurate musket fire burst in the water around them, but the cuirassiers managed to storm the other bank, put any opposition to the sword, and rode to Barbastro with the loss of 14 men in the retreat.[37] Habert had lost nearly a fourth of his infantry in the debacle, and the insurgents were only encouraged by their victory.[38] Guerrilla activity began to spread to the right bank of the Cinca, and Habert, fearing that he would be cut off from Zaragoza, fell back to Villafranca de Ebro. All of Aragon east of the Cinca and north of the Ebro had been lost to the guerrillas.[39]

The situation was no better for the French south of the Ebro River. While the guerrillas were hamstringing French forces in the north, *Capitán General* Joaquín Blake y Joyes was amassing an army in Valencia, intending to strike into Aragon from the southwest. Blake was born in Málaga in 1759, the son of one of many Irishmen who had fled to Catholic European nations after their defeats in their home and in England. A military man through and through, Blake first fought the French in 1795 as a *coronel* and was promoted to *brigadier* in 1802. The chaos of the French invasion let Blake, who had never personally led more than three battalions, shoot up in the Spanish military hierarchy as his superiors were either sacked, defeated, or even assassinated![40] While well-respected and intelligent, having authored a regulatory manual on infantry tactics, Blake was at times indecisive and lacked the ability to inspire his troops to charismatically harness their energy and push towards victory. Commanding the Army of Galicia, Blake was beaten by Bessieres at the Battle of Medina de Rioseco on 14 July of 1808. He then skilfully extricated his army from a French trap at the Battle of Zornoza on 31 October but was defeated by *Maréchal* Claude Victor-Perrin at the Battle of Espinosa de Los Monteros on 10-11 November. The weakening of French forces in Aragon opened up a promising opportunity to quench Blake's burning desire for vengeance after his humiliating defeats. In early 1809, Blake was appointed *Capitán General* of the *Coronilla* – Aragon, Valencia, and Catalonia. As supreme commander of all Spanish forces in Eastern Spain, Blake eagerly made the most of his powers and called together the broken remains of several Spanish armies on the promise of a renewed offensive under favourable conditions and liberation of Aragon.[41] There were no spare troops to be had from Catalonia, but at Tortosa Blake found the Marqués de Lazán's division, the last remnant of the original Spanish Army of Aragon. From Valencia came a division of 5,000 men, mostly recruits, led by *Mariscal de Campo* Pedro Escriba Roca. More battalions were hastily being raised in Valencia, but they would not be ready until June. This new field army, named the 2° Ejército de la Derecha (2nd Army of the Right), numbered less than 10,000

who makes the unsubstantiated claim that 'More however from humanity than a motive of ostentation, proposals for exchanging them were immediately made to Saint-Cyr, and accepted by him'.

37 Gonneville, *Recollections of Colonel de Gonneville*, Vol.I, p.327.

38 Don W. Alexander, *Rod of Iron: French Counterinsurgency Policy in Aragon During the Peninsular War* (Wilmington: Scholarly Resources Inc., 1985), p.8.

39 Gates, *The Spanish Ulcer*, p.160.

40 Jean Sarramon, *Contribución a la historia de La Guerra de la Independencia de la Península Ibérica contra Napoleón I* (Ministerio de Defensa: 2010), Vol.I, p.107.

41 Oman, *Peninsular War*, Vol.II, p.414.

men. Blake had hoped for more men: victory was by no means certain with so small a force, but he also knew that the French were stretched thin in Aragon.

Directly opposing Blake was Laval, a competent commander, but he had only five infantry battalions, the 4e Hussards, and a few guns centred around Alcañiz.[42] So many III Corps units had been loaned out to other provinces that the only reserve available was the 115e Ligne, under Junot's direct command in Zaragoza. Laval knew a major attack was impending as soon as Spanish scouts began to reconnoitre his positions in April, and he requested reinforcements from Junot. The 115e Ligne was dispatched from Zaragoza to Alcañiz to reinforce Laval, and with this, he drove back the Spanish scouts, only to find that the 2° Ejército was on the move against him. Laval abandoned Alcañiz and fell back to Híjar, pleading for more soldiers. Junot scrounged together three battalions and rushed to Laval's aid upon

Joaquín Blake. (Vicente Riva Palacio, *México a través de los siglos* (México: Ballesecá y comp., 1880), Vol III)

receiving his request for more reinforcements. The Spanish advance was temporarily halted and Laval retook Alcañiz, but Blake split his force to try and cut off the French, forcing Laval to retreat to Híjar once again on 18 May, the same day Suchet arrived in Zaragoza. It was in this distressful situation that Suchet would take command of Junot's III Corps.

---

42 Alexander, *Rod of Iron*, p.8.

2

The 1809 Campaign for Zaragoza

Suchet on the Scene

Général de Division Louis-Gabriel Suchet arrived at Zaragoza on 18 May, accompanied by a powerful escort comprising of a battalion of the 64e Ligne and a voltigeur company of the 40e Ligne, crack veteran units which he had led in his division at Austerlitz and Jena. Junot relinquished his position to the newcomer, none too sad to be offloading the burden of command. Suchet had no sooner settled into his new post on 20 May than he learned of Habert's disastrous expedition and Laval's situation. It was only his first day on the job.

The army which Suchet inherited was in a state of complete disarray, its men plagued by all the worst wartime ailments, from sickness to demoralization, as well as detachment assignments which weakened the regiments. III Corps still had not recovered from its ordeal in the Siege of Zaragoza, in which it had suffered the brunt of the casualties. In contrast to its more famous cousin of the same name under *Maréchal* Davout in La Grande Armée d'Allemagne, III Corps of the Armée d'Espagne was made up not of France's finest, but of battered and weary veterans and provisional regiments that lacked cohesion and experience. III Corps had been serving in the Peninsular War since the initial French takeover, first entering service under the name of 'II Corps of the Army of Observation of the Gironde,' led by *Maréchal* Moncey. The nucleus of III Corps were three veteran regiments: the 14e and 44e Ligne and a battalion of the 5e Légère. They were joined by a gaggle of 60 conscript depot companies who had been shoved together into provisional regiments, then later baptized into French military annals as the 114e (1er Régiment Provisoires de l'Armée d'Espagne), 115e (3e), 116e (5e), 117e (9e), and 121e (3e, 4e, and 5e Légions de la Réserve) Régiments d'Infanterie de Ligne.[1] The infantry complement was completed by the Polish 1er, 2e, and 3e Régiments d'Infanterie de la Légion de la Vistule, excellent troops, but badly worn out by the privations of the siege of Zaragoza. For the cavalry, Suchet had available to him the 4e Hussards, the 1/1er Lanciers de la Vistule, and the 13e Cuirassiers, formerly the 1er Cuirassiers Provisoires. The mounted units were something of a lone bright spot, having largely escaped the horrors of the Siege of Zaragoza and not in as poor of a shape

---

1   Edouard Detaille (trans. Maureen Reinertsen), *L'Armée Française* (New York: Waxtel & Hauser, 1992), p.37.

as the infantry.[2] III Corps naturally came with several support companies, such as sappers and miners, many of whom were leftovers from the siege. As for the artillery, Suchet was supposed to have eight companies of foot artillery and one company of horse artillery, but he found only 20 cannon. To make matters worse, many of the artillerymen and train personnel had left for Germany and had to be replaced with infantrymen.

On paper, III Corps numbered 20,000 men, but Suchet found out the hard truth soon enough. III Corps was nominally composed of three divisions, but much to Suchet's chagrin, his 3rd Division was virtually non-existent. Its commander, Morlot, had died in March and still no suitable replacement had been appointed–instead, the division had been dismembered and parcelled out to other Spanish provinces for various assignments. The 121e Ligne and 3e Vistule were on garrison duty in Navarre, while a brigade made up of the 116e and 117e Ligne was on prisoner escort duty at Valladolid. On reviewing the latter two regiments at Bayonne, *Maréchal* Kellermann wrote, 'The condition of their misery cannot be described,' compelling him to send medical personnel to Zaragoza to alleviate the plight of III Corps.[3] If this was the condition soldiers on relatively easy assignments were in, one could only imagine what the rest of III Corps looked like. The actual field strength of III Corps was somewhere around 10,000 men, not including artillerymen and engineers.

Yet Suchet's badly understrength divisions would prove to be just the tip of the iceberg. A lack of numbers can often be offset by the superior drill and veteran quality of an army, but Suchet was not even afforded this luxury. He found a much-neglected corps whose morale was at its breaking point. Junot's tenure as commander had done little to alleviate the situation, and, in the days leading up to his replacement, Junot had made himself scarce and disengaged from command duties, leaving III Corps to slowly disintegrate as the men continued to suffer from a lack of pay, proper supplies, and proper leadership. Engineer officer Maurice de Maltzen, attached to III Corps, remarked that 'I have not yet seen General Junot, he lives a Spanish league from Monte Torrero. I have gone to visit him three times without being able to meet him…The Duke of Abrantes is never visible, I have appeared at His Excellency's house ten times without having been able to deliver my letters.'[4] Neglected by their leaders, the men of III Corps suffered. Shoes were particularly lacking, and food had to be scavenged on a day-to-day basis. Suchet described the ragged patchwork uniforms worn by the troops as:

> White and blue uniforms of different shapes, which presented to the eye the offen-
> sive remains of a variety of alterations recently attempted to be introduced in
> the dress of the troops, actually occasioned in the ranks a confusion of colours
> which banished all sense of military consideration from the minds of an already
> desponding and weak soldiery. The appearance of misery degraded them in their

2   Jose Gómez de Arteche y Moro, *Guerra de la Independencia: Historia Militar de España de 1808 a 1814* (Madrid: Imprenta y Litografía del Depósito de la Guerra, 1886) Vol.VI, p.34.
3   Alexander, *Rod of Iron*, p.5.
4   Maurice de Maltzen and Emmanuel Henri Grouchy. *Correspondance Inédite Du Baron Maurice De Maltzen: Officier Du Génie à L'armée D'Espagne 1809-1810* (Braine-le-Comte: C. Lelong, 1880), pp.11,13.

own estimation, at the same time that it encouraged the pride and boldness of a hostile population.[5]

Besides offering a scathing review of the state of III Corps, Suchet's comments reveal his immense displeasure with Napoleon's failed effort in 1805-1807 to uniform the French infantry in the traditional white of the *Ancien Régime*. The reference here is likely to the one victim of this aborted experiment in III Corps, the 14e Ligne, still clothed in white with black facings. By the end of 1809, all of Suchet's infantry were more or less clad in blues and shakos.

For most of these young conscripts, the Spanish 'war to the knife' was their first experience in combat, and they had no memories of the glories of Italy, Austerlitz, Jena, or even Friedland as a handle for Suchet to grab onto and boost their flagging morale. The situation was no better moving up in the ranks, for many officers and generals had requested and received a transfer to escape the miserable Spanish war to join the campaign against Austria, where opportunities for glory and promotion abounded. But that meant leaving their men behind with inadequate leadership. Such was the case with Maurice de Maltzen, who despaired of languishing in plague-infested Zaragoza, while many of his comrades were transferred to the Austrian front. All around there was general disgruntlement, for the men of III Corps also believed that they had gone unrewarded for the Siege of Zaragoza despite taking the brunt of French losses, while V Corps had been showered with rewards.[6]

Suchet recognized that his new command needed good leadership and time to reorganize, but the latter he could not provide. Spanish forces were closing in on all sides, and, aside from a confrontation, the only other option was the safer, but career-ending decision to abandon Zaragoza. Amidst the chaotic collapse of the French occupation in Aragon, Suchet identified Blake's 2° Ejército as the greatest immediate threat. If Suchet waited for his forces to concentrate at Zaragoza, Blake could run rampant around the countryside and cause all sorts of havoc for the French. Too much had been lost already, and Suchet decided that he needed to salvage the situation by knocking out Blake in a single decisive blow.[7] On 21 May, Suchet marched south with his reliable escort troops and Musnier's division to join Laval, leaving a small garrison to hold Zaragoza. Habert was ordered to join Suchet, but his force was still on the way from Barbastro and would only reach Villafranca de Ebro on the 23rd, too late to participate in the coming battle. Suchet's force met Laval's troops at the hills behind Híjar on the 22nd, bringing his field force to a total of 7,292 infantry, 600 cavalry, and 18 guns crewed by 320 gunners. After assembling his army to harangue them with a motivational speech, Suchet set off that night for Alcañiz.

5   Louis-Gabriel Suchet, *Memoirs of the War in Spain From 1808 to 1814* (London: Henry Colburn, 1829), Vol.I, pp.11-12.

6   Suchet, *Memoirs of the War in Spain*, Vol.I, p.12. Suchet attributed this unfortunate discrepancy to an 'untoward misunderstanding between chiefs.'

7   Suchet, *Memoirs of the War in Spain*, Vol.I, p.18.

The Battle of Alcañiz

The men of Blake's 2° Ejército had been resting at Alcañiz from their march from Tortosa since 19 May. After forcing Laval to retreat, Blake dispatched on 21 May a scouting force of 80 troopers of the Húsares Españoles and 200 infantrymen of the Voluntarios de Valencia, led by *Coronel* Casimiro Loy, to watch the road to Híjar and reconnoitre the French movements. Blake was conscious of the French superiority in cavalry, and had taken care to negate that advantage by positioning his army on the hilly and rugged right bank of the Guadalope River. The city of Alcañiz itself was on the left bank nestled inside a loop of the Guadalope. The ground Blake had chosen was split in two by an irrigation canal. Above this were Santa Barbara hill, the Virgen de los Pueyos hermitage, and the Los Pueyos hill to their west. Below the canal was Alcañiz and the main bridge across the Guadalope, which led to the Las Horcas hill, and further south, the Perdiguer hill. The Spanish army of 9,331 covered a front of three kilometres, primarily concentrated in separate groups on the Los Pueyos, Las Horcas, and Perdiguer hills. Assigned to the Los Pueyos hill, the northernmost and lowest of the three, were 2,500 men in four newly formed light infantry battalions and a single 7-pounder howitzer mounted in the hermitage under *Teniente General* Juan Carlos Areizaga, to whom Blake stressed the importance of his position on the right flank of the Spanish line.[8] A successful French attack there would threaten Blake's centre and potentially cut him off from the bridge to Alcañiz. In the centre, the Marqués de Lazán commanded *Coronel* Pedro Hernández de Tejada's column of two battalions, with a reserve of four grenadier companies[9], and *Brigadier* Miguel Ibarolla's 365 cavalry was positioned astride the Zaragoza Road.[10] Two artillery batteries under *Brigadier* Martín García Loygorri were placed in front of the centre infantry line: these consisted of a total of twelve 4-pounders, one 8-pounder, and possibly one 7-pounder howitzer. Blake and his staff established their headquarters behind the centre. The Perdiguer hill formed the Spanish centre-left, held by 2,589 infantry under *Mariscal de Campo* Pedro Roca, made up of the columns of *Coronels* Andriani and Pírez. Further south were Coronel Martín González Menchaca's 1,261 light infantry, taking cover in an olive grove, and supporting Roca. Blake turned each hill into a formidable stronghold of infantry, but they were isolated, particularly the vital Pueyos hill. Blake also placed 829 men of the Tercio de Migueletes de Tortosa between Alcañiz and Caspe, and another 494 men of the 3/Voluntarios de Zaragoza at Castelserás to guard the far ends of the Spanish flanks, but these forces were too far away to play any part in the battle.

Historian Charles Oman criticizes Blake's deployment as being 'extremely dangerous when considered strategically; for Blake had been tempted by the strong ground into fighting with the river Guadalope at his back, and had no way of crossing it save by the single bridge of Alcañiz and a bad ford.'[11] Blake's deployment was not wholly without redemption, given that the high ground on the west bank of the river was an excellent defensive position, and fighting on the east bank meant giving up Alcañiz to the French. Undoubtedly involved

8   Blake's report, Arteche y Moro, *Guerra de la Independencia*, Vol.VI, p.427.

9   Nick Lipscombe, *The Peninsular War Atlas* (Oxford: Osprey Publishing, 2010), p.127.

10   Of the cavalry, only 422 were mounted. The count of 365 cavalrymen is after deducting the 80 Húsares Españoles who had been sent out by Blake as an advance guard.

11   Oman, *Peninsular War*, Vol.II, p.417

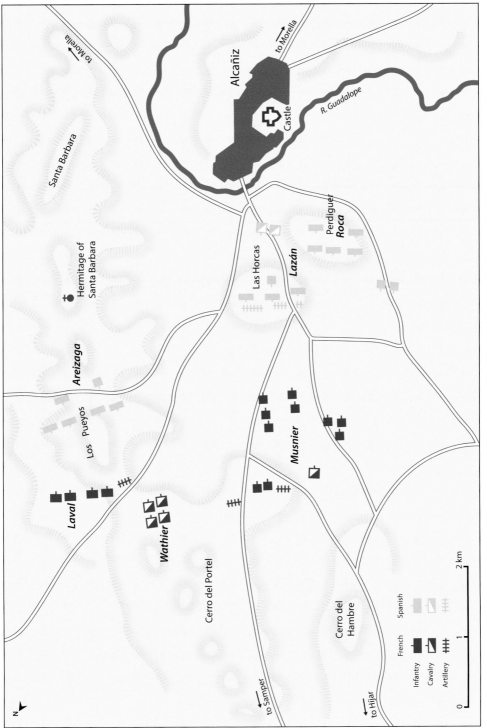

The Battle of Alcañiz, 23 May 1809.

in Blake's decision-making was a significant amount of confidence, given recent Spanish and allied successes not only in Aragon but all across the Peninsula. Nevertheless, it was truly a dangerous position. The desire to secure immediate tactical objectives led Blake to position his army with its back to a river, where defeat could easily turn into disaster. Blake had decided to play a high-risk all-or-nothing game; he had no real reserve other than four grenadier companies, and if pushed off the hills, he was flirting with disaster and the potential loss of his entire army.

The French encountered Loy's vanguard early on the morning of 23 May as they advanced on Alcañiz. Informed of the development, Blake sent his cavalry and two light artillery pieces to reinforce Loy, who steadily withdrew in the face of overwhelming French numbers. Loy retreated to take up position at the hermitage behind Areizaga, and Blake's cavalry returned to his left flank. The French force arrived before the Spanish position at around 6:00 a.m. and spread out into battle order. As they did so, Blake's artillery opened fire.[12]

It is uncertain if Suchet immediately recognized that he could break the Spanish right and then cut off Blake's escape, as he himself later claimed; it is more likely that he was unsure of the Spanish dispositions and the lay of the land and spent some time pondering.[13] In any case, Suchet decided to open the battle by sending Laval's single brigade of 2,044 to outflank the Spanish right and capture the Pueyos hill and threaten Blake's line of retreat across the bridge, just as Blake had anticipated.[14] On the other end of the battlefield, *Général de Brigade* Claude-Joseph Buget's brigade was to make an attack against Roca, but Buget was still moving into position when Laval began his attack. Areizaga's men levelled their muskets and unloaded a few steady volleys that sent the French into a retreat back to their starting position, harried by a few Spanish light infantrymen who opportunistically gave chase.

As Laval reorganized his columns for another attack, Blake sought to relieve the pressure on Areizaga and gave the order for Ibarolla's cavalry and Menchaca's light infantry to make a demonstration against the French centre.[15] Menchaca's two battalions, the Voluntarios de Zaragoza and the Cazadores de Valencia, duly formed closed columns and began to march from Perdiguer hill to the Pueyos, followed by Ibarrola's cavalry from the centre. This bold manoeuvre was only possible because Musnier's division, forming Suchet's centre, was still a good distance from the Spanish line.

Menchaca's manoeuvring failed to deter Laval, who mounted another attack on the Pueyos hill, which was just as easily repulsed as the first.[16] Blake hoped to capitalize on the failure of the second French attack and ordered Ibarolla's cavalry to charge Laval's inner flank. Though they had just been defeated twice, Laval's infantry still had some fight left in them – they reformed and promptly blazed away at the Spanish cavalry, wounding Ibarrola

12   Blake's report, from Arteche y Moro, *Guerra de la Independencia*, Vol.VI, p.428.
13   Suchet, *Memoirs of the War in Spain*, Vol.I, p.19-20.
14   Blake's report, from Arteche y Moro, *Guerra de la Independencia*, Vol.VI, p.428. In addition to being the divisional commander, Laval himself directly commanded one of his brigades.
15   Archivo Cartográfico de Estudios Geográficos del Centro Geográfico del Ejército, C.66-N.49: Partes de la acción de Alcañiz en 1809.
16   Suchet, *Memoirs of the War in Spain*, Vol.I, p.20. Suchet describes Laval's attack in his memoirs as a mere feint to cover for the attack in the centre, a claim which does not correlate with Laval committing 1,000 men in two failed attacks and the timespan of the battle. The attack on the Spanish centre is estimated to have taken place several hours after Laval's first attack.

and halting the charge. Not a moment later, Wathier's hussars launched a countercharge which saw the Spanish cavalry routed and out of the battle. Menchaca's infantry was left exposed by the flight of the cavalry and suffered heavy losses as it retreated.[17]

With no progress made on the attack against the Spanish right, Suchet decided it was time to launch his main attack on Blake's centre to break through the Spanish line and capture the Alcañiz bridge, which would doom Blake's army by seizing their line of retreat. The opportunity to completely wipe out Blake's 2° Ejército was here in his grasp, and Suchet was not apt to let it go. *Général de Brigade* Gabriel Jean Fabre's brigade of 2,700 men of the 114e Ligne (three battalions) and the 1er Vistule (two battalions) was formed up in two regimental attack columns and directed to advance down the Zaragoza–Alcañiz road that ran through Blake's centre. Fabre's advance was to be supported by the French artillery and the long-delayed diversionary attack by Buget's brigade against the Spanish left.

For many of Blake's recruits, it was their first time seeing the serried blue-coated ranks advancing steadily to the ominous beat of the *pas de charge*. For the Spanish veterans, they knew all too well that the unstoppable columns would march forwards under a withering and increasingly panicked fire from the defenders, then, at 100 paces, the battlefield would thunder with the shout of '*Vive l'Empereur!*' Shouldered arms would lower *à la charge*, a hedge of bayonets glimmering before their victims' eyes as the French broke into a sudden rush. Fabre's attack columns were met with a hail of musketry from Lazán's battalions and cannonballs from the Spanish artillery, but shook off the damage and continued their attack.

At the head of the attack was the French entomologist *Colonel* Pierre Francois Auguste Marie Dejean. Dejean was a coleopterist, a scientist who studies beetles, as well as an officer of the Empire and a prominent figure in Imperial academic circles. He often provided his men with glass vials to collect any beetles they saw, and for Dejean, the assault on Horcas hill was as good a time as any to find a new species. A beetle was spotted lounging on a flower – amidst the cannonballs soaring past him and ploughing into his column, Dejean deftly dismounted with the practiced skill of a former dragoon, scooped up the beetle and stuck it on a pin, then pinned it inside his custom cork-lined helmet and re-joined the attack.[18] Soldiers often used their shakos and helmets as extra storage space, but few would have imagined that one could be used to hold insect specimens!

Seeing the French closing in, the Spanish artillery switched to grapeshot. The Spanish gunners fought exceptionally well. Their commander Loygorri had only seen defeat after defeat despite he and his men giving their utmost at every battle, and the hope of victory at Alcañiz inspired them to fight harder, loading and firing their pieces without a rest. Blake showered deserved praise on his artillerymen, writing in his post-battle report:

> Surely if the officers who served it had not conserved the incredible serenity and courage to wait for the enemy, firing grapeshot until they almost touched the mouths of the cannons, perhaps they would have managed to break the line, despite the lively fire of a battalion of the 2° Regimiento de Saboya, another of América, and of the 1° Regimiento de Valencia, which was on the left of the centre.[19]

---

17   Blake's report, from Arteche y Moro, *Guerra de la Independencia*, Vol.VI, p.428.
18   Anon., *Annales de la Société Entomologique de France* (Paris: La Société 1845), Ser. 2, Vol.III, p.503.
19   Blake's report, from Arteche y Moro, *Guerra de la Independencia*, Vol.VI, p.429.

The French column faltered in the last stages of its charge, crumbling as the line of massed Spanish artillery on the Horcas hill unloaded deadly sprays of grapeshot, carving bloody swathes in the French ranks. Buget's brigade had failed to press the Spanish left flank, so Roca's Valencian infantry were free to pour effective enfilade fire into the right side of the attack column. Dejean's hat was peppered with holes, but both he and his specimen escaped intact.[20] A ditch across the French line of advance marked their 'high-water mark'; for all the frantic exhortations of their officers, the French were unable to advance beyond the ditch, and the attack columns disintegrated and fled down the slope. Suchet, who only briefly skimmed over the battle in his memoirs, claims that his attack was forced to turn back due to a broad ravine. Santiago confirms the presence of a canal at the time but asserts that the average canal could not have been as large as Suchet claims.[21] That Fabre's brigade suffered an estimated 350 casualties implies a much more heated engagement than being simply turned back for a want of crossing a ravine. Suchet most likely was searching for an excuse to explain his defeat and deny credit to the Spanish.

Only when the Fabre's brigade had retreated to their starting position was Suchet able to rally it. Five fresh battalions were called up, but Suchet decided against renewing the fruitless attacks and used them only to deter the Spanish from taking advantage of the precarious situation. He kept his troops on the field for a few hours more in order to gather the wounded and wait for the rest of the day to pass to conduct a night-time retreat. The French departed the battlefield that evening with the 64e Ligne, Suchet's bodyguard unit, deployed as the rearguard.

Demoralized and weary, Suchet's battalions had only managed to put up a sub-par performance against determined Spanish resistance. It became clear to Suchet, who had been wounded in the foot at the closing stages of the fight, that months of hardship without result had eroded III Corps' fighting spirit. After seven hours of battle, the French had suffered between 700 and 800 casualties, the Spanish 284.[22] Both Suchet and Blake, however, grossly exaggerated the casualty figures in their after-action reports to their own favour. Suchet wrote to Napoleon that he had merely conducted a probing action against Blake's army (whose strength he put at 19,000), and broken off the engagement at the cost of 40 dead and 300 wounded due to a lack of confidence in his troops and Spanish numerical superiority.[23] This is certainly a far cry from the concentrated assaults on the Spanish right and centre. Such deceitful reports to Paris were rampant by Napoleon's generals, who sought to both mask defeats as well as justify their requests for reinforcements. They truly took after their Emperor to 'lie like a bulletin.' On the other hand, Blake claimed to have found 500 French corpses and that another 1,500 of the enemy were wounded or missing.[24] The massive inflation of French casualties served to magnify the impact the battle would have on Spanish propagandists and recruitment. Despite the tactical and strategic errors Blake had made, his raw and untried army had stood fast and held their ground well. For Blake, the victory at

---

20   Dejean named the species of the beetle he had found at Alcañiz as *Cebrio ustulatus*, but much to his chagrin found that it was an already-identified species.

21   Suchet, *Memoirs of the War in Spain*, Vol.I, p.20; Santiago, *Alcañiz, María y Belchite 1809*, pp.31-32.

22   Santiago, *Alcañiz, María y Belchite 1809*, p.41.

23   Alexander, *Rod of Iron*, p.13.

24   Blake's report, from Arteche y Moro, *Guerra de la Independencia*, Vol.VI, p.429-430.

Alcañiz was redemption from his defeat at Espinosa de los Monteros and gave the Spanish nation hope at a time when victories were hard to find, in addition to reaping the general a knighthood into the Order of Calatrava. For his bravery and role in the battle, Loygorri was promoted to *Mariscal de Campo* on 1 June, not eight months after he had first become a *Brigadier!*[25] The victory energized Blake's volunteers, filling them with a hard-earned, but also potentially dangerous, confidence.

Suchet's army had put around 17 miles between themselves and the Spanish when the night-time retreat began to fall apart, for the same darkness which Suchet had hoped would provide cover now compounded the confusion and demoralization of his troops. The panic started amongst the leading 1st Division with a rumour that the Spanish were in hot pursuit, and their cavalry had intercepted and captured the entire 3e Vistule.[26] Word spread like wildfire, men fired blindly into the darkness, and the whole army hurtled in panic in a frantic retreat to Samper, where Suchet had planned to make camp. Only daylight revealed the non-existent threat, and the embarrassed soldiers were quickly rallied. The near-disastrous rumour was discovered to have been spread by a panicked drummer. A desperation to restore order set in among the French commanders, who set up a quick tribunal. After identifying the drummer as the primary instigator, they had the scapegoat executed by firing squad in front of the army. This macabre display evidently served its purpose, for Suchet felt confident enough to spend two days at La Puebla de Híjar restoring morale and waiting for Blake.[27] When the Spanish did not appear, the French continued their retreat to Zaragoza, arriving at the city on 30 May.

It had been risky of Suchet to conduct a night-time retreat, but that he did so shows both the necessity of the cover of darkness due to the dismal state of III Corps and how much the situation at Alcañiz warranted a pursuit from the Spanish. Blake, however, had declined to pursue, neither following Suchet immediately after the battle nor at a strategic level by advancing on Zaragoza that week. Blake had no way of knowing that French morale and discipline hung on a fragile thread. As far as he could see, their cavalry and rearguard were still in good order. Blake was always quite fearful of the French cavalry and had little faith in his own fickle cavalry to conduct a pursuit and follow up on his victory, let alone fight against their French counterparts.[28] The few victories the Spanish regular armies achieved by themselves in the Peninsular War were largely due to the steadfastness of their infantry and artillery, and such victories were usually unexploited due to the inability and unreliability of Spanish cavalry. On the other hand, countless Spanish defeats were due to the state of utter despair of the Spanish cavalry, which often broke and fled even before it engaged.

In any case, Blake did not have much cavalry to use – Ibarolla's horsemen were still recovering from their rude handling by the 4e Hussards. Additionally, Blake was expecting substantial reinforcements from Valencia and wished to fully consolidate his army before making another move against Suchet. Until they arrived, Blake held his position and spread

25   Arteche y Moro, *Guerra de la Independencia*, Vol.VI, p.42.
26   Suchet, *Memoirs of the War in Spain*, Vol.I, p.21. In Suchet's memoirs, it is stated that the unit rumoured to have been captured was the 2e Vistule, which was not present at the battle. Most likely the unit in question was the 3e Vistule.
27   Suchet, *Memoirs of the War in Spain*, Vol.I, p.22.
28   Oman, *Peninsular War*, Vol.II, p.420.

word of his victory to the population, content to let increasing guerrilla activities wear down the French until he could bring an overwhelming force against them. To advance north and put pressure on Suchet was to also risk giving battle, something which Blake was not inclined to do until his reinforcements had arrived. If he had learned anything from Alcañiz, it was that he could trust his army to hold their ground in prepared positions, but he had yet to see if they could go on the attack or fight on an open field.[29]

On the other hand, there is no denying that Blake lost a major advantage by making the cautious decision. Suchet admits that 'If general Blake had moved rapidly forward after the action of Alcañiz without allowing time for the 3rd corps to recover from its defeat, he would, perhaps, have compelled it to evacuate Aragon. It is probable, however, that this general was unwilling, by too much precipitancy, to compromise a success which he considered almost infallible.'[30] It was extremely fortunate for Suchet that Blake had declined to press on after Alcañiz, not knowing the disastrous state of III Corps. Blake's decision to rest on his laurels gave both sides a chance to rest and consolidate their forces, but the next engagement would show who had benefited more from the reprieve.

Preparations and Manoeuvres

If he had not been before, Suchet was now fully alerted to the dire state of III Corps and the French position in Aragon. As he shepherded his troops back to the relative safety of Zaragoza, Suchet began to seriously contemplate evacuating Zaragoza and informed Minister of War Clarke and Emperor Napoleon of his desire to abandon the city, a message which would take weeks to reach its recipients.[31] Abandoning Zaragoza came with dire consequences, and the decision weighed heavily on Suchet's mind, putting him into a 'very painful state of uncertainty as to the course which it was most advisable to adopt.'[32] A pile of rubble Zaragoza might be, it was of great strategic value in commanding the routes into central Spain from France. The loss of Zaragoza and Aragon would threaten French forces in central Spain and hamstring the already-strained lines of communication between Madrid and France. Additionally, if Suchet ordered his men to evacuate, nothing he could do would prevent the possible collapse of morale among his troops. Certainly, there would be a perception that the new upstart commander, who had just lost at Alcañiz, now saw it fit to abandon in a matter of weeks the city which had taken III Corps months and the lives of thousands of their comrades to capture. The only other option was to confront Blake in a decisive battle, whenever the Spanish general decided to advance. But Suchet did not want to run the risk of repeating Alcañiz, then have his line of retreat cut by a mass revolt in Zaragoza and thereby recreate the disaster of Bailén. Unless he received substantial reinforcements, the odds of victory were slim. Suchet accordingly dispatched urgent requests for more troops to Madrid, but King Joseph and *Maréchal* Jourdan were too preoccupied with the threat posed by the return of British forces to Portugal to pay much attention to

29   Oman, *Peninsular War*, Vol.II, p.421.
30   Suchet, *Memoirs of the War in Spain*, Vol.I, p.25.
31   Alexander, *Rod of Iron*, p.15.
32   Suchet, *Memoirs of the War in Spain*, Vol.I, p.22-23.

events in Aragon and waved aside Suchet's concerns as an exaggeration.[33] All that could be spared to Suchet was *Colonel* Louis-Benoit Robert's 3,000-strong brigade, which had originally belonged to III Corps to begin with! Robert was set to join Suchet by mid-June, but a single brigade was hardly enough to even the odds against Blake's exponential flow of reinforcements and recruits.

When Suchet finally reached Zaragoza on 30 May, he found the city in a state of panic, with wounded being evacuated, French soldiers selling their wares, and officers saddling up their requisitioned carriages to flee.[34] Suchet put a halt to the defeatist sentiments and resolved to wait in the city for Robert's brigade, hoping that it would arrive before Blake did, while in the meantime doing all that was possible to improve his state of affairs. All III Corps units were called in to take up defensive positions within and around Zaragoza, a measure which abandoned the rest of the Aragon, but a necessary one which allowed Suchet to affect a concentration of his forces. The only troops placed beyond the outskirts of Zaragoza belonged to a two-battalion force under Fabre at Muel, a small town 20 miles south of the Zaragoza. This body of troops was ordered to obtain information about Blake's movements. Suchet also dispatched daily cavalry patrols to range the countryside and keep watch for Blake's army. Soldiers stood yawning and at attention every day at 3:00 a.m. at their posts, manning the fortifications that Suchet had ordered to be dug in the outskirts of the city. Redoubts were built along the Huerva River and on Monte Torrero, and the Zaragoza suburbs were barricaded. Most important though, was Suchet's work in restoring III Corps to a standard of decency, and there was much work that needed to be done. Suchet ordered a review of his troops and for each of his regiments to state their grievances with the assurance that he would do his best to alleviate their woes. He 'thus acquired a knowledge of the causes to which the bad spirit prevailing in some corps was to be ascribed, distributed praises and punishments, and dismissed a few officers for neglectful or culpable conduct.'[35] Measures were also taken to ease tensions between the restless Zaragoza citizenry and the occupation force: 'The new commander-in-chief, Suchet, was far more severe on matters of discipline than his predecessor had been' wrote Brandt, 'and any junior officer who took a few eggs from a peasant would soon find himself before a court martial.'[36] The officer corps was shaken up and a number Suchet deemed not up to the task were dismissed back to France. The occasional firing squad was also employed to enforce discipline in the extreme cases, but a gentler approach was much more common – long overdue pay which had been left in careless arrears by Junot was seen to and tattered uniforms were mended. III Corps was not exactly *en grande tenue*, but looking the part of a soldier certainly helped restore the long-lost sense of professionalism. There was little idle time for the soldiers of III Corps. Constant reviews, unit manoeuvres, and firing drills helped restore discipline, while also making an impression on the Zaragoza citizenry that the III Corps was still a fighting force to be reckoned with. All of the reforms and fortifications did much for the condition of Suchet's men, but there was little hiding that the Spanish were converging on Zaragoza at any moment with superior forces, and Suchet made simultaneous preparations for the

---

33   Alexander, *Rod of Iron*, p.14.
34   Fuertes, *La ocupación francesa de Zaragoza*, p.63.
35   Suchet, *Memoirs of the War in Spain*, Vol.I, p.24.
36   Brandt, *In the Legions of Napoleon*, p.75.

worst-case scenario of evacuating Zaragoza. Anything and anyone that was vulnerable in the case of a revolt or an attack on the city, or would hinder a retreat – the artillery park, baggage train, and the sick and wounded – were pre-emptively evacuated to Tudela and Pamplona. The Aljafería palace within Zaragoza was restored to a state of defence to keep watch over the populace and function as a citadel the French could hold on to even if they had to evacuate the rest of Zaragoza.

With Suchet having concentrated all his troops in Zaragoza, the Spanish now controlled the countryside, and the only French holdings left north of the Ebro were the Zaragoza suburbs and Jaca. News of the French defeat at Alcañiz ignited a patriotic fervour in Aragon which fuelled a sharp increase in partisan activities. Blake was only too happy to provide aid to the guerrilla bands to keep the French occupied while he amassed his army. *Coronel* Ramón Gayán put together a poorly armed partisan band 1,000 strong and cut the lines of communication to Madrid. A young soldier named Martín Javier Mina was given leave to organize guerrillas in Navarre and further isolate the French in Zaragoza. Perena's guerrillas had active on the left bank of the Ebro, and they made campfires within sight of Zaragoza to encourage rebellion in the city populace. The partisans had grown bold, perhaps too bold. On the night of 7 June, six battalions were quietly dispatched to attack Perena's base at Perdiguera. The guerrillas had not bothered to put up a strong night-watch and were quickly overrun and scattered by the overwhelming French force, leaving their entire supply stores for the French to loot.[37] Despite the minor success, the guerrilla activities continued to increase, and the situation worsened daily for the French. The downside of concentrating III Corps in Zaragoza was that it became much more difficult to feed a large number of troops in a single area. Guerrilla warfare was taking its toll on French foraging parties, and starvation became a very real threat.[38] No amount of drilling and discipline could ward off the pangs of hunger, and undertaking large counter-guerrilla operations against the swarms of partisan bands roaming the countryside was impossible with Blake's 2° Ejército looming on the horizon. If the situation continued as it was, the Spanish threat to Zaragoza alone could drive the French out without a fight.

While Suchet was making his frantic preparations in Zaragoza, Blake had spent the last days of May at Alcañiz cleaning up the battlefield and resting his troops. On 30 May, Blake marched his army into Caspe for a victory parade.[39] The promised reinforcements from Valencia soon arrived in great numbers, comprising of both new regiments and drafts for existing ones.[40] A massive effort was also undertaken in Teruel to procure enough shoes, clothing, and supplies. Blake's advance was further delayed from waiting for even more reinforcements from Catalonia. The commander of the Spanish Ejército de la Derecha based in Catalonia, Theodor von Reding, had died of his wounds suffered at the Battle of

---

37   Brandt, *In the Legions of Napoleon*, p.75. Brandt took part in the raid and secured for himself a mule, which 'in spite of its nationality, served me well.'

38   Alexander, *Rod of Iron*, p.115.

39   Luis Antonio Pellicer Marco, 'La Batalla de Alcañiz', Asociación Cultural, <https://www. asociacionlossitios.com/batallaAlcañiz.htm#4>, accessed 14 April 2021.

40   Arteche y Moro, *Guerra de la Independencia*, Vol.VI, p.51. The Valencian Junta sent over 2 million reals raised in 15 days and 11,881 men to Blake's army. They commented that the only defenders left in the city of Valencia were armed with pikes!

Valls in April, leaving his shattered and leaderless units under Blake's charge. Blake lost no time claiming four of Reding's old battalions for his own 2° Ejército.[41] Two more artillery batteries, one of horse and one of foot, arrived from Tarragona to bolster Blake's already powerful ordnance. After three weeks of organization and preparation, Blake mustered an army of over 20,000 men, 1,000 cavalry, and 25 guns, organized into three divisions under Lazán, Roca, and Areizaga, the first two commanding mostly Valencian levies and the latter commanding the Aragonese with which Blake had won at Alcañiz.[42] The new 2° Ejército was over twice the size of the army Blake had fielded at Alcañiz – he was finally ready to finish Suchet off and drive the French from Aragon.

It had taken several weeks for Suchet's initial plan to evacuate Zaragoza to make its way around to the necessary people: Jourdan in Madrid, Clarke in Paris, and Napoleon in Vienna. The Imperial high command would hear none of it. Napoleon himself, at the time based in Schönbrunn Palace dictating his campaign against the Austrians, wrote to Joseph, criticizing him for putting operations in Aragon on a back seat and declared the province to be critical.[43] Clarke ordered *Général de Division* Laurent de Gouvion Saint-Cyr's VII Corps to support Suchet, though Saint-Cyr was preoccupied and could lend no aid. But by then, it was too little, too late – Blake had finally begun to move, and III Corps would be on its own against the 2° Ejército in the coming battle.

Blake launched his renewed offensive on 10 June, reaching Belchite on the 12th with the intention of manoeuvring and threatening Suchet's lines of communications so as to force him into a battle on ground of Blake's choosing or to abandon Zaragoza. At Belchite, Spanish morale soared after learning of the French defeat by the Austrians at the Battle of Aspern-Essling, which by the time word had reached Spain, had been exaggerated into a decisive defeat for Napoleon.[44] Such news only increased Blake's desire to get to grips with Suchet and continue the list of coalition victories. However, whether Blake truly needed to advance against Suchet or not is questionable. Historian Don Alexander criticizes Blake for this, writing that Blake was

> …mistaken in his belief that he needed to force Suchet's hand. Blake's mere presence at Belchite, in conjunction with the activities of the guerrillas, would have achieved his objective of compelling Suchet to evacuate Zaragoza or attack Blake's larger army on ground of its own choosing. Throughout the peninsular campaigns Blake underestimated the effectiveness of guerrilla warfare. Instead, he preferred to hazard a major battle with his regular forces.[45]

With hindsight, Blake should have kept his distance against Suchet and adopted a Fabian strategy of letting starvation and guerrillas take their toll while his elusive army maintained

41 Oman, *Peninsular War*, Vol.II, p.420.
42 Oman, *Peninsular War*, Vol.II, p.423. The official strength of the 2° Ejército was given as 25,000, but accounting for detachments and those hospitalized leaves Blake with around 20,000 infantry, 1,000 cavalry, and 25 guns.
43 Alexander, *Rod of Iron*, p.15.
44 Arteche y Moro, *Guerra de la Independencia*, Vol.VI. p.53.
45 Alexander, *Rod of Iron*, p.15

its distance. Alexander deems it inevitable that Suchet would have to abandon Zaragoza in such a scenario, giving the Spanish a bloodless and riskless triumph. But such a strategy would have been difficult to justify in light of the victory at Alcañiz and his vast numerical superiority over Suchet, especially since he had diverted precious troops away from fighting the formidable Saint-Cyr in Catalonia for his own campaign to liberate Aragon.[46] Blake also had little way of knowing the extent of the dire straits Suchet was in, which the French general revealed in his dispatches to Madrid and Paris. Blake's intention since the aftermath of Alcañiz had been to force Suchet out of Zaragoza with the sheer strength of his massive 2° Ejército, and weeks had been devoted to preparing for just that strategy. There was a renewed confidence in the fighting ability of Spanish troops both in themselves and their officers, so Blake saw little reason to sit back and wait, letting Suchet take the initiative, rather than best utilizing the resources available to him. Blake's strategy, which Oman astutely terms as simultaneously going on the 'strategic offensive' and 'tactical defensive', was a mix of both immediate military action and a prudent course of caution.[47] He did partially act along Alexander's prescribed strategy and was still rather cautious in his manoeuvres in front of Zaragoza, keeping to the hills instead of advancing directly against the open plains around the city and challenging the French to a pitched battle. If the opportunity for battle on his terms and on the ground of his choosing arose, however, Blake certainly would not shirk from it.

Such an opportunity emerged sooner than expected. Blake received intelligence reports of a small isolated French force around Cariñena (actually Fabre's force at Muel) and decided to strike at it and deal the first blow to Suchet.[48] The Spanish army left Belchite on the 13th in two columns; Blake took Lazán's 1st Division, Roca's 3rd Division, and most of the cavalry and artillery to march westward over the Huerva river to Cariñena and Longares, intending to attack Fabre from the front. The other column – comprised of Areizaga's mostly Aragonese 2nd Division, two squadrons of the Cazadores de Olivenza, and eight cannon – moved northwest to Botorrita, just 16 miles south of Zaragoza, to attack Fabre from the rear and cut off his path of retreat to Zaragoza. Areizaga crossed the Huerva near Botorrita on the 13th and captured a French convoy laden with supplies from Calatayud. Not only that, but Areizaga's surprise crossing put his 5,000 men directly between Zaragoza and Fabre's now isolated 1,200 men. After clashing with Blake's vanguard, Fabre realized he was in danger of being surrounded and retreated his men north to Plasencia del Jalón, further away from Suchet.[49] Suchet was informed of the dire situation and immediately dispatched Musnier to rescue Fabre. Nightfall prevented the French from re-establishing contact with

---

46   Oman, *Peninsular War*, Vol.II, p.420.

47   Oman, *Peninsular War*, Vol.II, p.423.

48   Southey, *History*, Vol.II, p.378. Southey is the only source that explains Blake's advance as an attempt to trap Fabre, while all other sources claim it was intended to cut Suchet's lines of communication to Madrid. Southey's version of events makes sense given that Blake ordered Areizaga to Botorrita. If Blake was maneuvering west solely for the intention of cutting Suchet's lines of communication, there would have been no reason for him to detach Areizaga. If Areizaga was to guard his lines of communication, Blake would not have advanced him so close to Zaragoza to risk being isolated and attacked. Blake's movements to María after driving off Fabre further indicate that he sought a decisive engagement.

49   Diversos-Colecciones, 195, N.68: Reseña de los alborotos en Lérida, muerte del general Reding y de las primeras operaciones realizadas por Blake en 1809.

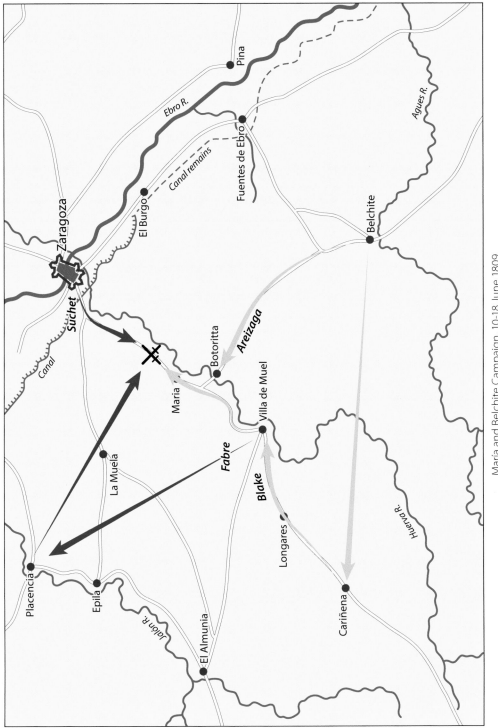

María and Belchite Campaign, 10-18 June 1809.

Fabre's detachment, which had managed to escape safely, but the determined Musnier could not have known of this and made his attack the next morning with the French advance guard.[50] He forced Areizaga's men back across the Huerva, but could not take Botorrita, for the arrival of Blake with the bulk of his army forced Musnier in turn to retire. Blake, remaining on the left bank, advanced on the town of María and encamped his army there, just twelve miles south of Zaragoza, while Areizaga's division remained at Botorrita on the right bank, around six miles south of Blake's main army.

Though Suchet was reluctant to engage in battle, Blake had forced his hand. To give up Zaragoza, the French general decided, would be a humiliating career-ending decision that would jeopardize all French operations in Spain. On 14 June, Suchet ordered the rest of his army to join Musnier at the Santa Fe Abbey, halfway between Zaragoza and María and confront Blake. He could not abandon Zaragoza without a fight, not when so much French and allied blood had been spilled to capture the city. Though he would have preferred to wait for Robert's brigade, which was due to arrive soon, Blake's army was too close, and Suchet did not want to fight the Spanish in or near Zaragoza, where they could likely count on the aid of the citizenry.[51] The reliable *Colonel* François-Nicolas-Benoît Haxo was given part of the 121e Ligne and several engineer and sapper companies to garrison Zaragoza and prevent the populace from revolting, a dangerous possibility given the close proximity of a massive Spanish army. Patrolling the Huerva river outside of Zaragoza was another detachment of the 121e Ligne.[52] Laval was posted at Monte Torrero with an infantry brigade of 2,000 and a battery of artillery as a strategic reserve and to guard Zaragoza in case Areizaga advanced on the city by way of the right bank.[53] That evening, Suchet established his headquarters at the Santa Fe Abbey and dictated his plans for the coming battle. Messengers were sent to hasten the march of Robert's brigade, which was but a few kilometres from Zaragoza, and to order Fabre to re-join the main army, which the latter was able to do. In all, Suchet had just 9,000 men and 12 guns to take to the field with, but he was counting on the timely arrival of Robert's brigade and hoping that his efforts had kindled the flames of French *élan* which had carried the Grande Armée from victory to victory, *le feu sacré*, in the hearts of the men of III Corps.

The Battle of María

The next morning, both armies met on a series of parallel ridges north of the town of María. Right of the ridges ran the road to Zaragoza from María, parallel to which ran the Huerva River, restricting manoeuvres on that side of the battlefield. Blake decided on a layered line of defence, placing his two infantry divisions on successive ridges. Roca's division formed his first line on the northernmost ridge, with most of the artillery dispersed along this line. Behind this ridge were several more ridges, on one of which Blake deployed Lazán's division

---

50   Arteche y Moro, *Guerra de la Independencia*, Vol.VI, p.57.
51   Suchet, *Memoirs of the War in Spain*, Vol.I, p.30.
52   Santiago, *Alcañiz, María y Belchite 1809*, p.49.
53   Suchet, *Memoirs of the War in Spain*, Vol.I, p.28. Laval's infantry brigade consisted of the 44e Line and 3e Vistule.

Sapeur of the 14e Ligne, by Pierre-Albert Leroux.
(Anne S.K. Brown Military Collection, Brown University Library)

as a second echelon. The entire Spanish cavalry, commanded by *Brigadier* Juan O'Donojú, occupied the open ground on Blake's right between the hills and the Huerva where they could be most effective – if they did not rout as they tended to do. At the town of Cadrete on the other side of the Huerva, Blake positioned *Coronel* Juan Creagh de Lacy's vanguard brigade in case Laval advanced out of Monte Torrero to flank the Spanish line. Blake also stationed two battalions of infantry and half a battery of artillery some way to the rear to guard the bridge to María over the Salado stream, which ran across the rear of the Spanish line. Once again Blake deployed his army with its back to difficult terrain, this time the Salado stream, a much lesser obstacle than the Guadalupe River, but still dangerous if his army was defeated – the Salado was fordable for infantry and cavalry, but nearly impossible for the artillery to cross. With the bridge so far to the rear of his right flank, Blake's centre and left would be left in danger if the Spanish army was forced to retreat.

Though a general engagement was most certainly about to occur, Blake made no attempt to order the 6,000 men of Areizaga's division, who were some of the best in his army, to join him. Oman estimates that it would have only taken two hours for Areizaga to arrive, leaving plenty of time for him to make a difference in the battle.[54] Instead, Areizaga was tasked with guarding Blake's rear and right flank, as well as observing Laval's brigade at Monte Torrero – a menial task to which far too many men were committed. Nor would Areizaga 'march to the sound of the guns' on his own initiative, or even attempt to break through Laval's position into Zaragoza; instead, his division sat idly at Botorrita for the entire day despite the sound of battle roaring to his front.

Both the sides deployed slowly, especially Suchet, who was stalling to give Robert's brigade time to arrive. Musnier's division was placed on the ridgeline directly opposite Roca's; they were separated only by the Cuarte Valley. On the extremity of the French right stood the 1/1er Lanciers de la Vistule. Wathier's cavalry formed up on the left on the open ground around the María road, while Habert's brigade was kept further behind by the Santa Fe Abbey. A reserve made up of a battalion each of the 64e Ligne and 5e Légère was placed behind Musnier. As Blake's army was deploying, Spanish skirmishers engaged the French all along the line but made a particularly strong show of force against the French left. This quickly escalated into a heated firefight where Spanish light infantry, supported by the cavalry of the Regimiento de Santiago, inflicted heavy losses on the skirmishers of the 2e Vistule and almost broke their skirmish line.[55] Only when the French called up an artillery bombardment did the Spanish retire. Suchet was still stalling when he received word around noon that Robert's men had arrived in Zaragoza and were en route to reinforce him. Now assured of the timely arrival of reinforcements, Suchet ordered Habert to move up in support of Wathier, while Robert would replace him in the left reserve position by the abbey. Suchet decided to fight defensively at first and ordered his cavalry to dismount and his infantry to rest, clearly passing the initiative to Blake.[56]

Sometime between 1:00 and 2:00 p.m., Blake decided that he would have to go on the offensive, dismayed that Suchet was showing no intention of doing so himself. Blake ordered the leftmost two battalions to outflank the French. Ironically, though, Suchet was

54   Oman, *Peninsular War*, Vol.II, p.426.
55   Oman, *Peninsular War*, Vol.II, p.425.
56   Suchet, *Memoirs of the War in Spain*, Vol.I, p.30.

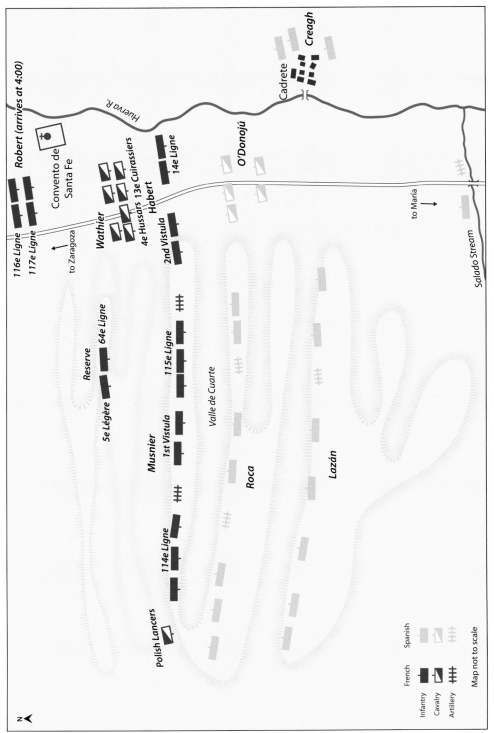

The Battle of María, 15 June 1809.

Infantry of the Légion de la Vistule.
(The Vinkhuijzen Collection of Military Uniforms, New York Public Library)

at that moment just about to make an attack himself, made confident by Robert's anticipated arrival within a few hours, but, seeing the Spanish battalions lumbering down the ridge and into the Cuarte valley, Suchet rode to the right flank to personally direct a counterattack. The Polish Lancers were dispatched to hit the Spanish in the flank, supported by a swarm of 200 voltigeurs who poured down deadly fire while the 114e Ligne formed an attack column to charge. The combined arms attack was too much for the Spanish, who retreated back to their lines in disorder. Suchet immediately ordered Musnier to attack before the Spanish could reorder themselves, rapidly swinging back the initiative to his favour.

Josef Chlopicki, Engraver unknown.
(Courtesy of José Arcón)

The 114e Ligne pressed the attack, supported by the 115e, while the 1er Vistule marched into the valley in columns, withholding their fire in shouldered arms, their *Colonel* Chlopicki at their head – in all some eight battalions of French and Polish infantry. The Spanish artillery fired a murderous barrage, to which *Colonel* Sylvain Valée's French artillery eagerly responded in turn to cover for the infantry. Still reeling from their failed attack, the battered Spanish left hastily regrouped and repositioned itself before the Franco-Polish attack could fall on them, while Blake recognized the dangerous situation and diverted troops from his centre-right to his left. Held up by rough terrain, the French columns were slowly being pulverized by concentrated Spanish artillery fire and musketry. While Suchet had done his best to bring III Corps back up to shape in the short time he was given, the memory of the humiliation at Alcañiz could not have been far from his mind. Seeing his attack faltering, he committed more men into the fray.[57] There could be no turning back with the offensive – he sent forward his chief of staff *Général de Brigade* Jean-Isidore Harispe with a grenadier company and ordered the 2e Vistule from Habert's brigade and the reserve battalion of the 64e Ligne to support the attack. Harispe was wounded the moment he arrived, but the presence of reinforcements sparked a renewed vigour in the troops stuck in the valley. The sudden eruption of a violent rainstorm (possibly even with some hail) brought a halt to the battle by reducing visibility for half an hour, giving temporary respite to both sides.

---

57   Suchet, *Memoirs of the War in Spain*, Vol.I, p.32.

During the storm, Suchet learned that Robert had arrived at the Santa Fe Abbey. Suchet had been withholding Habert's brigade as a last reserve, but with the arrival of Robert, he could commit it without worry. With Blake's centre fully occupied by Musnier's attack, Suchet decided to strike down the Zaragoza road against the weak Spanish right.[58] The storm was gone as quickly as it had come, leaving the French troops in the valley slogging in mud, but their situation had been stabilized enough that Suchet left his centre position and rode to Habert to oversee the attack. The 4e Hussards and 13e Cuirassiers were placed behind Habert's three battalions, and at 3:00 p.m. the entire French left was ordered forwards.[59] The 5e Légère led the attack deployed as a screen of skirmishers, followed by the 14e Ligne. The fire of the French infantry sufficiently disordered the Spanish right, and Wathier's hussars and cuirassiers seized the opportunity to ride out through the gaps between Habert's battalions to conduct their own attack. The sudden movement of the French cavalry combined with the fire of the French infantry left O'Donojú's men with no time to prepare to receive the charge. The entirety of the Spanish cavalry, demoralized and frightened by the mass of horsemen charging at them, scattered to the four winds in a terrified flight. The open ground along the Huerva was perfect hunting ground for the French cavalry, and Lazán's rightmost battalions quickly crumbled before the attack. His momentum unchecked, Wathier reformed his troopers and charged towards the María bridge, destroying Blake's reserves there. While the French cavalry continued their rampage, Habert's brigade wheeled in to attack the exposed Spanish flank.

Though his line of retreat had just been compromised, Blake kept his troops on the heights. For a man in his suddenly perilous position, it was the better of the few options available to him. Blake was well aware that his inexperienced army did not possess the discipline to disengage from Musnier's attack and retreat; under the conditions he was in it would be a difficult manoeuvre for even a veteran army. The best he could hope for was that his troops would repel the French attack as they had at Alcañiz, then slowly begin to withdraw without collapsing into a chaotic rout. The battle was not yet lost for Blake. He barked out a rapid series of orders to reposition his infantry to refuse the line against Habert's attack and committed Lazán's hitherto largely unengaged division into the battle line. The Spanish infantry redressed their lines, loaded their weapons, and steeled themselves against the onslaught.

Habert's brigade charged up the eastern slopes of the ridges and Musnier renewed his attack from the front, but the Spanish held their ground stubbornly. For the men of the III Corps, it was the first in a long time that victory was so close; they would show their Emperor that the glories of Austerlitz and Jena could still be replicated in their neglected campaign, and show Suchet that Alcañiz was behind them. Steadily the Spanish inched back

---

58   Suchet, *Memoirs of the War in Spain*, Vol.I, p.31; Arteche y Moro, *Guerra de la Independencia*, Vol.VI, p.65. Suchet congratulates himself in his memoirs for noticing at that moment that Blake's only line of retreat was the María bridge, which could easily be cut by an attack to the right. Arteche y Moro scathingly criticizes this claim, writing that Suchet likely intended to hold his cavalry in reserve and send them in when his infantry had stormed the heights, but Spanish resistance forced him to change his plans.

59   Santiago, *Alcañiz, María y Belchite 1809*, p.57.

Sylvain Valée, by F. Richer. (Rijksmuseum)

against the weight of the attack, and the balance of victory tilted in favour of the French.[60] The Spanish infantry gradually fell back down the ridge as III Corps pushed its attack with determination and élan.

By the time the exhausted French had pushed Blake's men off the ridge, it was late into the evening. The darkness was a godsend for the Spanish, who fled over the stream under the cover it offered, and Blake managed to keep his army in good order despite the perils and confusion of darkness and French harassment.[61] The 2° Ejército de la Derecha would survive to fight another day. French attempts at a pursuit proved futile, and Suchet was content to rest his men on their hard-fought victory. Suchet admitted to losing 800 men, against Spanish losses of 1,000 killed, 3–4,000 wounded, several hundred prisoners including *Coronel* Menchaca and *Brigadier* O'Donojú, and three standards of the 34 that the Spanish regiments brought to the field. Fifteen of Blake's 17 guns were also lost, having been unable

---

60   Arteche y Moro, *Guerra de la Independencia*, Vol.VI, p.68.
61   Diversos-Colecciones, 195, N.68: Reseña de los alborotos en Lérida, muerte del general Reding y de las primeras operaciones realizadas por Blake en 1809.

to cross the ridgelines and Salado stream; the two that he brought out had been in reserve behind the bridge.[62] Much to their credit, the rest of the Spanish reformed that night at the rally-point at Botorrita, where they were reinforced by Areizaga's division. Blake remained at Botorrita that night and the rest of the following day, for he hoped to give stragglers time to re-join their units and was undeterred by the close proximity of the French; despite the loss of nearly all his artillery, the Valencian recruits had conducted themselves with bravery and discipline at María.

The Battle of Belchite

III Corps took a much-deserved rest that night. Suchet, while relieved of a substantial worry, was as busy as ever, having ridden back to Zaragoza to secure the city and prepare for what tomorrow would bring. Laval's brigade, which had seen no action, was ordered to take up an advance position at Torrecilla de Valmadrid and threaten Blake's line of retreat. Though Blake had nearly been at the gates of Zaragoza and Perena's campfires could be seen on the other bank of the Ebro that night, the weary citizenry had not risen up, in no small part thanks to the presence of Haxo's garrison. The next morning, Suchet was surprised to find that Blake was still at Botorrita. He had fully expected Laval's advance to force Blake from his position.[63] Perhaps Blake had not noticed Laval. Upon re-establishing communication with Laval, Suchet learned that Aragonese guides had misled Laval and gotten his brigade lost, seriously delaying the flanking manoeuvre.[64] Undaunted, Suchet ordered his army to advance on Blake's left. The French were exhausted from yesterday's battle to the point where they were incapable of much more than merely walking, allowing Blake to break camp on the night of the 16th and retreat in good order towards Belchite.[65] Combined with the leisurely pace of his army and Laval's setbacks, Suchet's trap netted nothing, except at Torrecilla de Valmadrid where Laval did manage to capture a battalion of the 4º Infantería Marina – reinforcements en route to join Blake that had the misfortune to run into the French brigade.[66] Nevertheless, Suchet was determined to finish Blake off and complete his victory; he pressed the pursuit as far as Puebla de Albortón, where he encamped his army on the night of the 17th.

While Blake may have found much solace in the performance of his troops at María and conducted his retreat slowly, Blake's men evidently did not see eye-to-eye with their commander's opinion of the situation. The sudden reverse in Spanish fortunes had heavily demoralized Blake's army. They had been so close to liberating Aragon, yet turned away at the gates of Zaragoza. The poor road conditions and bad weather during the retreat worsened the despondent mood of the Spanish soldiers by ingraining the picture of a defeat,

---

62   Santiago, *Alcañiz, María y Belchite 1809*, p.61.
63   Suchet, *Memoirs of the War in Spain*, Vol.I, p.35.
64   Suchet, *Memoirs of the War in Spain*, Vol.I, p.36.
65   Gates, *The Spanish Ulcer*, p.164.
66   Diversos-Colecciones, 195, N.68: Reseña de los alborotos en Lérida, muerte del general Reding y de las primeras operaciones realizadas por Blake en 1809. Suchet, *Memoirs of the War in Spain*, Vol.I, p.36, mistakes this unit as Blake's rearguard, but Blake had in fact made clean his getaway.

and by the time Blake reached Belchite on the 17th, his force had been reduced by 3,000 deserters, mostly levies and sunshine patriots who had left the colours once hardship began to set in. Despite the demoralization of his army, Blake still felt confident enough to forgo the head start he had on Suchet to offer battle on ground of his choosing.

The next morning, Blake mustered just 12,000 cold and fatigued men from his original army of 20,000. He had only managed to save two guns at María, but there had been eight more with Areizaga, bringing his artillery up to a total of 10 guns. The battlefield Blake arrayed his army on was a low-lying plain dotted by orchards and olive groves. In the centre of Blake's position was the town of Belchite, which Blake garrisoned and fortified. Belchite was nestled between two low hills, the Calvario hill on the right and El Pueyo hill (a different hill to the one at Alcañiz) on the left, both of which Blake positioned his flanks on. The left was deemed the weakest point, for El Pueyo had a gentle slope and was open and exposed.[67] Thus, it was well protected by several lines of infantry and anchored on the far end at the fortified Pueyo Monastery. The Spanish cavalry, numbering only 300 and a negligible factor against Suchet's powerful regiments, was deployed in advance of the Zaragoza road. Remarkably, or perhaps by this point, expectedly, Blake deployed his army with its back to the Aguasvivas River, a tributary of the Ebro. Though the morale of his army may have been wanting, the Spanish position at Belchite was all in all quite defensible.

Against this, Suchet had nearly 13,000 men, including Robert's and Laval's fresh brigades. Arriving with his army in front of Blake's position on the morning of the 18th, Suchet commented that 'Those lines were connected by barns, loop holed houses and intrenchments. The whole ground in advance of our front, and especially of our centre, was lined with olive trees intersected by ditches and canals for irrigation which rendered it of difficult access.'[68] Suchet took one good look at Blake's position, then completely ruled out a frontal assault. He did quickly recognize that Blake's left was the weakest point and accordingly laid out a plan of attack.

Suchet decided to conduct a pincer movement and crush Blake's flanks. A screen of light infantry from the 5e Légère was deemed sufficient to pin the well-protected Spanish centre. Habert's brigade and the 13e Cuirassiers were to make a broad sweep around the Spanish right between Belchite and Codo to outflank it, while Musnier's division, supported by the 4e Hussards, would charge the Spanish left in battalion columns once the French artillery softened up the enemy. The preliminary bombardment and threatening advance of the French attack columns sufficed to compel the Spanish left to abandon the Pueyo Monastery and fall back to Belchite. Blake rode up and down the lines, rallying his men, and attempted to organize a combined-arms attack by his infantry in columns and cavalry, supported by his artillery, but the manoeuvre was countered by Wathier hardly before it had begun.[69]

Suddenly, a most unexpected stroke of luck swung what had thus far been a fairly even battle in the favor of the French. *Lieutenant* Auvray, one of Suchet's aides de camp, advanced two light cannon on the French right to engage in counter-battery fire against the Spanish

---

67   Arteche y Moro, *Guerra de la Independencia*, Vol.VI, p.74.
68   Suchet, *Memoirs of the War in Spain*, Vol.I, p.37.
69   Santiago, *Alcañiz, María y Belchite 1809*, p.66.

Trooper of the 4e Hussards, by Eunice Kiang. (Author's collection)

artillery.[70] One of his howitzers landed a freak shot into the Spanish ammunition reserve in the centre of the town – the shell's explosion ignited a caisson, setting off a chain reaction of massive explosions as the fire spread amongst the ammunition wagons. The nearby battalions of the Cazadores de Valencia and Provincial de Ávila, especially the latter, were greatly disordered and injured. As these units disintegrated and fled, they triggered a domino-effect rout of the surrounding battalions, which were likewise stunned by the massive explosion. Confusion ran rampant, as many believed that they were being attacked in the rear, and shouts of 'betrayal!' rang out as the Spanish tossed aside their muskets and bolted en masse.[71] Spanish morale, shaky to begin with, collapsed instantaneously as soldiers broke formation and fled only because they had seen the unit next over do so. In such a fashion, nearly the entire Spanish army was in full rout within a matter of minutes, running pell-mell through the streets of Belchite for the Aguasvivas River, hotly pursued by the French. A few soldiers who kept their heads managed to close the town gates to stall the pursuit, but it was not long before the French broke in. Only the Regimiento de América held together to attempt to put up a rearguard action in the town square, but they were instantly ridden down by 1/1e Lanciers de la Vistule. In spite of the total collapse of the 2° Ejército, relatively few men actually fell into the hands of the French, for Habert's brigade was still conducting its flanking manoeuvre and was unable to join the pursuit, which itself was stymied by the narrow town gates. Nonetheless, the French chased their fleeing foes over the Aguasvivas River for at least seven miles. When the 1° Regimiento de Valencia managed to rally on the plains below the river, it was surrounded, shot at, and forced to surrender with its flag.[72]

The action had lasted no longer than a few hours, in which the French had suffered 200 killed and wounded. The Spanish lost 2,000 killed, wounded, and captured, along with nine cannon, 23 caissons, a single standard, piles of small arms discarded in the rout, and all the munitions and stores in Belchite. Of the vast quantities of food that were captured, von Brandt estimated that only 10 percent ever reached Zaragoza, not due to guerrilla activity, but the unreliable civilian commissaries who sold the food to hungry civilians along the way at an inflated price.[73] The greatest consequence of the Battle of Belchite though, was that the 2° Ejército had scattered into virtual nonexistence. Some fled into the hills and for their homes, while others made it to the Spanish strongholds of Tortosa, Morella, and San Mateo. By 1 June only 10,000 badly demoralized troops remained of the over 20,000 who had originally set out on the crusade to liberate Aragon.[74]

With the complete rout of the 2° Ejército de la Derecha, the 1809 campaign for Aragon came to an end. All the progress Blake's army had made in May and early June had been lost in the course of several decisive days. Blake's decision to make a stand at Belchite was wholly unnecessary. After María, the wise decision would have been to make a retreat to

70   Brandt, *In the Legions of Napoleon*, p.79. Brandt curiously warns of Suchet's overdramatization of the battle. He himself had personally escorted Auvray's artillery to its position, and commented that 'The whole affair did not last long enough for him to carry out the various dispositions which he details,' that is, the flanking attacks did not develop fully by the time the battle ended.

71   Brandt, *In the Legions of Napoleon*, p.79.

72   Santiago, *Alcañiz, María y Belchite 1809*, p.69.

73   Brandt, *In the Legions of Napoleon*, p.79.

74   Oman, *Peninsular War*, Vol.II, p.430.

Tortosa and regain strength, not fight another battle. The French pursuit was lax and Blake had had ample time to make a retreat to Tortosa in good order. Had he done so, he would at least still have an army. For five long years, 1809 was as close as the Spanish would get to retaking Zaragoza. In analysing the operations of both Blake and Suchet, Suchet had managed to triumph through the tactical supremacy of his troops, particularly the cavalry, and his reconstruction of III Corps into a viable fighting force was undoubtedly a major factor in his victory. For Blake, French tactical superiority and the constant inability of his own cavalry to stand up to their French counterparts, or do anything for that matter, had cost him the campaign. That Blake received criticism for failing to pursue in the aftermath of Alcañiz, only for a similar move to be deemed unwise in hindsight when he decided to force a battle with Suchet three weeks later, shows the fine balance Blake had to walk with regard to operational strategy. However, Blake himself was not entirely blameless. His failure to recall Areizaga's division on the 15th, and Areizaga's own complacency, lost him his best chance to retake Zaragoza by winning the Battle of María. It is also astounding that in all three battles Blake deployed his army with its back to a river, which would theoretically have hampered his retreat, yet managed to avoid annihilation. On the other hand, Suchet had been a hair's breadth away from defeat. His resolution to hold onto Zaragoza was a huge risk considering Blake's numerical superiority, an advantage which Blake squandered by failing to concentrate all of his available forces for the Battle of María. Suchet had thrown the dice and won, but there was still much work ahead. By no means had Suchet conquered Aragon by defeating Blake; he had only just managed to restore the situation.

3

The Occupation of Aragon

Counter-Guerrilla Operations in Aragon

Though Blake's army no longer posed a threat, various armed groups and fortified towns still contested Suchet's control over Aragon. Many elements of the dispersed 2° Ejército now joined up with guerrilla bands and carry on the struggle. While this made the guerrilla bands larger and easier to hunt, the addition of trained soldiers and officers made them much more powerful than they had ever been. These guerrilla bands were everywhere, striking at French detachments and besieging small garrisons.

Suchet's first order of action was to organize a force to relieve the garrison at Jaca, where *Commandant* Antoine Lomet's poorly supplied garrison had been bottled up since May. His troops were mostly National Guardsmen, heavily demoralized to begin with, and they had the audacity to desert *en masse* in large groups (as protection from guerrillas). Executions hardly deterred the deserters and by June, Lomet had but 432 of his original 1,036 soldiers left. Foraging parties were harassed to no end, and, running low on supplies, Lomet could only write to Suchet a terse message of bravado: 'I will hold firm until extinction.'[1]

Suchet dispatched *Colonel* Louis-Augustin Plicque with 830 men and two cannons to assist Lomet, but the situation in the Upper Ebro was far worse than anticipated. Guerrilla bands ran rampant throughout the countryside, and on 7 July Plicque's force was attacked by guerrillas en route to Jaca, forcing the French column to sprint the remaining few miles in a frantic rush to escape the trap. However, Plicque had not brought any extra supplies with him to Jaca and Lomet determined that the extra troops would far exceed the cost-benefit ratio of the manpower needed to defend the fortress and the consumption of the scant rations at hand. Thus, Plicque returned to Cincovillas on 10 July with nothing to show for his efforts.

This dismal failure caused Suchet to realize that the guerrilla threat was larger than first anticipated, and that he needed to address it before Blake could raise another army. Suchet decided to renew the offensive to clear Upper Aragon of guerrillas and dispatched both Habert and Plicque. Habert attacked Perena, who had been moving against Barbastro, forcing him to retreat into the Pyrenees, while Plicque returned from the Roncal valley with nothing but empty promises of peace from the peasantry – more needed to be done to pacify Upper Aragon.

---

1   Alexander, *Rod of Iron*, p.23.

The arrival of 1,200 reinforcements from France in July and August finally allowed Lomet to conduct offensive operations. On 7 August he unleashed a column of 1,500 men under *Chef de Bataillon* Lapeyrolerie to Saliente, where Perena's band was headquartered. The guerrillas put up a stubborn resistance but were driven off with some losses. Saliente was plundered, and as Lapeyrolerie continued his march, any villages where weapons were found were burned. The raid also bagged 6,000 sheep and 200 cattle.[2] Suchet also dispatched Musnier with 1,800 infantry, 250 cavalry, and four cannon to escort a supply convoy to Jaca and destroy Miguel Sarasa's band at their base in the San Juan de la Peña convent, a well-protected monastery in the mountains and home to the tombs of the old kings of Aragon. On 23 August, the 30-man regimental band of the 115e Ligne and their 40-strong escort party were ambushed and massacred at the village of Bernues with no survivors. Upon hearing of this, Musnier immediately marched from Jaca to Sarasa's base.[3] Despite the formidable position and symbolic status of his base – even the Moors had failed to take the position in their conquest of Spain – Sarasa avoided battle and retreated. The French subsequently destroyed all but the tombs.[4]

With the situation around Jaca somewhat stabilized, Musnier turned his attention west to the Echo, Anso, and Roncal valleys in the north western most point of Aragon, where Renovales' guerrillas were active. For this operation, 1,650 men of the Jaca garrison were sent to guard the eastern routes at Broto and Viescas, while Plicque struck from the southwest, converging with Musnier onto Roncal.[5] Renovales, who was a regular army officer, decided to make a stand. His guerrillas fought hard at the mountain passes, but were gradually pushed back, and in their wake Plicque and Musnier enacted a punitive scorched-earth policy, shooting any peasants found with weapons. French terror campaign had worked its effect. When the French were before Roncal itself, the guerrillas and their supporters realized that further resistance was futile. They sent a delegation to surrender – all weapons would be relinquished and the French would take hostages to ensure cooperation. As part of the surrender terms, Renovales himself was permitted to leave to Lérida with some of his men, while the rest of his force dispersed. Two French battalions remained to secure food and livestock contributions levied on the inhabitants.[6]

With Roncal pacified, the French turned their attention to the bands of Perena, Pedrosa, and Baget in the east. These bands were chased beyond the Cinca river after several small skirmishes, during one of which Habert is said to have sacked the town of Fonz, with disregard for the property of supporters of the French.[7] Lapeyrolerie pursued a Catalan band westwards, where the guerrillas fought a rearguard action at Graus before fleeing further west. Lapeyrolerie thought he had the guerrillas cornered when he came upon their campfires; however, he soon found that his position was surrounded by defiles, and that the

---

2   Alexander, *Rod of Iron*, p.24.
3   Suchet, *Memoirs of the War in Spain*, Vol.I, p.63. His forces were one battalion each of the 5e Légère, 115e Ligne, and 64e Ligne, and part of the Jaca garrison.
4   Fuertes, *La ocupación francesa de Zaragoza*, p.43; Suchet, *Memoirs of the War in Spain*, Vol.I, p.64. Fuertes believes the tombs were saved not by the orders of Suchet, as the general claims, but simply because the French did not think them worth destroying.
5   Alexander, *Rod of Iron*, p.25.
6   Suchet, *Memoirs of the War in Spain*, Vol.I, p.64.
7   Arteche y Moro, *Guerra de la Independencia*, Vol.VII, p.34.

guerrillas were massing all around him. Lapeyrolerie ordered his men to break out with their bayonets. The guerrillas were caught off guard, their confusion further confounded by the darkness, allowing the French to retire safely to Graus, while the guerrillas, perhaps unnerved by the ordeal, continued their retreat.[8] By October the French had secured the entire left bank of the Ebro, establishing garrisons at Fraga and Monzón to guard Aragon against forays from Mequinenza and Lérida. The French commanders claimed to have inflicted some 1,000 casualties in the pursuit.[9]

Meanwhile, French forces had also been engaged in operations on the right bank of the Ebro. Suchet first targeted Gayán's *partida*, which numbered at around 3,000. A strike force of 3,000 infantry in four battalions, 100 cuirassiers, and two guns was assembled at Longares under Laval. On 20 July they surrounded Gayán's fortified camp at the Nuestra Señora del Aguila convent and stormed it. The guerrillas fled with little resistance and the French destroyed the base and all the supplies stored there. To follow up, *Colonel* Klicki was sent to subjugate Daroca with his lancers and a regiment of Poles, while Laval continued on to Calatayud.[10] There he found that the *afrancesado* officials appointed by Suchet had been kidnapped when the guerrillas took control. Laval pressed on in a search-and-destroy mission in Northwest Aragon, but found little and simply retired. The moment Laval withdrew, Gayán returned, now reinforced by a new powerful force under the leadership of *Mariscal de Campo* Pedro Villacampa. Villacampa's command was mostly composed of regulars from the 2º de Princesa and 2º de Soria regiments, but this did not prevent him from being driven out of Calatayud with 130 casualties by *Colonel* Henriod. However, after forcing Villacampa to retreat, Henriod simply went back just as Laval had, leaving a small detachment of the 14e Ligne at El Frasno to guard the road to Zaragoza. The French had yet to realize that their careless assumption that driving away the guerrillas equated to defeating them was flawed; Villacampa returned with 4,000 men and overwhelmed the detachment at El Frasno on 25 August, taking 65 prisoners.[11]

Suchet was frustrated at the ineffectual goose chase his subordinates had been running and ordered Henriod and Chlopicki to attack Villacampa. The guerrillas escaped the trap and retreated to the town of Molina. With nothing left to do, the Franco-Polish troops sacked Calatayud. This time though, Suchet ordered Chlopicki to garrison and hold the key towns of Calatayud, Daroca, and Calamocha with the 1er Vistule, part of the 2e Vistule, and the 13e Cuirassiers.[12] On 12 October, Chlopicki's force intercepted a guerrilla band under Molina which had been attempting to unite with Villacampa, and forced it to retreat.

It seemed at first that the guerrillas had been all but driven out of Upper Aragon during the summer operations, but Sarasa returned in November to harass the Jaca garrison, which had been reduced under an air of false security and the *marche* battalion dispersed to join the regular infantry regiments of III Corps. Without their prior numbers, the garrison had little offensive capabilities, and Suchet duly shifted a battalion of the 64e Ligne to the area. The new commander of Jaca, Maurice de Roquemorel, brigaded the

---

8   Suchet, *Memoirs of the War in Spain*, Vol.I, p.67.
9   Alexander, *Rod of Iron*, p.26.
10   Alexander, *Rod of Iron*, p.29.
11   Arteche y Moro, *Guerra de la Independencia*, Vol.VII, p.29.
12   Suchet, *Memoirs of the War in Spain*, Vol.I, p.69.

reinforcements with the Chasseurs de l'Ariege mountain troops and placed them under the capable Lapeyrolerie's command. The town and fortress of Benasque controlled a communication route to France and was the last Spanish stronghold in Upper Aragon, and the French aimed to capture it in their operation against Sarasa. The French pursued Sarasa, but having failed to catch him within a week, stopped at Matidero and turned northwest to the Benasque valley. They pushed into the valley, driving back the 1,500 guerrilla defenders and reached the Spanish-held Benasque fortress on 23 November, surprising the garrison there. Fearing for their lives and wanting little part in the coming storm, the civilian population of Benasque sent a delegation to Lapeyrolerie to ask that the town not be harmed. Lapeyrolerie arrested the delegation and demanded that the Benasque garrison surrender immediately, with threats to execute the delegation, storm the fortress, and massacre the garrison if a surrender was not forthcoming.[13] Terrified, the demoralized garrison capitulated. The fall of Benasque left Mequinenza, a small riverside town with an imposing castle, as the last Spanish stronghold in all of Aragon.[14] Lapeyrolerie continued his conquest of the Pyrenees towns, but on 7 December, his troops encountered Sarasa's band at Novales. The French attacked immediately but faced heavy resistance from the insurgents; among them were Polish deserters who faced execution if captured.[15] Despite this, the guerrillas broke and fled to Lérida. The French lost around 20 casualties, the guerrillas 30 or more.

In Lower Aragon, Belchite and Caspe came under attack on 16 October, the former by a small band of guerrillas but the latter by five battalions from Mequinenza. Nonetheless, both attacks were repulsed. Throughout early October Villacampa's force had largely remained quiet outside of a few probing skirmishes with Chlopicki – the guerillas were massing at Orihuela del Tremedal just 42 miles northwest of Teruel. The Aragonese Junta had banked all their hopes on Villacampa's *partida* in the form of vast resources and funding, and the guerrillas received 4,000 uniforms, 800 muskets, 200 horses, and 80,000 reales.[16] Realizing that Villacampa's concentration equated to having a full Spanish division operating in Aragon, Suchet sent orders for Henriod to strike first. Henriod took a force of 2,100 men and three guns from Daroca, and his skirmishers engaged Villacampa's advance guard on the early morning of 25 October at the Ojos-Negros pass and turned their flank, forcing them to fall back to Orihuela del Tremedal.[17]

Villacampa then decided to give battle to the French. His force totalled several thousand well-armed troops, supported by armed peasants, and outnumbered the French by at least two-to-one. Additionally, the Spanish general placed great confidence in his defensive position on the mountain of Tremedal. The rocks lining the slopes provided excellent cover, but Villacampa thought it wise to add ditches and an abatis. The extreme terrain would also negate the powerful French cavalry. Henriod arrived in front of Villacampa's position at

13   Alexander, *Rod of Iron*, p.26.
14   Alexander, *Rod of Iron*, p.26.
15   Alexander, *Rod of Iron*, p.26.
16   Alexander, *Rod of Iron*, p.30.
17   Suchet, *Memoirs of the War in Spain*, Vol.I, p.70. Suchet gives the order of battle for Henriod's force as the 14e Ligne, eight companies of the 2e Vistule, the 13e Cuirassiers, two cannon, a howitzer, and 150 Aragonese civilians managing the wagon train.

11:00 a.m. on the 25th. Instantly realizing the futility of a head-on attack, Henriod opted to try to force the Spanish position by other means. For most of the day he conducted feints against Villacampa's right flank on the road to Albarracín with the bulk of his forces, hoping that Villacampa would commit his reserves forces in the mountain church of Santuario de la Virgen del Tremedal to the left.[18] Villacampa took the bait and reinforced his right, but still no attack was forthcoming. This farce carried on until dusk, when the French baggage column and a part of the infantry began to retreat back to Daroca. At the same time, six voltigeur companies of the 14e Ligne and the Légion de la Vistule, plus a cannon and howitzer, were seen moving into Orihuela, whose inhabitants had fled before the battle.[19] Villacampa rapidly shifted his reserves back to the centre as a precaution, but the French artillery merely fired several ineffective shots in what seemed like a rearguard action. While the flashes of the artillery in the darkening sky fixated the attention of the Spanish,

Pedro Villacampa. (Courtesy of José Arcón)

the unseen voltigeurs clambered up an unguarded section of the rugged slopes in total silence. The French artillery ceased fire to complete the impression that Henriod's withdrawal was now fully underway. Suddenly, the French elite companies rushed out of the darkness to roll up the Spanish position. The abrupt shock of the attack sent the guerrillas reeling, and, despite his best efforts at rallying his men, Villacampa was swept away in the rout. Casualty figures are disputed for both sides, but were light for the French and light to moderate for the Spanish. In any case, Villacampa's force escaped largely intact due to the French being unable to field their cuirassiers, though the Spanish stockpile of supplies and arms was captured. Unable to transport the loot back to Daroca, Henriod opted to destroy it using fireworks and gunpowder found in the church, and the resulting explosion

18   Suchet, *Memoirs of the War in Spain*, Vol.I, p.71.
19   Suchet, *Memoirs of the War in Spain*, Vol.I, p.72.

also destroyed the church.[20] Afterwards, the French descended into the abandoned town to loot it.

While Villacampa's band was by no means destroyed as it had preserved most of its manpower, the defeat at Tremedal substantially reduced his scope of operations for the rest of 1809. His men regrouped near Molina to lick their wounds and continued to receive supplies from the Aragonese Junta, but some of the Junta's members sought to replace Villacampa for his failures. November saw several raids by various detachments of Villacampa's force, such as on 24 November, when a detachment under *Capitán* Antonio de Val ambushed three companies of the 44e Ligne that had been on tax collection duty at Berge, inflicting some casualties.[21] The retreating French were attacked by the villagers of Cella during their escape, for which the French retaliated by returning and hanging the mayor. However, minor skirmishes such as these did little to weaken the tightening French hold on lower Aragon.

December saw a renewed effort by the French to rid Lower Aragon of Villacampa for good. *Général de Division* Edouard Milhaud's dragoon division of three brigades was sent from Madrid to assist Suchet, who had been operating without outside assistance since he took command. Milhaud arrived at Calatayud on 16 December, but his presence was only made known to Suchet when he arrived, and it would only be momentary as Milhaud had orders to join IV Corps in Castille. Seeking to make the most of the temporary reinforcements, Suchet organized a massive sweep of Lower Aragon. On the 18th he massed five battalions, part of the 13e Cuirassiers, and 10 guns at Daroca under his personal command for the coming operation with Milhaud, which would also be supported by part of Musnier's division.[22]

Suchet moved southwards from Daroca to Teruel. However, Milhaud moved southwest and away from Suchet's force towards Castille, leaving the western routes open for Villacampa to escape through. Musnier had been suddenly attacked by elements of the Tortosa garrison and was unable to support Suchet's operation. Lacking the manpower for a concentric entrapment of Villacampa, Suchet simply arrived at Teruel on 22 December, obtained oaths of allegiance from the city officials, and departed on the 30th.[23] Several days later on 3 January, Villacampa returned to reoccupy the city until the next time he was chased out. It should be noted that this was actually the only counter-guerrilla operation Suchet would lead in person, and a wholly unsuccessful one at that.

---

20   Anon. 'Santuario Virgen del Tremedal', *Orihuela del Tremedal*, <http://www.orihueladeltremedal. es/turismo/que-puedes-visitar/santuario-la-virgen-del-tremedal/>, accessed 29 December 2021; Suchet, *Memoirs of the War in Spain*, Vol.I, p.73. Brandt, *In the Legions of Napoleon*, pp.102-103. Accounts differ with regards to what happened in the final stages of the battle. As a participant in the attack, Brandt claims that the Spanish munitions had been kept in a separate building instead of the church, and that the fleeing guerrillas had deliberately detonated it in a small series of explosions. While Suchet writes that the town of Orihuela del Tremedal nearly caught fire from the sparks of the explosion, Brandt refutes this by saying that he saw no fire and that Suchet was likely misled by exaggerated post-action reports. The appearance of the town on fire probably stemmed from French-Polish troops who demolished some furniture and wooden structures to create bonfires for warmth.
21   Alexander, *Rod of Iron*, p.31.
22   Alexander, *Rod of Iron*, p.33.
23   Alexander, *Rod of Iron*, p.34.

Suchet's next adventure lay in the neighbouring province of Navarre, for on 17 December, Napoleon placed Navarre under Suchet's supervision, the consequence of Suchet's incessant squabbling with *Général de Brigade* Louis-Annibal de Saint-Michel d'Agoult, the Governor of Navarre. Throughout the second half of 1809, d'Agoult's meagre garrison had proved insufficient in suppressing the Navarrese guerrillas, and the problem became Suchet's too when these guerrillas raided into Aragon. Suchet had been forced to send 2,500 of his own troops into Navarre to secure lines of communication, all the while arguing with d'Agoult, whom Suchet regarded as old and ineffective.[24] In November, Suchet's forces suffered two major setbacks when a counter-guerrilla operation headed by Plicque and Buget was defeated, and later that month Javier Mina managed to raid the French base at Tudela. Suchet come out the victor over d'Agoult in their spat, and Napoleon gave Suchet authority over Navarre. In the first days of January 1810, Harispe, who had been left in charge of Navarre while Suchet wrapped up his joint operation with Milhaud, launched an elaborate multi-column operation to destroy Javier Mina's *partida* at Sangüesa. This failed miserably, with one column reporting to have nothing to show for their efforts but a single guerrilla killed, and the French commanders playing their favourite blame game in the aftermath.[25]

Suchet learned of the fiasco in Navarre at the same time he received a letter from Napoleon criticizing him for not sending enough troops into Aragon. The vexation of the Emperor was enough to goad Suchet into action, and declaring that he would decapitate Javier Mina, hang his subordinates, and deport his captured soldiers, Suchet committed all available resources to running the Navarrese guerrillas to the ground.[26] Joining Suchet were troops under *Général de Division* Jean Reynier, which had just arrived in Navarre. In contrast to his clumsy efforts to trap Villacampa in December, Suchet strategically placed his battalions to seal off escape routes and launched several columns to break the guerrillas. Faced with overwhelming French forces, Javier Mina ordered his guerrillas to scatter and hide, and the French too split up their force to maintain the pursuit on the guerrillas and prevent them from regrouping.[27] Javier Mina managed to escape to Lérida, but the power of the guerrillas in Navarre had been temporarily broken.

Suchet and III Corps fumbled their way through learning the ropes of counterinsurgency warfare in 1809, not suffering any major defeats but struggling to achieve any *partida*-ending decisive victories. In light of the total defeat of Blake's army, however, Spanish resistance in Aragon had been left a wreck, and the few successes Suchet enjoyed against the guerrillas was just enough to secure the province. Despite the failure of multi-column operations and a perpetual habit of failing to garrison captured towns, on balance, Suchet could safely say that he had achieved enough success against the guerrillas in Aragon to be able to lay down the groundwork for a French regime. Sporadic guerrilla activity still occurred on the fringes of Aragon, even in areas that were thought to have been pacified such as the Roncal Valley, but by the end of December most of the guerrillas had been pushed out to these frontier

---

24   Alexander, *Rod of Iron*, p.36.
25   Alexander, *Rod of Iron*, p.38.
26   Alexander, *Rod of Iron*, p.40.
27   John L. Tone, *The Fatal Knot*, (Chapel Hill: University of North Carolina Press, 1994), p.80.

regions. While the dispersion of the guerrillas did not entail their complete defeat, their dislodgement enabled Suchet to implement his administrative policies without interference.

In order to fully understand Suchet's role in French counter-guerrilla operations, it is imperative to understand guerrilla warfare in the Peninsular War and its antithesis, counterinsurgency practices. The Peninsular War is perhaps most famous for being one of the birthplaces of modern guerrilla warfare. Common usage of the word 'guerrilla', which has become well ingrained in the English language, actually originated from the Peninsular War. Looking at the etymology of the word, 'guerrilla' is a Spanish diminutive for 'guerra' and thus roughly translates into 'little war.' After the Peninsular War guerrilla warfare would be used in many ways – by regular armies to supplement their operations, by freedom fighters to wage war against oppressive invaders, and by rebels to overthrow legitimate governments, among others. While guerrilla warfare was nothing new to mankind's long struggle of perfecting the art of killing one another, the Peninsular War did mark a turning point in terms of the frequency of such wars, in part due to its extreme compatibility with a rising tide of popular nationalism, followed by ideological war, all across the world.

So what was guerrilla warfare in the Peninsular like? The typical Spanish guerrilla of the time generally conjures up images of patriotic citizens and peasants outraged at French excesses, who wore their Sunday best or colourful work clothes to battle, armed with whatever weapons were on hand, be it daggers, fowling pieces, or farm implements. Driven into a patriotic fervour by rousing and heartfelt speeches given in the town square by prominent locals or monks, the assembled mob of civilians, numbering anywhere from a dozen to a hundred, would form a guerrilla band under the singular leadership of a charismatic figure and set off to kill the occasional unfortunate French straggler, ambush couriers, attack convoys, and such. When all was said and done, the guerrillas would melt back into civilian life until the time came to strike again.

Certainly, in the first months of the French invasion the typical Spanish guerrilla fits the above stereotype, and it was this image of popular resistance that appealed heavily to nationalist sentiments that came in the years after the war which fuelled a disparity in reality and perception of guerrilla warfare in the Peninsular War. The mythos of the 'Spanish guerrilla' has grown into a legend of its own, fuelled by hero-worship of notable individuals such as Julián Sánchez, the two Minas, and Juan Martín Díez, better known as 'El Empecinando'. Of course, legends and stereotypes are distinct from actual facts, and the true nature of the Spanish guerrilla was much more complex.

As the war dragged on and the guerrillas became a more prominent force in the Peninsular War, the guerrilla bands themselves underwent an evolution into two distinct types. The first were the 'popular resistance' and 'insurgency' the aforementioned local patriots, brigands, or fanatics, who were insurgents in the truest sense, living hand-to-mouth and on the run or disguised amidst the local populace, engaging in ambuscades and assassinations. This first type of guerrilla truly exemplified the idea of an 'enemy in plain sight', and it was these that Suchet's administration was most effective at suppressing. The second type of guerrilla was an evolution from the armed wing of a popular revolt to what were essentially highly mobile regular army units, which for the purposes of this book, will be referred to as guerrillas, separate from the common insurgency, though the two often worked together. It is these that feature most prominently in the counter-guerrilla sections of this book, for it was guerrilla units of this type that were powerful enough to undertake operations signifi-cant enough to enter historical records and inflict damage on the French.

There are three reasons as to how and why the Spanish guerrilla movement became highly organized and militarized. The first cause of evolution was the product of the Spanish government's attempts to harness and control an increasingly anarchical popular war. When the guerrilla war first began in 1808, the violence was spearheaded by local militias and spontaneous rebellions, and, on the worst side of the spectrum, opportunists and bandits who made little distinction in killing French soldiers or fellow Spaniards. The negative effects of this guerrilla movement for Spain were twofold: the often-lawless nature of the guerrillas diminished the authority of the Central Junta and the guerrillas sapped manpower from the recruitment pool for Spain's regular armed forces. Early attempts to corral the guerrillas were unsuccessful, but as the war progressed, the Spanish were able to incorporate many guerrilla units into the regular army structure, organizing them into regiments. The end product of this was the creation of independent light divisions, called the *Divisiones Volantes*, the official title given to many guerrilla groups such as those of Joaquín Durán and Villacampa.

The second reason was the growing relationship between Spanish regular and insur-gent forces. As opposed to being led by flashy individuals or religious fanatics, the most successful guerrilla bands were organized and led by regular Spanish army officers (who still needed to be charismatic). For example, Villacampa was a regular army officer, and his 'guerrilla band' was centred around the remnants of line regiments 2° de Princesa and 2° de Soria. He was also operating under direct orders from Blake to conduct irregular warfare and incite rebellion in Aragon. Here one can see the blurring of the lines between inde-pendent guerrilla groups and regular army forces. Another notable who fought in Aragon was Felipe Perena, an army officer and former governor of Huesca, whose group was organ-ized as a regiment of volunteers. These guerrilla units operated out of Spanish fortresses and worked in close conjunction with Spanish field armies, on which they were reliant for supplies and arms.

The third and final reason was in regard to changes in methods and tactics. As the guer-rilla bands grew bigger thanks to influxes in recruits, they lost the mobility and flexibility of small, hard-hitting bands, and were easily located and destroyed by the French. The best example of this is Espoz y Mina. After having his band virtually annihilated at Belorado, Mina decided not to downsize his *partida* and stick to hit-and-run warfare, but to raise a formidable force that could match the French in a fair fight.[28] Instead of utilizing purely guerrilla tactics, Mina trained his men to fire a disciplined volley, then charge in with the bayonet. In general, the *Divisiones Volantes* tended to operate as guerrillas strategi-cally and operationally, but fought in linear formations when facing the French in battle. Correspondingly with the tactical developments, many guerrillas were organized into regi-ments, and uniformed to mark their status as regular troops – usually this was just a simple brown uniform jacket and a black top hat, with more elaborate hussar-style uniforms for the light cavalry.

---

28   Charles J. Esdaile, *Fighting Napoleon: Guerillas, Bandits, and Adventurers in Spain 1808-1814* (New Haven: Yale University Press, 2004), p.39.

For the insurgency as a whole, the strategic objectives were to deny the French access to towns and villages, harass lines of communications, and, when coordinating efforts with regular armies, to cause enough damage to force the French to divert troops from the front lines. Guerrillas frequently targeted French outposts, but, in the absence of artillery, developed their own unique means of siege warfare with explosives and mining. Besides the standard tactics of ambushes and raids, the greatest value of the guerrillas was in preventing the establishment of French rule. Religious propaganda condemning the French as infidels for their disrespect of Spain's Catholic institutes was a crucial element in alienating the French occupiers, and many of Spain's clergy played an active role in leading the insurgency. Those suspected of supporting or even associating with the French were publicly denounced, or at worst, murdered, and such actions invariably deterred other civilians from supporting the French. Brandt relates a story about how a local magistrate he befriended at Monzón was assassinated in broad daylight before his family, guilty of performing his magisterial duties under French rule and joining the Polish Legionnaire in a guitar duet.[29] The effectiveness of such tactics is only attested to by what followed the magistrate's assassination:

> The clerk and the treasurer, with whom I had now to liaise for lack of a magistrate to issue the rations, both suddenly absconded to the country…In the space of the next twenty-four hours all the other inhabitants played the same trick or went into hiding. On the next day, which was market day, not one peasant appeared in town and only a few women and children could be seen in the streets. Things were looking decidedly sinister…[30]

If the Peninsular War was one of the keystones of the history of guerrilla warfare, it was also the birthplace and testing ground of many counter-insurgency strategies and tactics. For an army whose strength was its prowess in conventional warfare, the fluid and complex nature of guerrilla warfare was an unfamiliar world to the Empire's military strategists.

In his work 'The Centurions vs the Hydra: French Counterinsurgency in the Peninsular War (1808-1812)' Major Philippe Gennequin establishes the difference between the terms 'counter-guerrilla' and 'counter-insurgency':

> [C]ounter-guerrilla will be used to define military operations conducted to attack the insurgency directly. And counterinsurgency will be understood as the combination of all instruments of war to break the link between the insurgency and the population. In a nutshell, the two concepts can be differentiated through their application: counter-guerrilla aims at the enemy, whereas counterinsurgency targets the population.[31]

---

29   Brandt, *In the Legions of Napoleon*, p.70.
30   Brandt, *In the Legions of Napoleon*, p.71.
31   Philippe Gennequin, 'The Centurions vs the Hydra: French Counterinsurgency in the Peninsular War (1808-1812)', U.S. Army Command and General Staff College (2011) <https://apps.dtic.mil/dtic/tr/fulltext/u2/a547277.pdf> accessed 29 December 2021. p.4.

In some ways the distinction between the two mirrors the differences between strategy and tactics. Counter-guerrilla operations form one part of a larger counterinsurgency strategy, which often involves simultaneous administrative efforts, varying on the objectives of the occupation force. In the case of the First French Empire, the goal of its counterinsurgency efforts was to pacify the Spanish provinces to allow for the establishment of local governments loyal to the Josephian regime.

All French commanders in the Armée d'Espagne struggled with the guerrilla war, and, with the exception of Soult and Suchet, nearly all were miserably unsuccessful at defeating the guerrillas. It is no surprise that many French commanders failed at counterinsurgency. Left to their own devices by Napoleon's creation of military governments under their charges, many of these French generals simply lacked the ingenuity and experience needed to provide leadership over all aspects of counterinsurgency – economic, political, social, and military – in the region under their charge, and failed to understand their opposition. French authorities were quick to place the causes of the Spanish insurgency on an unwillingness to accept the 'progressive' and enlightened Josephian regime by a largely backwards population whose motivations were simplified to religious fanaticism. Religious influence was only a small factor amidst the sea of reasons that drove ordinary civilians to risk their lives and join a war of brutality and hardship. The guerrilla war in Spain was a complicated affair, and motivations for resistance differed for every individual, but its root causes can be generalized as thus:

- The flames of rebellion had existed in both Spain and her overseas colonies for some time, due to discontent against the Bourbon monarchy due to its corruption and inability to stop Spain's geopolitical decline and flagging economy.
- Opportunities for personal gain arose amidst the disorder and chaos of war.
- The invasion and occupation of Spain by a foreign force and the overthrow of Spain's traditional rulers, the Bourbon monarchy, left a power vacuum in many regions.
- The strain of an invading army which lived off of the land broke the resources of an already-impoverished Spanish population
- The deprivations, abuses, and atrocities inflicted upon Spanish civilians by French troops.

A successful counterinsurgency strategy needed to address all of the following, and Suchet was able to do just that. Suchet was successful because of his adoption of a successful counterinsurgency programme in its entirety to cover all the key aspects of counterinsurgency, not just counter-guerrilla warfare. Against the difficulties posed by the new challenge of guerrilla warfare Suchet rose above his peers through the implementation of a counterinsurgency programme which effectively eliminated popular resistance from Aragon. His administration of Aragon was as close as Napoleon's Empire ever got to establishing full regional control over any part of Spain. While the neighbouring provinces of Navarre, Castille, and Catalonia were flaming with rebellion, Aragon's French administration managed to cleverly utilize limited resources to successfully pacify the province. Suchet's studies in business and administration back in his youth undoubtedly provided him with the skills and knowledge necessary to develop a counterinsurgency programme which addressed not just the military aspect, but the political and economic aspects as well.

Counter-Guerrilla Warfare

The first part of Suchet's counterinsurgency programme was counter-guerrilla tactics, the purely military aspect. From 1809-1810, Suchet possessed roughly some 25-30,000 men to act as both a field army and internal security force with which to control a province of around 560,000 people and 48,000 square miles.[32] This was well above Gennequin's recommended ratio of 25 counter-insurgent soldiers for every 1,000 locals.[33] As Suchet's 1809 operations would prove, military success against the guerrillas was the result of micro-management, careful planning, leadership, and tactical innovations. At the tactical level of Suchet's counter-guerrilla operations were mobile 'flying columns.' They were exactly as their name describes them – highly mobile ad-hoc formations, typically consisting of cavalry, infantry, and light artillery. To compensate for his thinly-stretched units, Suchet used mobility as a force multiplier, so that a smaller, agile formation could cover more ground. Suchet's mobile columns numbered anywhere from a hundred to a few thousand men, depending on the mission. Flying columns had long been a feature of Napoleonic French armies as a means to rapidly secure objectives, and Suchet had employed them early in his career in the War of the Second Coalition.

Flying columns in the Peninsular had to be well organized and well-led; small and quick enough to match the guerrillas in speed, but still bring substantially more firepower than the enemy. When marching along the winding roads which stretched through the rocky hills of Aragon, a flying column was typically screened by a group of hussars, followed by the main body of infantry and artillery. At the rear of the column was a troop of pack mules, laden with supplies for 10 days and doubling as transports for the wounded.[34] This last purpose was significant for morale, as previously, wounded and stragglers from French columns were often simply left behind to be murdered by guerrillas once the column had passed. At an operational level, multiple flying columns often conducted joint efforts to target and destroy a single guerrilla band–search and destroy missions. Destroying a guerrilla base or retaliation against villages suspected of harbouring guerrillas was not enough – new bases could always be established, and atrocities against Spanish civilians only furthered local support for the guerrillas. The objective of such missions was usually the complete annihilation of a guerrilla band through encirclement or a breakthrough assault followed by a relentless pursuit. Such operations were cumbersome and required intricate planning for the movement and coordination of different mobile columns operating on multiple axes, converging from different points. Without the luxury of modern telephones or radios, mobile columns had little way of instant communication with each other to coordinate reactions to situational changes. Operations were made even more difficult if the columns belonged to different regional commanders. And, more often than not, the guerrilla bands often scattered and escaped the French 'search and destroy' missions. The long pursuits easily exhausted the men and frayed their morale, often for little to no results to make them worthwhile. What these missions did do was scatter the guerrillas for long enough to buy

---

32   Alexander, *Rod of Iron*, p.56. Aragon had numbered around 620,000 people pre-war, but by the time Suchet consolidated his hold in 1809, the population had decreased by at least 10 percent.

33   Gennequin, 'The Centurions vs the Hydra', p.99.

34   Gennequin, 'The Centurions vs the Hydra', p.65.

time for the establishment of French rule and/or destroy the guerrilla bases of operation. When a guerrilla base was captured, its defences were destroyed and supplies looted. French soldiers tore apart the walls of villages suspected of harbouring guerrillas, for the guerrillas were known to wall up their stockpiles of weapons and supplies.

Suchet was an opportunist in victory, squeezing out every last drop of advantage from his successes by keeping the momentum going and quickly moving on to take other targets. The same was for guerrilla warfare. In the aftermath of a battlefield victory or a siege, Suchet capitalized on the immediate damage his conventional victory may have had on guerrilla forces by immediately engaging in counter-guerrilla offensive in the hopes of catching the guerrillas while they were still stunned and wrong-footed by the impressive speed of his conventional victories.

Supporting the mobile columns and key to any occupation force was the establishment of garrisons both small and large all across Aragon. Large garrisons were posted at key urban areas such as Zaragoza, Alcañiz, and Huesca, later Lérida and Tortosa, turning those cities into French strongholds. Suchet went to great lengths to ensure that the garrisons were up to strength and well supplied.[35] The imposing presence of a large body of French troops ensured the security of *afrecescados* and acted as a 'muscle' for the establishment of French administration. Beyond simply holding the cities, the garrisons also coordinated with mobile columns to launch offensive operations against the guerrillas and secured the lines of communications, allowing for a safer movement of supply convoys. While this strategy of using strongholds tied down a large number of Suchet's troops, it was much more effective in consolidating French gains in the long term in comparison to other provinces where garrisons were much more dispersed. At a strategic level Suchet moved step by step, securing an area and garrisoning it before advancing to attack the next objective. The effectiveness of such a strategy was in no small part due to Suchet's incredible skill in conducting successful operations with a reduced field force.

The paradox of occupation was that larger garrisons provided more security and could partake in offensive actions, but required large amounts of supplies. On the other hand, smaller garrisons scattered throughout the land (in Aragon typically 50-200 men) freed up more troops for campaign use and consumed less supplies in a single region, but were tempting targets for guerrilla bands and could do little on their own until relieved. The main strategic difference between the two was as such: small garrisons dispersed across towns and villages were extremely useful in security duties and asserting French control over wide areas in a province where the main font of resistance had already been broken by counter-guerrilla operations. The dilemma of small or large garrisons was something that would haunt French commanders in Aragon as the guerrilla war went on, an issue whose benefits and detractions are further explored in later chapters.

Suchet used smaller garrisons to secure key points in rural areas. Numerous blockhouses were constructed along French lines of communication all throughout the Peninsula. The blockhouse was an enclosed polygonal building (often square, but some had more sides to offer a better field of fire), that stood anywhere from one to three stories tall, and was

---

35   Gennequin, 'The Centurions vs the Hydra', p.57.

typically made of wood or masonry.[36] But in most small-town garrisons, existing buildings deemed suitable for defence, such as castles, churches, or monasteries, were repurposed to create a fortified compound. The prevalence and tactical importance of churches as a part of the garrison system was not lost on French officers. Nearly every Spanish town and village had one of these large, towering structures, perfect for placing sentries, who used the church bells as an effective alarm system.[37] Time and time again throughout the Peninsular, a few dozen gendarmes and infantrymen hunkered down in their fortified posts to repulse attacks by hundreds of guerrillas. The tactical weaknesses of this system were that these large and easily defensible buildings were rarely isolated within the town, and as such, it was easy for the guerrillas to fortify the neighbouring houses to fully blockade the garrisons. The roofs of these buildings were a target for the guerrillas, whose favourite, but usually unsuccessful, tactic was to set the roof on fire.

The threat posed by guerrillas prompted unique innovations at the small-unit level, especially with ordnance. Mobile columns preferred the 4 and 8-pounder guns of the old Gribeauval System than the heavier 6 and 12-pounder field guns of the Year XI System implemented in 1803, for the lighter Gribeauval guns were easier to transport on the poor Spanish roads.[38] French artillerymen also experimented with portable artillery pieces that could be disassembled and carried on several pack animals and quickly reassembled for rapid action. Howitzers proved to be especially useful in counter-guerrilla warfare, as their elevated range allowed them to bombard guerrilla positions in hills and mountains.[39] The French gendarmes made good use of wall guns in defending their isolated outposts against guerrillas. The wall gun (*fusil de rempart*, also known as an amusette) was an oversized musket hurling a terrifying one-inch calibre lead ball, typically mounted on ramparts. Its effective range of 250 yards made it an effective sniping weapon.[40] Such wall guns were sometimes concealed in French wagons in convoys, giving guerrillas the impression of a vulnerable soft target, only to reveal a nasty surprise in an ambush.

As for cavalry, only six percent of the terrain in Aragon was deemed ideal for textbook cavalry charges, but this did not restrict the use of cavalry for other means.[41] III Corps' cavalry component had no dragoon regiment until 1811, surprising considering the predominance of dragoons in French armies of the Peninsular War. Suchet's 4e Hussards filled the role of an all-purpose cavalry. Their mobility made them effective in engaging in traditional light cavalry duties – scouting, patrolling, and pursuing – but they also learned to fight like dragoons, dismounted with carbines in skirmish order. Trumpet-call orders were simplified to adjust to the spontaneity of guerrilla warfare. Even the 13e Cuirassiers – armoured battle cavalry typically held in reserve for smashing the enemy line on the field of glory – found a place in counter-guerrilla warfare. Suchet did not have the luxury of affording functional distinctions amongst his mounted units and the cuirassiers were thrust into the heart of

---

36   Jean-Denis G.G. Lepage, *French Fortifications 1715-1815: An Illustrated History* (Jefferson: McFarland & Company, 2009), p.168.

37   Gennequin, 'The Centurions vs the Hydra', p.64.

38   John R. Elting, *Swords Around a Throne* (New York: The Free Press, 1988), p.262.

39   Gennequin, 'The Centurions vs the Hydra', p.56.

40   Elting, *Swords Around a Throne*, p.489.

41   Gennequin, 'The Centurions vs the Hydra', p.50.

counter-guerrilla warfare. True to their status as elite troopers, they adapted well to fighting in mobile columns, though it caused heavy attrition in their ranks. Counter-guerrilla operations also made Suchet's soldiers adept at night fighting, something that would greatly aid Suchet in his siege operations. Out of this *'petite guerre'* emerged a new breed of junior officers – men such as Robichon of the 13e Cuirassiers, Brandt of the 2e Vistule, Lecomte of the 14e Ligne, Foison and Martin of the Gendarmes, and Desbouefs of the 81e Ligne just to name a few – aggressive, determined, courageous, and extremely adept at small-unit tactics, for counter-guerrilla warfare was not for the weak of heart.[42] Desbouefs remarked:

> The Spanish war was an excellent school for the French officers. They were charged with commanding garrisons and detachments on the march, in a country where fighting was daily, where the eye of the enemy followed them everywhere, where the smallest negligence was often paid for with one's life. They performed manoeuvres that were not in the ordinance and acquired knowledge that only experience can teach.[43]

Suchet kept a close and fond eye on these prized junior officers, fully knowing that low-level leadership skills were the heart of successful mobile columns or garrison posts. Crucial to any counter-guerrilla operation was intelligence, information on the movements and whereabouts of the guerrillas. This could be acquired by good scouting, but it was far easier to come by through spies and sympathetic peasants. At a local level, Spanish supporters of the French regime rendered invaluable services to French counterinsurgency efforts as translators and guides. As acceptance of French control over Aragon grew, so did Suchet's intelligence network. Local French commanders often relied on bribing Spanish guerrillas to spy, defect, or even assassinate guerrilla leaders. Some even offered guerrilla leaders generous rewards to entice them to lay down their arms and even join the French administration, though the effectiveness of bribery was very much contingent on the perception of French power.

As for the Spanish efforts at propaganda, well, it was a game two could play. Suchet dedicated immense energy to propaganda efforts and the conquest of the mind. He espoused the deeds of his forces and administration, while widely publicizing crimes by insurgents committed against the Aragonese. It helped that Suchet heavily censored the press, though contraband Spanish newspapers still circulated and even French troops found them useful for news on the rest of Europe, as the Spanish papers were faster than the French ones.[44] The guerrillas were depicted as little more than bandits and criminals in French-run newspapers. The deprivation and hardships brought on by conflict were skilfully transposed onto the guerrillas, while the good behaviour of his troops and tangible benefits of French administrative policies naturally served to reinforce that point and undermine guerrilla libel against Suchet. There were even times when Aragonese would actively take up arms

---

42   Gennequin, 'The Centurions vs the Hydra' p.62. The 81e Ligne would enter Suchet's command later in the war.

43   Marc Desbouefs, *Souvenirs du capitaine Desboeufs: les étapes d'un soldat de l'Empire (1800-1815)* (Paris: Alphonse Picard et Fils, 1901), p.174.

44   Brandt, *In the Legions of Napoleon*, p.96.

against the guerrillas. Surprisingly, these incidents were not rare. They occurred not out of a love for the French, but out of spite against the excesses of the desperate guerrillas, who would steal supplies and forcibly recruit men from villages.

So successful was his propaganda campaign against the guerrillas that in March of 1810, Suchet was able to recruit enough locals passionate about the French cause to organize two companies of Aragonese Gendarmes, totalling around 150 men, specifically for counter-insurgency purposes, placed under the command of Pedro Garcés de Marcilla, Barón de Andilla. Andilla was a former Spanish Army officer, as were many of the Aragonese Gendarme officers. The Aragonese Gendarmes were tough men, employed specifically for counter-insurgency purposes and prisoner escort duty. Each gendarme had their hand tattooed so they could be easily caught if they deserted. They would be followed in 1811 by four companies of Aragonese Fusiliers. While this small and often unreliable group of several hundred men was all that Suchet managed to raise in terms of militarized collaborationist forces, French regional commanders in other provinces could only dream of such cooperation from the local populace, and it speaks for the moderate effectiveness of Suchet's counterinsurgency policies as a whole.[45]

Breaking the Cycle of Violence

It was one thing to defeat the guerrillas militarily through counter-guerrilla operations, but another to eradicate them completely. The key to this was in separating the guerrillas from the Spanish population to deprive the guerrillas of manpower, resources, and shelter, and to do this, Suchet had to quell the popular insurgency. One of the main reasons why the Spanish population was rising up against the French was not because of some overarching love for the monarchy or country, but simply because the French soldiers behaved atrociously towards Spanish civilians. At the root of this problem was the French inclination to forage and live off of the land, a method which increased their military effectiveness but garnered them few friends among the locals. III Corps troops had behaved no differently than other French units and saw the entire country as open for forage and plunder. Such a policy was much less viable in impoverished Eastern Spain than it may have been in the rich farmlands of the Rhine, and as such, the impacts of the French practice of living off the land greatly impacted an already-starving population. The guerrilla war also began to breed a deadly cycle of violence. Frustrated at the exhaustive and attritional nature of the guerrilla war, French soldiers looted and burned villages accused of harbouring guerrillas or murdering French soldiers, their inhabitants shot indiscriminately. In turn, more Spanish were incentivised to join or aid the guerrillas out of sheer outrage at French excesses and atrocities.

Suchet realized that he first had to reign in his men, for all of the other elements of his counterinsurgency programme would be meaningless if the cycle of violence between his troops and the Spanish civilians continued. The foraging and confiscations which the Grande Armée so excelled at were incompatible with Suchet's goals. The practice was banned, and

---

45   Rollet, 'Conqueror and Administrator', p.25.

all supplies requisitioned from locals were to be paid for in cash. Any complaints of miscon-
duct were subject to investigation. Given the haphazard nature of soldiers' salaries, looting
had become a source of income for many soldiers. To address the problem from all ends,
Suchet quickly enacted reforms to the III Corps finances and created bakery and butchery
departments to ensure that his men would want for nothing. Suchet was always meticulous
in ensuring that he had enough reserve supplies stored up to prosecute a siege, and, at least
compared to other French commanders, was timely with his soldier's pay.

Discipline was tightened in III Corps, and those who committed crimes against Spanish
civilians were dealt with harshly, such that some soldiers even felt that their own officers
were too quick to side with Spanish civilians in a dispute![46] Von Brandt relates an incident where a cuirassier had been sentenced to be executed for looting. *Colonel* d'Aigremont
evidently did not see eye to eye with Suchet and saw it fitting enough to put the thief before
a firing squad loaded with only blanks, however, the man died simply from shock the
moment the squad 'fired'![47] Nonetheless, the men of III Corps soon found that the ban on
their 'freedom' to tread all over the Spanish citizenry reaped great rewards in the form of
not having to watch every window for a sharpshooter and every alleyway for an assailant.
Suchet successfully ended the violent excesses of his troops, which allowed them to conduct
operations freely without the strain of a popular insurgency, and showed the Aragonese that
they could live peacefully and prosper under French rule.

However, this is not to say that Suchet was all carrots and flowers. Suchet's work in
breaking the cycle of violence was more pragmatic than humanitarian, for Suchet was quite
capable of utilizing calculated violence, as seen in his targeted bombardment of civilians at
Lérida and the sack of Tarragona (though these occurred in operations outside of Aragon).
Woe to those who continued to resist French rule. In the aftermath of Belchite, a proclamation was issued granting full amnesty for any guerrilla who surrendered and returned
home. Those who failed to heed the call had their property confiscated and, if captured,
would be immediately executed. Non-violent resistance was dealt with harshly as well, and
by the end of the year, dozens of rabble-rousers and others who spoke out against Suchet's
regime had been deported to prisons in France. Several people who had mocked some guerrilla deserters were immediately arrested – four were deported to French imprisonment, and
two were even shot on Suchet's orders![48] But what set Suchet apart from all the other French
commanders who similarly employed summary executions, reprisals, burning of villages,
and other terror tactics in a frustrated attempt to deal with the guerrillas was that Suchet
offered the Aragonese an appealing package of order and peace under a stable administration as a viable alternative to resistance and death.

---

46 Jacques-Abraham Graindor, *Mémoires de la Guerre d'Espagne 1808-1814* (Éguzon: Points d'ancrage,
    2002), p.78.
47 Brandt, *In the Legions of Napoleon*, p.89.
48 Alexander, *Rod of Iron*, p.54.

Previous Administration

In order to understand the administrative and economic aspects of Suchet's counterinsurgency policies, it is necessary to examine the situation of the province of Aragon prior to Suchet assuming command. The province of Aragon was once the Kingdom of Aragon, and played a key role in unifying the many kingdoms of the Iberian Peninsula to form modern Spain. Like all the other Spanish provinces, it had a unique culture and history derived from its time as an independent kingdom. Aragon was broken up into 13 administrative districts, known as *corregimientos*: Tarrazona, Borja, Calataud, Daroca, Albarracin, Teruel, Alcañiz, Benavarre, Barbastro, Huesca, Jaca, Cincovillas, and Zaragoza. Each was managed by a magistrate known as a *corregidor*, who was responsible for most tax duties, while towns were governed by an *alcalde*.

The battles of 1808-1809 had left Aragon impoverished and in utter financial ruin. As the French stranglehold in the province tightened, local officials had carted away three million francs to Seville and many had deemed it wise to flee with their valuables. Never wealthy to start off with, the war had devastated the economic situation in Aragon. Aragon had little in the way of industry and its economy was agriculturally based. About half of farmland was dedicated to wheat and grass crops, while the other was used for fruit, vegetables, or livestock grazing.[49] Despite the predominance of agriculture, harvests yielded little in the unforgiving terrain, at best no more than 25 percent of the seeds that were laid, and farming techniques were noted to be inefficient.

Prior to the creation of Suchet's military government, Aragon was managed by the Josephian government, headed in Aragon by one of Joseph's intendants, Luíz Menche. Authority in Aragon was split between Joseph's Royal Administration, mostly made up of former Bourbon officials, and administrators and commanders of III Corps. In theory the two sectors worked together under one government, with the Spanish handling civilian affairs and the French military. The expectation had been that the regional government would supply III Corps and provide auxiliaries and a police force, however, the Spanish bureaucrats were reluctant to support an occupation force and did little to provide for French troops.[50] Joseph's bureaucrats aimed to revitalize the economy and govern Aragon, while the priority for the French administrators was to keep III Corps supplied through local resources, so both goals ended up competing with each other for limited resources. Not surprisingly, the government of Aragon quickly split along these two factions and a power struggle broke out between the Spanish bureaucrats of Joseph's regime and Imperial French administrators. It was a one-sided affair though, for the existence of the Josephian government was wholly dependent on the security provided by III Corps, and the tenuous communications between Madrid and Zaragoza meant that Joseph's bureaucrats were often without policies or instructions from Madrid. Junot had ended the arguments by imposing martial law to wrest away the last bits of government power into the hands of the French military, in spite of his orders to cooperate with the Spanish government.

---

49   Alexander, *Rod of Iron*, p.56.
50   Alexander, *Rod of Iron*, p.50.

Fortunately for Suchet, by the time he had crushed Blake and was afforded the time to dabble in administrative duties, the situation had improved. Joseph had given Suchet official control over the entirety of Aragon, which entailed the destruction of Menche's floundering bureaucracy, but Joseph's well-placed trust would be richly rewarded.[51] Despite having to clean up the messy aftermath of the imploded Royal Administration and Junot's tactless power grab, Suchet managed to begin the implementation of his new administrative ideas and counterinsurgency policies as part of the royal administration, later on his own by leading the Second Military Government as Governor of Aragon. On 9 February, 1810, Suchet received a decree from Napoleon dated 11 January, which established the Second Military Government in Aragon, of which Suchet was governor. Impatient with the lack of progress and victories in the Peninsular War, Napoleon had decided to shake up governmental organization in Spain with the establishment of military governments and viceroyalties in several Spanish provinces; Aragon, Catalonia, Navarre, and Andalusia, to name a few. The military governments were independent from Joseph's regime, and answered only to Napoleon. For Suchet, this meant that his authority was greatly expanded with his new position as the Military Governor of Aragon. The creation of the Second Military Government was in some ways symbolic, as Joseph had already given Suchet virtual *carte blanche* over affairs in Aragon. While this gave Suchet and his fellow military governors a greater freedom of movement in achieving local successes, the order was detrimental to French grand strategy in Spain, for they were now without centralized leadership. The consequence of stripping Joseph of his authority was that now French-occupied Spain was essentially ruled by various warlords who jealously guarded their armies and territories instead of a single commander-in-chief who had the authority to coordinate operations between multiple corps.

Suchet's Governance

Many Spanish, particularly those in the educated middle and upper classes, welcomed the Josephian government as bringing an era of enlightenment ideas to a Spain they believed had been weakened by the ineptitude of the Bourbon Monarchy and had fallen behind its continental neighbours. Those who supported the Josephian administration, throwing their lot in with their French at risk to their own lives and that of their families, were known as *afrancesados*, (meaning 'the Frenchified') and mostly concentrated in urban areas.[52]

For Suchet, it was these people who became the heart of his government, for the *afrancesados* who would fill the ranks of native bureaucrats and administrators were more likely to be listened to than any French official by the Aragonese people. Suchet correctly surmised that the Aragonese would be more willing to swallow rule under their fellow Aragonese than from the foreign invaders. The basis of Suchet's administration was the creation of a primarily Aragonese bureaucracy under minimal French supervision, which kept most

---

51   Alexander, *Rod of Iron*, p.50.
52   Max Boot, *Invisible Armies* (New York: Liveright Publishing Corporation, 2013), p.85.

elements of the former Spanish government and allowed a degree of self-governance.[53] While such a policy may seem like common sense for occupational forces today, it was a fairly novel concept at the time. Supporting the Aragonese bureaucracy was a team of around 200 French civilian and military officials, headed by a French-born Spaniard named Francois Larreguy (Francisco Larregui) who served as Secretary General. Utilizing the framework of existing systems of governance allowed Suchet to focus his main efforts on military campaigns, rather than on state-building.

Suchet focused on gaining the support of the prominent Aragonese elite, who could more easily command the respect of the general populace and potentially spark a bandwagon movement. But the dynamic between French occupation forces and *afrancesados* was often weak, and, at first, Suchet struggled greatly in utilizing the support of the *afrancesados* effectively and finding enough people to fill the ranks of his administration. Suchet complained that 'there are hardly any of them who want to serve us.'[54] It was no surprise that few wished to do so. When French forces were unable to provide effective protection for the *afrancesados*, support for the Imperial administration inevitably dropped, as many of those who supported it went into hiding for fear of retaliation. After the French captured a town, the *afrancesados* would come out to greet the French and in turn many were appointed as local administrators. However, the French forces would soon depart elsewhere, and the French-appointed mayor and bureaucrats suddenly had no one to back their decrees, and found themselves at the mercy of the guerrillas, who fled at French approach and returned at their departure. This was the reason why the Royal Administration failed at a local level, for all of their appointed officials were either kidnapped or murdered. It was only after Blake's defeat at Belchite that the French could gradually provide soldiers to protect local officials by establishing small garrisons to perform security duties.

The lack of competent officials was solved by the success of Suchet's other counterinsurgency initiatives. The gradual stabilization of Aragon convinced many of the wealthy Aragonese who had initially fled to return, at which Suchet greeted them by returning their confiscated property, and those hesitant to join hands with Suchet eventually did so, won over by his well-meaning policies or for a lack of choice thanks to French military victories.[55] The image that Suchet carefully cultivated, that government employees would not so much be working for the French as for the good of the Aragonese people, convinced many competent and skilled officials who had worked to resist occupation to seek employment with the new administration. Mariano Domínguez, who had managed Spanish supplies in the Siege of Zaragoza as Palafox's commissariat officer and was knowledgeable on Aragon's resources, was appointed as director of the police, a task he proved to be effective at. Others included the Spanish judge José Villa y Torre, who served as head of the Royal Court of Justice. The cadre of government officials tasked with leading and managing the province was selectively hand-picked for their merits and skills by Suchet himself.

---

53   Carlos Franco de Espés, 'La Administración Francesa en Aragon: El gobierno de mariscal Suchet, 1809-1813', *Revista de historia Jéronimo Zurita*. 91 (2016), p.100.
54   Suchet to Clarke, 7 June 1809, cited in Alexander, *Rod of Iron*, p.51.
55   Suchet, *Memoirs of the War in Spain*, Vol.I, p.325.

Despite his Republican beliefs, Governor-General Suchet had something of a flair for the grandeur and splendour of royalty, and built himself a court, ruling 'as if he were a king by proxy'.[56] Numerous banquets and balls were held, and in July of 1810, Suchet ordered the construction of a garden in the archbishop's palace, completed on 1 August, just in time for Honorine to enjoy upon her arrival in Zaragoza the following day.[57] In addition to satisfying Suchet's extravagant tastes, these lavish displays and social events help ease the citizens of Zaragoza back into the civilian life they once enjoyed prior to the war. Honorine ushered in a softer, more personal side to Suchet's administration, as a young socialite who could connect with the people. When she became pregnant in 1811, she travelled back to France in April on a custom-built Sedan chair and a massive escort described as a 'small army' that existed solely for the purpose of protecting Honorine and her unborn daughter Louise-Honorine Suchet, an honour that befit the wife of the Governor-General.[58]

Placating the Population

The genius of Suchet's counterinsurgency programme was that all it asked of the average Aragonese was not so much to actively support the French regime – that would be done by *afrancesados* and grow in time as the long-term benefits of Suchet's policies took hold – but simply to submit to French rule and not actively take up arms against the French. Suchet set realistic expectations from the start: he did not expect to endear himself to the Aragonese nor did he demand widespread support. All he had to do was portray submission to French authority as a better alternative to resistance, and ensure that French authority was acceptable enough. Suchet took the utmost care to ensure that his regime did not attempt to impose too much onto the daily lives of the Aragonese. Suchet's objectives necessitated measures that were tyrannical enough, but whenever it could be helped, Suchet was inclined not to burden the Aragonese with the hallmarks of heavy-handed foreign occupation. All of Suchet's policies, from recruiting Aragonese to government posts, retaining existing laws and bureaucratic systems, and emphasizing Aragonese culture, served to subvert expectations that the occupation force would impose its own beliefs onto the Aragonese and created the illusion that all Suchet's regime was doing was returning self-governance to Aragon, to be as it had once been as a proud and powerful independent kingdom, thereby giving his government a semblance of legitimacy.

To that end, Suchet incorporated a tactful understanding of Aragonese culture into his policies. Suchet took the effort to educate himself on the particular history and customs of Aragon, as distinct from the rest of Spain. Armed with that knowledge, Suchet painted himself as a contrast to the cumbersome and inefficient previous administrations, French and Spanish alike, and as an enabler of Aragonese independence and exceptionalism. Non-Aragonese were barred from civil service positions, for both the Bourbon and Josephian government had employed officials from Madrid to govern Aragon, something that had prickled the pride of the Aragonese. Seemingly minor actions, such as preventing

---

56   Fuertes, *La ocupación francesa de Zaragoza*, p.68.
57   Fuertes, *La ocupación francesa de Zaragoza*, p.83.
58   Fuertes, *La ocupación francesa de Zaragoza*, p.119.

the removal of church treasures from the Notre Dame du Pilar church in Zaragoza to Madrid further impressed upon the Aragonese that the French administration had the interests of the people in mind as well. Suchet ordered the creation of the 'Academy of the Friends of the Province of Aragon', an institute overseeing cultural development and preservation, and symbolically made himself Director of the Institute. Higher education programs were revived or created, for example, a school of arts and mathematics for 150 students. Suchet's emphasis on Aragon's uniqueness had twofold gains – it served to both create the image that his regime was culturally sensitive, and to alienate Aragon from the rest of Spain and the war for its independence. The latter theme appealed heavily to the Aragonese rivalry with Catalans, something which even resulted in outright violence during the war. The rich theatre scene in Zaragoza was also one way for Suchet to access the population, and on days meaningful to the French Empire (news of the victories at Wagram and Ocaña, the anniversary of Napoleon's coronation), theatre tickets were free.[59]

The Church

In addressing matters of culture, it was of the utmost importance that Suchet also addressed the role of the Catholic church in promoting the insurgency, and he likewise conducted this task with tact. In the deeply Catholic nation of Spain, the clergy was a cornerstone of society and culture, and thus held immense power, especially over the religious peasantry. Many priests and monks joined guerrilla groups against the French invaders, and the Zaragoza monks became famed for their fierce resistance in the siege of the city. The Revolution, and then Napoleon, had damaged Catholicism in France and Europe. Not only did Napoleon imprison Pope Pius VII, but he also ordered the abolishment of the Inquisition and all religious orders in Spain, as well as the confiscation of Church property, which led several thousand unemployed and disgruntled monks available to actively resist the French occupation.

Suchet realized the power of the Spanish church which the French had neglected and abused, and extended an offer of cooperation. All the priests needed to do was preach peace and order in their sermons, without necessarily becoming mouthpieces of the military government as someone less tactful than Suchet may have ordered. In exchange, Suchet would reconstruct the churches destroyed in the war, guarantee a regular salary for clergymen, and protect the church, though the nationalized church property remained under his control in a futile attempt to squeeze a few more drops of cash by selling it.[60] Suchet's astute offer of a neutral position proved to be easier to swallow than a demand for full support, and the policy did much to quell the popular insurgency. In fact, one of the first of the prominent Aragonese to join Suchet was the Bishop of Zaragoza, Miguel de Santander, who was renowned for his oratory skills and served Suchet well in espousing the need for peace. The two would become friends, collaborating in carefully selecting clergy whom they trusted would follow Suchet's mandates. However, any priest who called for resistance against the French faced deportation to a prison in France. Suchet himself attempted to ease

59   Fuertes, *La ocupación francesa de Zaragoza*, p.215.
60   Rollet, 'Conqueror and Administrator', p.11.

tensions by participating in a public ceremony on 12 October, 1809, dedicated to the Virgen del Pilar, an act which surprised and pleased many Spanish.[61]

An odd way the power of the church in Aragon was used to aid the French was in overcoming the language barrier. In his survey of Aragon, Suchet remarked that,

> Although there existed no colleges, nor public schools, teachers of Latin were to be met with in every direction; the poorest workman could easily, and at a cheap rate, procure his children a knowledge of that language, which was sufficient for the admission into a convent of monks. This mode of education is evidently owing to the wealth and preponderating influence of the clergy.[62]

While the influence of Catholicism in France had suffered during the Revolution, it was still very much prevalent, particularly in rural communities, and the allied nations of the Grand Duchy of Warsaw and the Kingdom of Italy were deeply Catholic. Many French, Polish, and Italian soldiers suddenly found their Latin education invaluable in communicating with the Aragonese, an all-too-important task in establishing a positive dynamic between occupier and occupied.

Despite Suchet's successful creation of a working relationship between the church and the French administration, many French officers and soldiers still held the Spanish clergy in deep suspicion, largely in part due to tales leading to monks as being linchpins of guerrilla and resistance movements and the legacy of the Inquisition. Brandt, his own prejudice heightened by his consumption of sensational novels such as *The Monk*, attempted to publicly expose misdeeds by the Spanish monks, whom he referred to as his 'sworn enemies.'[63]

Economic and Taxation Policy

Alongside a comprehensive administrative system was a robust economic policy designed to both exploit Aragon of its resources and revitalize the local economy. The dire economic state of Aragon could not be emphasized enough. The looting which followed the fall of Zaragoza is estimated to have robbed Aragon of at least 11 million reales, and in 1809 the French were able to collect just 600,000 reales in taxes. The war had deprived Aragon of over 10 percent of its taxable population, either dead, fled, or actively fighting the French.

French logistical policy in the Peninsula had been for the bulk of equipment and money to be sent from France. As an administrator, Suchet was quite content with this arrangement, for that meant most of the war effort was being funded by France, and Suchet only really needed to collect the taxes demanded by Joseph's government.[64] But the establishment of Suchet's military government changed that, and with his increased authority came greater responsibilities for Suchet. The decree of 11 January 1810 read in part:

---

61 Fuertes, *La ocupación francesa de Zaragoza*, p.96.
62 Suchet, *Memoirs of the War in Spain*, Vol.I, pp.307-308.
63 Brandt, *In the Legions of Napoleon*, p.103.
64 Suchet, *Memoirs of the War in Spain*, Vol.I, p.295.

[Y]ou should employ the revenues of the country, and even impose extraordinary contribution, if necessary, with a view to provide for the pay and subsistence of your corps d'armee, it being no longer in the power of France to defray these expenses… the country which you occupy, and which is possessed of abundant resources, must henceforth supply the wants of your troops.[65]

To the Emperor, Spain was a sideshow to his campaigns in Central Europe: the war in Spain needed to utilize as few resources as possible, and to that end, III Corps had to become self-sufficient. Napoleon correctly surmised that in spite of the Imperial coupon-clipping, the competent Suchet would somehow find the means to continue to supply his men. This entailed extracting an annual sum of 14 million kilograms of grain, 19,250 livestock, and 7,530,720 francs from an impoverished Aragon.[66]

In order to meet these demands, Suchet retained much of the existing tax system, but enacted numerous reforms upon it to reduce corruption and increase efficiency. Former state monopolies on certain goods such as salt, tobacco, gunpowder, and even playing-cards, were done away with, payment of taxes was permitted in goods useable by the army such as leather or food in lieu of specie to allow for flexibility and accommodation in payment, and those communities which paid their taxes on time were given tax breaks.[67] Suchet also streamlined and increased the efficiency of the old *condatoria*, the Spanish accountability office. Through strenuous efforts Suchet managed to collect enough grain to feed his troops, and he solved the livestock problem by sourcing them from France, funded by selling confiscated property.[68]

The entry of a massive entity into Aragon in the form of the French army brought untold hardship upon the Aragonese people, but Suchet saw potential in it as a new factor which could potentially shake up the economy. At a microeconomic level, one of Suchet's most simple, but effective, policies was the issuance of immediate pay to his troops every five days. This ingenious scheme had the double impact of raising morale among French soldiers and stimulating the local economy. Suchet was once an infantryman in the ranks himself: it may have been many years ago, but the habits of soldiers had changed little – pay was spent quickly for luxuries and necessities, and little was saved. After all, who knew what tomorrow would bring? Soldiers posted at garrisons blew their money in town, and the extravagant taxes the Aragonese paid found its way back into their pockets. Suchet wrote:

The inhabitants were soon convinced that the tax levied upon them was no more than an advance, which would shortly revert to their hands by bringing supplies to our cities and camps. Upon the same principle, every article manufactured in the country for the clothing or equipment of troops was carefully sought and paid for to the furnishers in ready money.[69]

---

65   Napoleon's decree of 11 January, in Suchet, *Memoirs of the War in Spain*, Vol.I, p.295.
66   Alexander, *Rod of Iron*, p.59.
67   Gennequin, 'The Centurions vs the Hydra', p.69.
68   Alexander, *Rod of Iron*, p.56. By January of 1810, the sheep population in Aragon had dropped from pre-war numbers of 1,900,000 to 100,000, and cattle from 100,000 to 8,000.
69   Suchet, *Memoirs of the War in Spain*, Vol.I, p.316.

Pay was not only issued promptly to soldiers but native civil employees as well. The punctual efficiency of the Suchet's military bureaucracy was in stark contrast to his corrupt Bourbon predecessors and even the ineffective Josephian administration.

Suchet's tax collection efforts were not without irregularities and hurdles. It was one thing for taxable income to be available, but another to actually be able to obtain it. The French often found themselves fighting the guerrillas just as much for the right to tax the locals as over territory. In his comprehensive analysis of the revenues of Aragon under the Second Military Government, historian Don Alexander deems that the single most important factor in the amount of taxes the French reeled in was simply their ability to collect them:

> Alone, the imperial administration could not collect specie or grain; therefore, Suchet had to employ powerful columns throughout the province in order to secure the resources required to support his corps. By these means, his administrative combination of Spanish bureaucrats working under the supervision of Bondurand and his handful of military administrators had largely accomplished Napoleon's primary directive of making the war support itself.[70]

Tax collection in pacified areas was done by French-appointed Spanish officials, but in areas where guerrillas were known to operate, French tax collectors were sent under the escort of a mobile column. The French had to fight hard to harvest the grain and collect the taxes, but when they were in force, this could be done successfully. Corruption was a rampant problem, so much so that Napoleon sent a direct letter to Suchet warning him that officers who requisitioned more than was needed to sustain their troops 'must be punished severely.'[71]

As Aragon was largely an agrarian economy, the income of most of its people was dependent on the harvest – money was most plentiful in the fall when the crops had been reaped and sold, while it was short in the summer.[72] Food shortages were a frequent problem, which Suchet had much difficulty addressing. This meant that Suchet sometimes was unable to collect enough revenue, especially in the summer of 1810, when most of his force was engaged outside of Aragon in blockading Tortosa. Even when the farmers reaped their harvest and got their taxable income in the autumn, Suchet's men were still in the field, now preparing to besiege Tortosa and thus unavailable for tax-collection duties. In those six months from July to January of 1810 the French managed to collect just 2,554,799 francs in taxes from Aragon, and Suchet's men had not been paid since March. But in the months after Tortosa fell, Suchet managed to collect 5,034,603 francs and give his troops their back pay as well as recoup the costs of the siege.[73] What history takes for irregularities could easily have become full-on challenges under the management of a lesser leader, but such potential challenges remained as just irregularities thanks to Suchet's incredible logistical feats and effective suppression of guerrillas. Suchet's prudent economic measures bore fruit

70   Alexander, *Rod of Iron*, p.101.
71   Letter 16702 to Suchet, 22 July 1810, from Bonaparte, *Correspondence de Napoléon*, Vol.XX, p.614.
72   Alexander, *Rod of Iron*, p.100.
73   Alexander, *Rod of Iron*, p.101.

when he became the only French commander to see an increase in revenue between 1810 and 1811 and achieve almost total financial independence from France.

Infrastructure

Yet if Suchet was squeezing Aragon for all its cash, how did he prevent the local economy from collapsing? The answer was through infrastructure projects and the forced marriage of the Aragonese economy to the French war effort. Suchet's economic revival and infrastructure policy was conducted with the goal of making Aragonese prosperity dependent on Suchet's administration and French occupation forces. Suchet's reconstruction of local infrastructure had a strong bearing of a military-industrial complex. A saltpetre factory in Zaragoza and gunpowder factory in Villafeliche were created to supply III Corps' munitions as well as reduce unemployment, though these projects and many of the repairs in Zaragoza had to be funded by Madrid due to a lack of extra revenue in Suchet's administration. Local industry was much encouraged, particularly when its output was usable by the army, as with textiles. Suchet's public works efforts occurred in the major cities of Aragon. The construction or refurbishment of hospitals in Teruel, Huesca, and Zaragoza serviced injured French soldiers and locals alike; the French medical system was one of the best infrastructure developments Suchet created in Aragon.[74] In the countryside, the decrepit Royal Canal, first constructed by the Holy Roman Emperor Charles V but later abandoned, was restored to both help irrigation of farmlands and expand water-based trade routes, which were taxed for revenue.[75] The construction of a road from Jaca to the French city of Oloron improved communications and supply routes with France, and facilitated the export of local goods. Suchet also dabbled in civil and non-military related infrastructure projects, almost making urban planning his pastime. However, Suchet's efforts to repair Zaragoza beyond fortifying the city were incomplete, especially in the outer suburbs, for in 1812, *Colonel* Jean-Baptiste Morrin would comment:

> The surroundings of Saragossa, so beautiful in the past, are now nothing but a desert, the beautiful olive groves which were the wealth of this country have all been cut down during the siege… everything has been destroyed… In the trips I have made to the overthrown districts, even though three years have passed since this memorable siege, I have still seen the frightening remains of the resistance put up by the besieged; some of the convents are filled with the skeletons of monks still wearing their habits.[76]

Ultimately, the nature of Suchet's economic development project meant that the French military machine became the number one customer of Aragonese food and material industries. Despite working to turn Aragon into a dependency of the French Empire and exploiting

---

74   Suchet, *Memoirs of the War in Spain*, Vol.I, p.324.
75   Gennequin, 'The Centurions vs the Hydra', p.71.
76   De Neef, *Devils, Daggers, and Death*, p.343-344.

its resources, Suchet appears to have held a genuine interest in the prosperity of the region under his control.

Assessment

It is difficult to discern how effective Suchet's policies, particularly his ventures in infrastructure and public relations, actually were, as most works on them are from the French perspective, with Suchet's own memoirs and communications as the primary source of information. Suchet's counter-guerrilla strategies did not achieve decisive victories or annihilate the guerrilla threat. Rather, it was Suchet's conventional military successes that weakened the guerrillas enough so that Aragon was no longer a safe haven. While a few guerrilla bands managed to elude French pursuit forces, they no longer enjoyed widespread support from a now largely apathetic Aragonese population. Suchet's tireless policies had the increasing effect of closely tying Aragonese interests to the success of the French administration and III Corps. By 1810, Suchet would succeed in all of his goals: virtually eradicating the guerrillas from Aragon, ensuring that III Corps was self-sufficient, and establishing French administration in the province.

Suchet's success in counter-guerrilla operations must be attributed to his quick understanding that the key to defeating the guerrillas was to ensure that the populace did not support them. While depriving guerrillas of local support is recognized today as one of the key principles of counterinsurgency warfare, Suchet had little in the way of guerrilla warfare theorists or books to teach him that, just his personal experiences and observations. To that end, Suchet's comprehensive counterinsurgency programme succeeded in alleviating the key grievances of the Aragonese against the French, while simultaneously reducing support for the guerrillas. Suchet was successful because he adopted a successful programme to cover all the key aspects of counterinsurgency, not just counter-guerrilla warfare as most French generals did.

The result of Suchet's successful counterinsurgency programme and governance was that III Corps became mostly self-sufficient and the guerrillas were constantly forced on the move and faced with decreasing local support. Deprived of a solid base of operations in Aragon, the major guerrilla bands were forced out of the province and made to establish their bases elsewhere. This created a unique situation in that, after 1809 until 1811, French counter-guerrilla operations rarely faced homegrown guerrillas from within Aragon, but, rather, dealt with guerrilla incursions from the neighbouring provinces of Navarre and Catalonia, though these groups often recruited from the Aragonese. For the early years of the war, Suchet's counterinsurgency programme sufficed in keeping these guerrillas at bay too, until the French were challenged by increasing Spanish tactical capabilities coupled with a decrease in the number and quality of French troops dedicated to counter-guerrilla warfare. Unable to continuously innovate beyond their initially successful methods, the French would ultimately lose control of Aragon in 1814. But for the most part, Suchet's counterinsurgency programme succeeded in internal pacification and maintained uncontested French control within Aragon for nearly two years between 1809 and 1811.

4

Campaign into Catalonia

Adventures in Valencia

As 1809 turned to 1810, the situation was looking far more auspicious for the French Armée d'Espagne. The ending of the war with Austria now allowed for French efforts to be concentrated in the Peninsula; while Napoleon himself would never again enter Spain, he was now in Paris where he could better coordinate the war effort. The Spanish autumn offensive to retake Madrid had ended in complete disaster at the Battle of Ocaña, where the 50,000-strong Spanish Ejército de La Mancha under Areizaga had been annihilated by a French army two-thirds its size led by the formidable *Maréchal* Jean-de-Dieu Soult.[1] A week later, another Spanish army under Duque del Parque was badly beaten at the Battle of Alba de Tormes. In Catalonia, Augereau had finally managed to take Girona, receiving its surrender on 12 December. Suchet, too, began the new year with fresh hopes. While Javier Mina, Perena, Villacampa, and other guerrillas still menaced Aragon, the counterinsurgency operations of late 1809 had done much to reduce their capabilities, and they were further suppressed by an influx of drafts mostly in the cavalry and regiments of the Légion de la Vistule that brought up III Corps' strength to 24,000 men (30,000 on paper).[2]

As his troops were mopping up the Navarrese guerrillas, Suchet paid a visit to Pamplona, to inspect the powerful French siege train parked there that would be available for him to employ in future operations. Just as Suchet was leaving Pamplona, he received new orders from Paris, relieving him of command of Navarre, for there was a new plan of campaign for III Corps: to capture Lower Catalonia. Suchet was to work in tandem with Augereau's VII Corps to capture either Lérida or Tortosa. However, no sooner had Suchet returned to Zaragoza was that order contradicted by another one on 15 February, this one from King Joseph, which ordered Suchet to rush Valencia and seize the city. Joseph and Soult had been attempting to capitalize on their victory at Ocaña by an offensive into Andalusia, and wished Suchet to support it by taking Valencia and finishing what Moncey had failed to do in 1808. Soult and Joseph assured Suchet that Valencia was heavily demoralized and that

---

1   Lipscombe, *The Peninsular War Atlas*, p.145. This is the same Areizaga who had commanded the Aragonese division in Blake's 2° Ejército; he had been promoted to command the Ejército de La Mancha.

2   Letter 16040 to the Prince de Neuchatel, 9 December 1809, from Bonaparte, *Correspondence de Napoléon 1er*, Vol. XX, p.65.

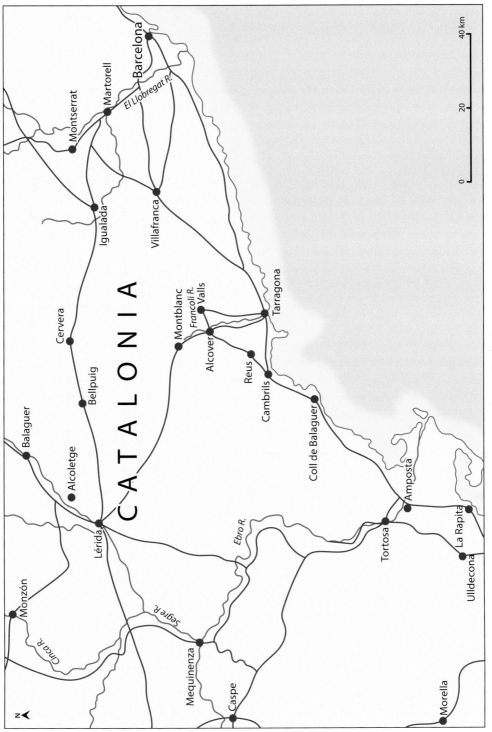

Lower Catalonia.

the city would surrender immediately – all Suchet had to do was to make a strong showing. Suchet's letters to Napoleon were intercepted by the Spanish and as a result, he was left to his own devices as to what to do.[3] Despite harbouring some doubts, Suchet decided that Joseph's orders took precedence.

The Valencia expedition was risky, for it required Suchet to make a foray deep into enemy-held territory with insecure lines of communications. Suchet had no siege artillery available to speak of, so his only real chance of success was that the city would give itself up as Joseph claimed, or that it was weak enough that it could be taken by storm. To clear the way for the expedition, Laval was sent with 3,000 infantry and 200 cavalry to secure the Zaragoza-Teruel-Valencia road from Villacampa. On 10 February, Laval entered Teruel, while Villacampa retreated south to Villel and took up a highly defensible position of fortified houses linked by entrenchments.[4] Laval pursued, beating the 800-strong Spanish vanguard at Villastar, then marched on Villel. Despite Villacampa's expectations and his frontline leadership, the double-layered defensive position was stormed and he was forced to retreat while Laval's men plundered Villel and Albarracín.[5]

With Villacampa seemingly neutralized for the moment, Suchet proceeded to Teruel on 26 February, assembling there Laval's division, Pâris's brigade from Musnier's division, and some cavalry (the 13e Cuirassiers, two squadrons of the 4e Hussards, and the lone Polish Lancer squadron) which was led by the recently-arrived *Général de Brigade* Andre-Joseph Boussart, a veteran dragoon officer of Walloon extraction. This was to be the main column for the Valencian expedition. A second column under Habert of two hussar squadrons and six battalions from the 116e and 117e Ligne and 5e Légère was assembled at Alcañiz and ordered to march to Morella and be past Castellón de la Plana by 2 March. This was a dangerous and ill-advised venture, for the distance and nature of terrain between Habert's and Suchet's lines of march were so great that if Habert's smaller force came under attack, there was no way for Suchet to assist him; in fact, such was the separation that Habert would be 'no longer in communication with the army' for some time![6] An expected reinforcement batch of some 4,000 conscripts in 10 march battalions en route from France under *Général de Brigade* Louis François Élie Pelletier Montmarie was given pre-emptive orders to advance to Daroca to guard Suchet's lines of communication to Zaragoza. Musnier was left in charge of Aragon with eight battalions and 250 cavalry, his force split between Jean-Marie Vergez on the Cinca and Buget on the right bank.

Habert made a head start, for he had the longest distance to travel, and was completely out of touch with Suchet by the time the latter departed from Teruel on 1 March. But the moment Suchet had stepped out of the city he received a dispatch from Berthier containing some very important news. First, was Napoleon's decree declaring Aragon to be in a state of siege and under a military government headed by Suchet. With that, there was a letter dated 18 February that ordered Suchet to besiege Lérida and Mequinenza instead of going to Valencia. On 17 February, Napoleon had written to Berthier:

---

3   Suchet, *Memoirs of the War in Spain*, Vol.I, p.94.
4   Brandt, *In the Legions of Napoleon*, p.111.
5   During the action at Villel, our erstwhile protagonist von Brandt was wounded while leading the French assault.
6   Suchet, *Memoirs of the War in Spain*, Vol.I, p.97.

My cousin, make known to General Suchet that I reiterate the order to him to make the siege of Lérida and Mequinenza, and to use the remainder of his troops to contain Aragon, by holding a body of troops on the border of the kingdom of Valencia; that I am especially keen to overcome Catalonia quickly. Tell him that the Duke of Castiglione [Augereau] has been as far as Barcelona, and that he is trying to get in touch with him. Let General Suchet know that, if he received orders from Madrid contrary to mine, he must regard them as null and void, especially as regards the administration.[7]

In fact, Napoleon had already ordered 1,400 pack animals to Zaragoza to haul Suchet's siege train, made ready from Pamplona! But any operations against Lérida were not feasible at the moment. Events were already in motion, and if Suchet changed the plan there and now, then what of Habert, with whom there was no way of communicating this new development? Suchet could stay in Teruel and enact the operation against Lérida, but that meant that Habert, upon arriving at his destination, would find himself deep in enemy territory isolated and alone. Thus, there was little choice for Suchet but to ignore the orders from Paris and carry on with the Valencian expedition, or otherwise risk the destruction of Habert's column at the hands of the 2° Ejército.

Habert had faced no opposition on his march; Suchet had only been met by a single brigade at the pass of Albentosa, but the French stormed the position and the Valencians retreated with the loss of four cannon. Suchet reunited with Habert at Sagunto on 5 March. Much to Suchet's delight, the town officials of Sagunto presented Suchet with the keys and pledged loyalty. Suchet spent a bit of time sightseeing the ruins of the ancient Roman fortress and amphitheatre of Sagunto, little knowing how important that location would be to him a year-and-a-half later. So far the expedition had gone well, and Suchet continued his march on Valencia, arriving before the city the next day. But contrary to what Joseph and Soult had told Suchet, Valencia had prepared a welcome reception of an entirely different kind. The city was under the governance of the authoritarian *Capitán Général* José Caro y Sureda, who had withdrawn the 12,000-strong 2° Ejército behind the city walls rather than face the French in the field.[8] Any attempts at scouting the city were met with heavy artillery fire. Within Valencia, patriotic fervour had taken hold in the population, which was determined to put up a fanatical defence in the vein of Zaragoza. Under Caro's dictatorial rule, any pro-French sentiments were rapidly suppressed, and several people were even lynched on mere accusations of harbouring such beliefs. For five days Suchet lingered outside of Valencia, with neither a siege train nor the numbers to take the city. He busied himself with beating up some small fry – partisan bands in the area – but could do little against the walls of Valencia. While Suchet was embarked on this fruitless expedition, the guerrillas struck hard in Aragon, managing to cut Suchet's lines of communication. This was enough for Suchet, who ordered a retreat back to Aragon on the night of 10 March.

Villacampa had been unexpectedly quick in his recovery after his tussle with Laval – the extent of which the latter had greatly overstated, claiming Spanish losses of 400 whereas the

7   Napoleon to Berthier, Letter 16267; Bonaparte, *Correspondence de Napoléon 1er*, Vol.XX, p.266.

8   It should be noted that Caro's official military rank was that of a *mariscal de campo*; *capitán general* was a titular rank conferred on the commander of a province.

Spanish had actually retreated in good order – and on the morning of 8 March Villacampa struck at Teruel. As the Spanish entered Teruel, *Colonel* Plicque's 400-strong Franco-Polish garrison conceded the town after taking 31 casualties and locked themselves inside the fortified seminary. However, the Spanish managed to occupy the bell-tower and church adjacent to the seminary: it was rumoured that some monks whom the French had permitted to stay had let Villacampa's men in.[9] The bell-tower was recaptured in a sortie, but the French situation remained critical. Lacking artillery, Villacampa dug a mine to try and blow the French out. Before he detonated the mine, Villacampa called a truce and permitted the French to inspect the mine in the hopes of obtaining a bloodless surrender. Engineer *Capitaine* Leviston, who had thus far been leading the defence due to Plicque's inactivity, judged that the Spanish lacked the gunpowder to breach the walls and refused to surrender; nonetheless, the garrison evacuated the threatened part of the seminary as a precaution.[10]

Informed of a convoy approaching from Daroca, Villacampa left a regiment to keep an eye on the Teruel garrison and marched on the convoy while it was in the open, handily destroying the 160-man escort and capturing two mountain guns. These could have very well been put to use bombarding the Teruel garrison, but the escort had fought hard and used their last breaths to destroy the munition wagons. Fresh from this victory, Villacampa returned to Teruel and proclaimed that Suchet was defeated at Valencia, and, after threatening to blow the garrison to smithereens, redoubled his mining efforts to lay down three more mines. Leviston was unfazed however, for Villacampa's actions and threats only revealed his bluff by giving credence to Leviston's original theory that the Spanish lacked the gunpowder needed to make a mine. Why else was it that Villacampa had yet to fire any of his mines despite the continued French refusals to surrender?

On 11 March, Villacampa marched to Albentosa and the vital pass around it, where Suchet had left a company of Poles and some cavalry. Despite being in a highly defensible position, the badly outnumbered Franco-Polish force foolishly marched out to face the Spanish in the open, and was annihilated with the loss of 170 men. However, by this time Suchet was quickly retreating from Valencia and relieved Teruel on 13 March, much to the joy of the garrison. Chlopicki was dispatched to chase away Villacampa, who had retreated to Cuenca to deposit his many prisoners.

As for the rest of Aragon, the guerrillas in the north attempted to seize advantage of Suchet's absence, but they were all beaten by French columns save for Perena, who was able to raid Monzón. In the west, Javier Mina moved into Cincovillas with 700 men, managing to defeat the *marche* battalion of the 121e Ligne near Exea. However, the young guerrilla had used up all of his luck. On returning to Aragon, Suchet immediately deployed his field force in counter-guerrilla operations, and Javier Mina found himself pursued by a column under Harispe and blocked in the north by the Jaca garrison. As Javier Mina retreated back to his base in Navarre, he was forced to disperse his *partida* against a powerful French force concentration. On 29 March, Javier Mina was captured with some of his men at Labiano. Suchet wanted him immediately executed, but Berthier rationally forbade it.[11] Javier Mina was out of the picture for the rest of the war, locked up in a French prison, but his mantle

---

9   Brandt, *In the Legions of Napoleon*, p.115.
10   Brandt, *In the Legions of Napoleon*, p.116.
11   Alexander, *Rod of Iron*, p.71.

would be taken up by another Mina, his uncle, Francisco Espoz y Mina, who would surpass his nephew and enter the annals of great Spanish heroes.[12]

The main consequence of the utterly useless Valencian expedition was that Napoleon was infuriated. This had quite an impact on Suchet, who would from that point on be meticulous about adhering to Imperial grand strategy as dictated by Napoleon, for better or for worse. Suchet found little respite after the Valencian expedition. When he returned to Zaragoza on 17 March, waiting for him were orders from Napoleon dated 1 March, dictating that Lérida be besieged at once, with assurances that Augereau's VII Corps would deal with the Spanish 1º Ejército of Catalonia. The end goal of French military operations in Eastern Spain was of course, the complete subjugation of the Levante and that meant the capture of the inland Catalonian fortresses, Tarragona, and Valencia. This was the long and arduous journey ahead for Suchet, and it was to begin with besieging Lérida by 1 March. The actions requested in Napoleon's message was a month overdue, but Suchet nevertheless resolved to carry them out. Despite Napoleon's orders for a coordinated operation against Lérida, Augereau rendered no aid to Suchet.

The Siege of Lérida[13]

In accordance with his orders, Suchet immediately transitioned his focus to the conquest of Catalonia by amassing a formidable army with which he would take to the field. This came with corresponding logistical problems, the first of which was that Suchet estimated that his operations in Catalonia would require at least 30,000 men, whereas he only possessed an army of about 23,000, of which many would have to remain in Aragon to maintain French authority. Aware that the guerrilla threat had not been completely extinguished and could badly hurt his lines of communications, Suchet decided to leave Laval in charge of Aragon with 10,000 men, which left him with a field force of 13,000 men in two divisions. While these were the cream of III Corps, it was far short of the required 30,000. Even with these sacrifices on both ends, Laval still did not have enough men to conduct security duties in the occupied province, so Suchet decided to abandon much of southern Aragon and concentrate security efforts in the central and northern areas. Suchet had requested reinforcements, and in March the Aragon garrison had been bolstered by the arrival of the 2e Légion des Gendarmes, made up of the 9e, 10e, 11e, 12e, 13e, and 14e Escadrons, totalling 1,158 men and 451 horses, but this was not enough, for the Gendarmes could only be positioned according to a set deployment from Paris rather than how Suchet saw fit as according to the situation.[14] A pervasive lack of manpower was not the only problem that haunted Laval and Suchet. A significant portion of the troops charged with defending Aragon were second-rate troops,

---

12   Tone, *The Fatal Knot*, p.72.Espoz y Mina had been part of the Jaca garrison, and escaped before its capitulation. Francisco Espoz y Mina will be henceforth be referred to as Mina in this narrative.

13   Unless otherwise cited, narrative background is summarised from: Arteche y Moro, *Guerra de la Independencia*, Vol.VIII, pp.308-338; Belmas, *Journaux des sièges*, Vol.III, pp.75-177; Oman, *Peninsular War*, Vol.III, pp.301-308; Suchet, *Memoirs of the War in Spain*, Vol.I, pp.110-155.

14   Emmanuel Martin, *La gendarmerie française en Espagne et en Portugal (campagnes de 1807 à 1814)* (Paris: Léautey, 1898), pp.328-329.

consistent with a general attitude in the French army of relegating unwanted but often vital garrison and patrol duties to such units. Nearly all of Laval's division on the left bank of Aragon was made up of 'conscripts, national guardsmen, and overaged gendarmes.'[15] The low quality of the occupation force was only exacerbated by the tendency for Suchet to rotate his men out of areas they were familiar with. Fortunately for Suchet, his work in pacifying Aragon in the past year had paid off tremendously, as many of the guerrilla bands were too busy licking their wounds and reorganizing to take advantage of Suchet's absence and his flawed garrison deployment, and there would be little disruption to his lines of communication by Spanish regular or irregular forces.

The transportation of the siege train itself was another issue. Consisting of 24 heavy cannon, 10 mortars, and six howitzers, with 700 rounds for each gun, the corresponding amount of gunpowder, and 12,000 entrenching tools, this impressive arsenal would render Suchet invaluable service, but at the same time was extremely cumbersome.[16] First gathered at Pamplona in Navarre, the siege train made its way to Zaragoza, a process that required multiple convoys and took up much of March.[17] From Zaragoza, the siege train had to be escorted to Monzón. Suchet opened his operations in late March by ordering Habert and Musnier to begin to converge on Lérida.

Habert undertook some preliminary operations against a Spanish force under *Coronel* Perena. Perena had been dispatched from Lérida with four Aragonese battalions totalling 2,000 men to watch the northern approaches to the city between the Segre and Cinca Rivers. These troops, along with five cannon, were fortified in Balaguer, guarding the stone bridge over the Segre, which Habert reached with a portion of his division on 4 April. Perena prepared to contest any crossing the French general attempted; however, he was outflanked by Robert's 117e Ligne, which had crossed the Segre at Camarasa eight miles north of Balaguer.[18] Perena withdrew in good order to Alcoletge, quickly crossed the Segre through Lérida, and made his way back north to the town of Corbins to secure the Noguera river crossing there. As for Musnier, he came up through Alcañiz and crossed the Ebro to approach Lérida from the south on the left bank of the Segre. His march was largely uneventful, only making a feint against the Tortosa garrison along the way. By sheer chance Musnier also made brief contact with two battalions of the VII Corps under *Colonel* Villatte while on his march to Lérida.

With Laval's division distributed in garrisoning Aragon, Suchet gave orders to the divisions of Musnier and Habert to march on Lérida itself, while he himself took Vergez's brigade (from Musnier's division), the 13e Cuirassiers, six companies of artillery, one company each of pontoniers and miners, and two companies of sappers to the stronghold of Monzón on the 10th and made the city his base of operations for the upcoming siege.[19] A hospital, bakery, and storehouses were established there.

---

15   Alexander, *Rod of Iron*, p.74.
16   Jacques Vital Belmas, *Journaux des siéges faits ou soutenus par les Français dans la péninsule, de 1807 à 1814* (Paris: Chez Firmin Didot frères et cie, 1837), Vol.III, p.77-78.
17   One such convoy was captured by Javier Mina.
18   Suchet, *Memoirs of the War*, Vol.I, p.114.
19   Suchet, *Memoirs of the War*, Vol.I, p.114.

Grenadier of the 44e Ligne, by Pierre-Albert Leroux.
(Anne S.K. Brown Military Collection, Brown University Library)

The citizens of Lérida looked out of their windows on 13 April to the ominous sight of blue-coated columns winding down the north-west road from Almacelles. Spanish soldiers scurried through the streets to their positions while civilians rushed to the safety of their homes. From atop the walls of the citadel, the garrison could see the French battalion flags billowing in the breeze, topped by gilded Imperial eagles which glimmered in the sun, heralding the arrival of the French III Corps. Suchet and his column were the first to arrive within sight of the city and Musnier's division arrived later that same day. Habert's division arrived the next day, having been the only column to be met with any opposition. He had run into Perena's troops at Corbins while marching on the right bank of the Segre. One can imagine that Habert was surprised and somewhat irritated to encounter Perena once more, after previously forcing him to withdraw on the other bank! Nevertheless, he pressed on. Under fire from the Spanish defenders, *Lieutenant* Monvel led Habert's detachment of the 4e Hussards in fording the Noguera River.[20] The engagement was brief, and though he could have taken his men to flee into the mountains, Perena ordered a retreat back into Lérida, and Habert advanced to take up a position on the San Rufo heights north of the city.

Lérida was no stranger to sieges and war. It had been besieged by Julius Caesar in 49 BC, then in 1644 during the Reaper's War, in 1647 by Louis de Bourbon, the Great Condé, and then besieged again in 1707 during the War of the Spanish Succession. The city's historical success rate was mixed, having been taken in 49 BC and 1707, but repulsing the other two sieges. Lérida was situated on a largely sparse and open plain on the western bank of the Segre, marked by two steep hills which formed the foundations for the city's formidable defensive works. There was nothing on the left bank of the Segre, not even suburbs, save for a small *tête-de-pont* consisting of a small lunette surrounded by a ditch which guarded the bridge into the city. Lérida's fortifications consisted of the typical fortress design of the time – a wall and bastion system with several towers – but it lacked ditches or exterior works beyond the main walls, even a glacis for that matter.[21] Suchet's greatest concern was the citadel, which was on a hill 150 feet above the rest of the plain and had a full field of fire into the town and its vicinity. The citadel had a storehouse with an abundance of food and water, and the terrain was such that it was only easily accessible from its western face, which faced into the city.[22] Three quarters of a mile south of Lérida, beyond the city walls, was the second hill, a plateau upon which several forts had been built, the most prominent being Fort Gardeny, an old Templar castle dating back to the twelfth century. The fort had been refurbished with new hornworks and was well protected with ditches and escarpments. At the end of the plateau were two redoubts, named del Pilar and San Fernando.[23] The outworks on the plateau presented great challenges for Suchet, as they would force his besieging army to stretch their siege lines in order to cover both the city and the fortified plateau, or take the plateau by force before investing in the city. In addition, their field of fire made it impossible for the French to close their blockade lines at the banks of the Segre south of Lérida.

20   Suchet, *Memoirs of the War*, Vol.I, p.115.
21   Suchet, *Memoirs of the War in Spain*, Vol.I, p.119.
22   Arteche y Moro, *Guerra de la Independencia*, Vol.VIII, p.310.
23   Oman, *Peninsular War*, Vol.III, p.301.

It was not only the fortifications of Lérida which concerned Suchet but also the large garrison and populace which stood firmly behind the walls of the city. The governor of Lérida was *Mariscal de Campo* José González, a sickly old man, but, fortunately for the Spanish, all command authority was vested to *Mariscal de Campo* Jayme García Conde, a far cry from the antiquarian generals whose careers had peaked in the eighteenth century that the French were so used to facing.[24] García Conde was young and spirited, his ambition for victory only matched by his ardent patriotism. He was fully intent on dragging the siege out for as long as possible to do as much damage as he could to French operations. García Conde had every reason to hope for a favourable outcome. Including Perena's force, the Lérida garrison numbered over 8,000 to Suchet's 13,000 – highly favourable odds for a siege. Many of the city's 18,000 citizens had mobilized in the defence of their city and would prove to be a major factor in maintaining the morale and resolve of the Spanish defenders. Including assorted irregular troops and civic militias, the Spanish total could go as far as 10,000 men. Perhaps the one failing of the garrison was that there were only 100 gunners to serve the 105 cannon lining the city's bastions and walls, so they were supplemented by 250 civilian volunteers, who lacked uniforms or even proper training.[25] At a strategic level, the French hold on Catalonia was tenuous at best, so García Conde could expect assistance from other Spanish forces. Despite the multitude of factors against him, Suchet resolved to invest in Lérida and began preparations. Suchet was not entirely without a few assets. He was confident that his men had gained experience in siege warfare from Zaragoza and could perform well. Suchet went to great lengths to describe Lérida's history in his memoir, and it is plausible that he had studied to some extent the previous sieges of the city prior to conducting his own in order to weigh into consideration what had worked and had not for his predecessors.[26]

Suchet established his headquarters at the village of Villanueva del Picat and set about his investment of Lérida. His decision not to officially begin besieging the city was more of a matter of circumstance, as he was operating without the expected support of VII Corps and still awaiting the siege train.[27] This did not stop him from ordering his engineers to immediately reconnoitre the city walls and make gabions and fascines. Meanwhile, the French infantry took positions on strategic roads to cut the city's supply lines. The 121e Ligne (three battalions) covered the westward roads leading to Mariola and Varcalas. Covering the northwest roads were elements of the 114e Ligne (two battalions) and 3e Vistule (one battalion) under *Général de Brigade* Buget. To his left on the San Rufo heights were the 5e Légère (two battalions) and the 116e Ligne (two battalions) under Habert, covering the northern roads leading to Balaguer and Corbins. A battalion of the 114e and two artillery pieces were entrenched on the Sierra de Canelin to screen Fort Gardeny and the redoubts. All that could be done was to maintain the French blockade along the Segre was a loose screen of cavalry patrols far out of the reach of Fort Gardeny's guns.[28]

24   Belmas, *Journaux des siéges*, Vol.III, p.80.
25   Nafziger Order of Battle Collection, 810DSAR: Spanish Garrison of Lerida, 1 April–1 May 1810.
26   Suchet, *Memoirs of the War*, Vol.I, pp.116-19.
27   Suchet, *Memoirs of the War*, Vol.I, p.123.
28   Gates, *The Spanish Ulcer*, p.290.

The French forces on the left bank of the Segre were connected by the rest of the army only by a portable bridge; the next nearest bridge was at Balaguer. The Spanish *tête-de-pont* on the left bank was surrounded by the 117e Ligne (three battalions), detached from Habert's division and placed under Harispe's command for the siege. Suchet also created a 'Corps of Observation' to serve as a mobile reserve force, and stationed it at the heights and village of Alcoletge, several miles northeast of Lérida. This formation consisted of the 115e Ligne (three battalions), the 1er Vistule (two battalions), and Boussart's cavalry, under the overall command of Musnier. While unable to fully cut off the city without dangerously overstretching his troops, Suchet's dispositions were meticulously planned to maximize the utility of the few units he could commit to the siege, even ensuring that Harispe's division had a route of escape to Balaguer if the communication bridge was damaged in the seasonal overflow of the Segre.

The situation rapidly escalated rapidly in the coming days. No sooner had the French settled in than a Spanish officer was captured while attempting to enter Lérida, and it was speculated that he was a messenger from a relief army. Rumours began to float that *Mariscal de Campo* Enrique O'Donnell was assembling an army at Montblanc to relieve Lérida, armed peasants were on the move, and that a division under Luis González Torres de Navarra, Marqués de Campoverde, was in Cervera.[29] Rumours or not, Suchet took no chances in his precarious situation, and on the 19th personally led the Corps of Observation – five battalions and the 13e Cuirassiers (four squadrons) – to the city of Balaguer to oversee the fortification of the north-eastern approaches to Lérida. This entailed fortifying Balaguer and destroying the bridge over the Segre at Camarasa. Hoping to take advantage of the absence of the French reserves, García Conde launched an energetic sortie from the bridgehead onto the left bank, but it was driven back by Harispe. Most importantly though, García Conde also dispatched a messenger to find the rumoured relief army and inform them of the French departure, a well-intentioned action which would inadvertently have great implications. The rumours had actually predated the action, for while O'Donnell was indeed planning to relieve Lérida, he was still in Tarragona and would depart on the 20th.[30] As it turned out, Augereau had failed to keep O'Donnell in check due to the withdrawal of his forces from Barcelona to Girona on 11 April, on the grounds that it was becoming impossible to supply Barcelona.[31] Augereau himself had a fair share of problems to contend with, but the 50,000 men he possessed should have been enough to secure the lines of communication between Barcelona and France, while maintaining a formidable field force to keep both Campoverde and O'Donnell in check. Instead, O'Donnell was left free to turn his attention to rescuing Lérida.

After securing or destroying the bridges over the Segre above Lérida, Suchet marched the Corps of Observation southeast on 21 April to scout the roads near Tarrega, some 30 miles east of Lérida. He was seeking to gather intelligence not only about O'Donnell, but about Augereau as well – a testament to the perilous lack of coordination and communication between French regional commanders seen throughout the Peninsular War. Suchet

---

29   Suchet, *Memoirs of the War in Spain*, Vol.I, p.125.
30   Arteche y Moro, *Guerra de la Independencia*, Vol.VIII, p.314.
31   Oman, *Peninsular War*, Vol.III, p.301; Gates, *The Spanish Ulcer*, p.290.

testifies to the obstinacy of the Catalans in their refusal to assist the invaders, writing that the French

> [H]ad great difficulty in employing spies in a country so new to us, in which every inhabitant was our enemy. We were everywhere hated, and everywhere deceived, unless when pride or the confidence of success in the enemy led them to involuntarily betray their intentions. In general however, all promises or threats were equally unsuccessful in eliciting any secret that one might turn to advantage.[32]

Such was the state of French intelligence efforts that Suchet admits that it was only due to sheer luck that he learned that O'Donnell had left Tarragona with two divisions and was on his way to Lérida.[33]

Though he was sceptical of the titbits of information and rumours he had obtained, Suchet would take no chances and on 22 April force-marched the Corps of Observation back to take up a reserve position on the heights of Alcoletge. On that same day, O'Donnell and his divisions reached Vinaxa, some 25 miles southwest of Lérida. O'Donnell's force consisted of the División de Reserva under *Mariscal de Campo* Miguel Ibarrola Gonzalez and the 4ª División under *Coronel* Ramón Pírez y Pavía, totalling some 7,000 regular infantry, 1,500 militia, 400 cavalry, and a single battery of artillery. They were reported to be the best troops in the 1º Ejército.[34] García Conde's messenger had made it through the loosely guarded French lines, and informed O'Donnell that a portion of the French infantry and their entire cavalry had maneuverer away from the siege. Though the message was a few days old and Musnier had since been ordered back to his encampment to prepare for O'Donnell's arrival, O'Donnell placed his optimistic faith in the message, and lulled himself into a false sense of security. Attempting to take advantage of the perceived absence of a large part of Suchet's army, O'Donnell endeavoured to hasten his arrival.

On the morning of 23 April, O'Donnell's troops broke camp from Vinaxa and set out on the Tarragona road towards Lérida, stopping at 10:00 a.m. for a two-hour rest in the village of Juneda, 12 miles southeast of Lérida. Still believing that the French were unaware of his approach, as he had yet to encounter any French scouts, the Spanish general planned to break Suchet's siege lines from the south, where the bridgehead could be used by the garrison to support his operation. Leaving Pirez's 4ª División at Juneda, O'Donnell sent Ibarrola's División de Reserva of 4,000 men ahead to Lérida at noon.

As Ibarolla's men resumed their westward march along the Tarragona road to Lérida, O'Donnell had failed to recognize the badly exposed position of his infantry in march columns on the low-lying open plateau the road ran on.[35] The plateau was devoid of any

---

32   Suchet, *Memoirs of the War in Spain*, Vol.I, p.126.
33   Suchet, *Memoirs of the War in Spain*, Vol.I, p.126.
34   Andreas Daniel Berthold von Schepeler, *Histoire de la révolution d'Espagne et de Portugal, ainsi que de la guerre qui en résulta* (Liège: J. Desoer, 1829), Vol.II, p.615; Jose Luis Isabel Sanchez, 'Ramón Pírez Pavía', Real Academia de la Historia, <https://dbe.rah.es/biografias/137372/ramon-pirez-pavia>, accessed 1 January 2022. Pírez was nominally second-in-command of the 4ª División, but had been in command since the wounding of its commander at the Battle of Vich in February.
35   Suchet, *Memoirs of the War in Spain*, Vol.I, p.128.

cover for the Spanish while placing any attacking force coming from the north below and out of their line of sight. Ibarrola had deployed his two brigades into three columns: *Brigadier* Pedro García Navarro's vanguard of his infantry brigade and a company of Spanish cuirassiers marched down the high road, flanked some ways to the rear by *Brigadier* Despuig's brigade formed up in two columns preceded by skirmishers, so that the entire formation vaguely resembled an elongated arrowhead.[36] While Ibarrola himself may have taken some precautions in screening his attack with a vanguard, it can be inferred from his strung-out line of march that O'Donnell himself expected nothing more than sweeping aside French outposts and making a quick and triumphant entry into Lérida, and was thus utterly unprepared for anything else. With a miles-long gap growing between them, neither Ibarolla's nor Pírez's divisions were in any position to quickly support one another if one or the other came under a concentrated attack. Why O'Donnell split his forces so dangerously is uncertain, be it hubris, ignorance, or a poorly-executed intention to keep Pírez's division as a reserve force.

Ibarrola's vanguard soon bumped into the advance pickets of Harispe's small French force of two squadrons of the 4e Hussards and three battalions of the 117e Ligne, tasked with screening the *tête-de-pont*. As the French pickets fell back and Navarro's men crossed over the bridge over the Segundo Canal, Harispe himself arrived on the scene at the head of the 4e Hussards, followed by several voltigeur companies of the 117e and 115e Ligne. Emboldened by the knowledge that Musnier could reinforce him within an hour, Harispe shook his men out in battle order and energetically engaged the Spanish.[37] Though Ibarrola's division as a whole outnumbered Harispe's immediate force, the bulk of his men were in marching order, and Despuig's brigade was a considerable distance behind Navarro and thus unable to lend any assistance. The Spanish were also stuck in an unfavourable position, being in the process of crossing the Segundo Canal. Upon realizing that he only directly faced the Spanish advance guard, Harispe boldy launched the hussars in a wild charge which badly mauled the Spanish light infantry and sent them back over the bridge with heavy casualties.

The French had not been the only ones to notice the arrival of O'Donnell's army. The inhabitants and garrison of Lérida also spotted the relief army and cheered vivaciously, watching from windows and rooftops as Navarro's brigade pushed towards the city. García Conde prepared to launch a sortie from the fortress bridgehead under the cover of a bombardment to support Ibarrola. Screening the bridgehead was the stalwart *Colonel* Robert and the 117e Ligne, keeping a wary eye on the sortie party as they filed out of the bridgehead to make their attack. Yet the cheers of the Spanish proved premature and soon died down as Navarro's light infantry fled back across the bridge, the French hussars at their tails. That the Lérida garrison saw the arrival of Navarro's brigade also meant that they saw its repulse, and Robert seized the opportunity to launch a counterattack.[38] The demoralized sortie party withdrew in the face of the French charge back into Lérida.

Musnier had heard the gunfire and acted decisively, immediately rousing his men to march to join the battle. The Corps of Observation hurried off of the Alcoletge heights

---

36 Navarro's testimony on the battle, from Suchet, *Memoirs of the War in* Spain, Vol.I, p.351. A company of cavalry usually refers to half a squadron.
37 Oman, *Peninsular War*, Vol.III, p.304.
38 Suchet, *Memoirs of the War in Spain*, Vol.I, p.129.

and force-marched roughly four miles to intercept O'Donnell's army, the five battalions of infantry having to accelerate their march speed to keep up with Boussart's cuirassiers.[39] O'Donnell had neglected to order his cavalry to screen his flanks, thus, Musnier's advance was only noticed when 'a thick cloud of dust was seen at a distance on the right'.[40] By now, O'Donnell himself had arrived on the scene and set up his headquarters in the ruined village of Margalef, six miles southeast of Lérida. Upon receiving news that Musnier was moving onto Ibarolla's right flank to cut his line of retreat, O'Donnell sent orders for Ibarrola to fall back, hoping to reunite Ibarrola's division with Pírez's division, which was still at Juneda. Navarro's brigade struggled to disengage from Harispe's hussars, while Despuig's men made good their retreat.[41] But Musnier followed in hot pursuit, and it was not long before his men caught up with the Spanish. It dawned on Ibarrola that any

Jean-Isidore Harispe, Engraver unknown. (By kind permission of the Eusko Ikaskuntza (Basque Studies Society))

further retreat was futile and would end in certain disaster with the French being so close, so he formed Despuig's brigade in a battle line along the Tarragona road on the coverless open plateau. Despuig's infantry was positioned in a line along the Tarragona Road, with 300 cavalry holding the right flank and a half-battery of three cannons on the left, waiting nervously as the columns of the 115e Ligne and 1er Vistule snaking onto the plateau led by 500 French cuirassiers, the most feared cavalry in Europe at the time.[42] Ibarrola's only hope was to hold out until the rest of the army, still four miles away, could arrive.

---

39   Suchet, *Memoirs of the War in Spain*, Vol.I, p.129.
40   Navarro's testimony on the battle, from Suchet, *Memoirs of the War in Spain*, Vol.I, p.351.
41   Navarro's testimony on the battle, from Suchet, *Memoirs of the War in Spain*, Vol.I, p.351.
42   Oman, *Peninsular War*, Vol.III, p.304. There is disagreement as to whether the Spanish cavalry was positioned on Despuig's left or right and thus, exactly which flank the cuirassiers attacked. The account given follows the recollection of Navarro, and substantiated by Oman and Arteche y Moro. Suchet, *Memoirs of the War in Spain*, Vol.I, p.130, writes that the Spanish had 'the artillery on its right, and the cavalry on its left,' a claim echoed by Belmas. Navarro's account, written in 1810, while Suchet's memoirs were written after the Napoleonic Wars, is likely correct, though the deployment given by Suchet may make more sense. Ibarolla's artillery was most likely marching towards the rear of the column, so it is logical that they would be on the Spanish right, lest they have fallen behind in the retreat. It is within the realm of possibility for the 13e Cuirassiers to have broken the Spanish left if the Spanish cavalry was there, then wheeled eastwards to roll up Despuig's brigade down the Tarragona road.

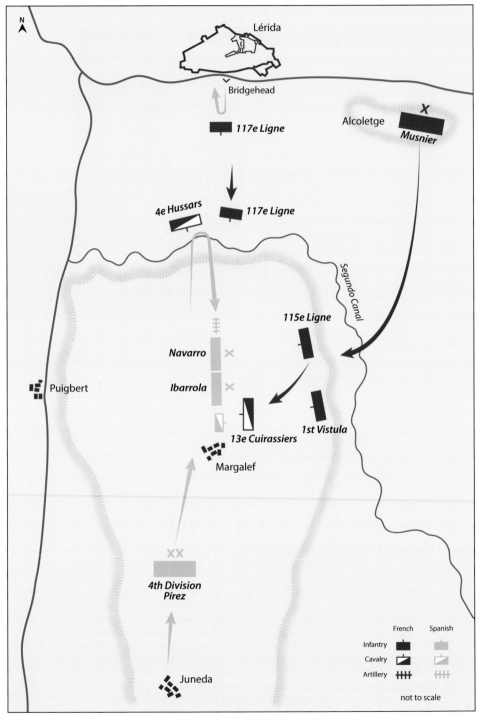

The Battle of Margalef, 23 April 1810.

Trooper of the 13e Cuirassiers, by Pierre-Albert Leroux.
(Anne S.K. Brown Military Collection, Brown University Library)

Trumpeter of the 13e Cuirassiers, by Pierre-Albert Leroux.
(Anne S.K. Brown Military Collection, Brown University Library)

Trooper of the 13e Cuirassiers in campaign uniform, by Pierre-Albert Leroux.
(Anne S.K. Brown Military Collection, Brown University Library)

Observing the Spanish deployment, Musnier began his attack by unleashing the 13e Cuirassiers against Despuig's line. The Spanish artillery fired upon the armoured horsemen as they deployed, but were quickly met with counter-battery fire from a battery of French horse artillery that had moved up to provide close support to the cuirassiers. Around this time, the rest of Navarro's brigade, after losing one of its battalions to the French hussars, caught up to deploy on Despuig's left in an attack column, just as Boussart began his attack.

No self-respecting cavalry general would fail to be found at the head of a charge, and Boussart was no exception. With their general leading them on, the cuirassiers began a slow trot towards the Spanish right, their entrance heralded by the strident call of the 13e's wine-clad trumpeters and the razor-edged blades of their massive heavy cavalry swords glimmering in the Iberian sun as they bore down upon their hapless opponents. Directly opposing the French cuirassiers were not only Spanish light cavalry, but ironically, also a company of Spanish cuirassiers. Yet there was a marked difference in quality between the two 'elite' units. The Spanish cavalry made a move of advancing to meet their foes in a charge, but the cuirassiers were upon them before they could react. Outnumbered and outmatched, the Spanish cavalry broke and routed in panic before the cuirassiers even made contact. The flight of the Spanish cavalry left the infantry exposed and with little time to react before the cuirassiers ploughed into them. The battalion of the Guardias Valonas attempted to form a square as the Spanish line crumbled from the raw shock power of the charge, but it was to no avail and they too were ridden down. Boussart wheeled his men right to roll up the disordered Spanish line. Infantrymen were bowled over and trampled underfoot by the massive French cavalrymen, who quite literally rode through their ranks, hacking and slashing as Ibarrola's entire division dissolved into a panicked rout. Spanish infantry dropped their weapons and fled as the cuirassiers followed in a relentless close pursuit, and O'Donnell himself was even swept away in the rout.

As the battle rolled towards Juneda, the lead elements of Pirez's division waiting there now bore witness to the butchery that was unfolding. Realizing the battle was lost, O'Donnell ordered his troops to retreat, deploying a battalion of the Regimiento de Kayser 3° de Suizos from Pírez's advance guard as a rearguard. Ibarrola's scattered troops rushed to the safety of the Pírez's division, hoping to escape the onslaught. The Swiss briskly marched forwards in their customary tight discipline to hold against overwhelming foes as their ancestors had so famously done at Rome and the Tuileries. There would be no glory for the Swiss at Margalef, however. The French cuirassiers re-formed and charged once more, riding down Spanish fugitives and smashing into the Swiss rearguard in spectacular fashion. The blue-coated Swiss were trampled and broken as hundreds of armoured cavalrymen crashed into their ranks. Though many of them were captured, the Swiss' sacrifice did buy time for many men from Ibarrola's division to escape and for O'Donnell to retreat his force to the town of Les Borjas Blanques.[43] *Chef d'Escadron* Saint-George led his squadron in pursuit, but, much to O'Donnell's credit, the Spanish rallied quickly and retreated in good order. O'Donnell was evidently satisfied with the conduct of his men, for he wrote in an after action report, 'The Reserve Division in particular, has covered itself with glory, and its example should serve

43   Rebolledo i Bonjoch, Francesc, 'La Guerra del Francès al Pla D'Urgell, Quaderns de El Pregoner d'Urgell, 32 (2019), p.56.< https://raco.cat/index.php/QuadernsPregonerUrgell/article/view/356293> accessed 8 February 2023.

as a model for those who appreciate military virtues: although this Division was beaten, the fourth, which supported it, with the greatest order, has withdrawn without a single man lost [sans the Regimiento de Kayser 3° de Suizos].'[44]

Margalef was a stunning victory for the French, who inflicted around 500 casualties, took an estimated 2,000 prisoners including eight colonels and *Brigadier* Despuig, and captured four flags and three cannon.[45] French casualties were light at 23 killed, 82 wounded and 60 horses killed, most of them sustained by the 13e Cuirassiers, which had borne the brunt of the fighting.[46] Trooper Tartarin was credited with taking one of the Spanish flags. Characteristically, Boussart himself was wounded in the fight.[47] The likelihood of success for a relief army of 7,000 against a besieging force of 13,000 was chancy, and O'Donnell would have been better off collecting more men before attempting to relieve the city, though this had been difficult due to the need to simultaneously defend Tarragona. His greatest error, however, was allowing his force to get split up in such a way that one half of it was completely crushed before the other could even come to its aid.

Suchet intended to fully capitalize on his decisive victory at Margalef, convinced that the destruction of O'Donnell's relief army had significantly demoralized the armed citizenry and regular garrison. Hoping that another blow immediately after the battle would shatter the garrison's morale, Suchet hobnailed together a plan for simultaneous night-time assaults by a battalion each of the 114e and 121e on the del Pilar and San-Fernando redoubts, respectively, in order to threaten Fort Gardeny. Debouching the Spanish from their outer works and taking the plateau would allow the French to tighten their siege lines.

The attack took place at midnight on the night of the 23rd-24th under the direction of *Général de Brigade* Vergez. The sentries in the redoubt del Pilar failed to notice the shadowy figures darting towards them, and, before they knew it, French soldiers were clambering over the earthworks and rushing into the redoubt. The redoubt was taken by total surprise, and its garrison fled after only a token resistance. The attackers of San Fernando faced greater difficulty however. Though numbering no more than 50 men under *Subteniente* Juan Puig, the San Fernando's garrison had been fully alerted by the commotion in del Pilar, and steeled their resolve to defend the redoubt. San Fernando was larger and better fortified than the del Pilar redoubt, and the French assault party found itself stuck in the ditch around the redoubt. Efforts to break down the gate were futile, for the French sappers had only parade axes, and the attackers eventually withdrew.[48]

The del Pilar redoubt was untenable without capturing San Fernando, as the garrison of the latter was in a position to fire on the French occupying del Pilar. The men of the 114e

---

44   O'Donnell's Orders of 26 and 27 April from Arteche y Moro, *Guerra de la Independencia*, Vol.VIII, p.505.

45   Suchet, *Memoirs of the War in Spain*, Vol.I, p.132, claims to have taken the impossibly high figure of 5,600 prisoners. Ibarolla's division numbered no more than 4,000, and Pirez's division was barely engaged.

46   Suchet to Berthier, 26 April 1810; from Belmas, *Journaux des siéges*, Vol.III, p.136.

47   Aristide Martinien, *Tableaux, par corps et par batailles, des officiers tués et blessés pendant les guerres de l'Empire (1805-1815)* (Paris: Henri Charles-Lavauzelle, 1899), p.20.

48   Suchet, *Memoirs of the War in Spain*, Vol.I, p.133, claims that his men were permitted to withdraw under a truce offered by the Spanish defenders, who lacked grenades and were fearful of being overwhelmed if the French attempted a desperate push.

withdrew from del Pilar, after disabling a captured 12-pounder cannon by rolling it off the plateau. Suchet's preliminary assault on the outer works of Lérida was a dismal failure, mostly a result of hasty planning. The French storming parties had been poorly equipped for the task before them, and the flaws in the attack plan were further compounded by the complications of a night-time assault. Nothing had been gained, and the Spanish reoccupied del Pilar the next day.

Desperate to end the siege by discouraging the Lérida garrison, Suchet sent a message to García Conde, inviting Spanish officers to inspect the field of battle and the vast number of prisoners the French had taken. The shock of the rout at Margalef had been partially eased by the repulse of the night attack on the redoubts, and García Conde's reply was short and determined:

> General, this town has never reckoned upon the assistance of any army. I beg to assure you of my distinguished consideration.
> Signed,
> Jayme García Conde[49]

The resolve of the defenders had been demonstrated. Unable to coerce a quick surrender, Suchet's hopes for a rapid victory quickly disappeared, leaving him with no other option than to open a siege. This process would require Suchet to slowly batter the fortress walls down with heavy siege guns and take the city by storm. A proper siege was set in motion in short order: the massive siege train arrived from Monzón, an artillery park and engineer quarters were constructed on the San Rufo heights, field hospitals were established, and a suitable breaching point was chosen. The planned point of attack was the northern face of the city, the same section that the Duc d'Orléans had stormed 103 years before in the 1707 siege. The Carmen bastion was deemed to be the weakest point of the city, for it was adjacent to the Segre River and therefore lacked the support of another bastion to its right (west). Like much of the city, it also lacked the protection of a covered way.

Springtime rain on the 26th and 27th flooded the roads and caused delays for the artillery convoys. Though the heavy rains postponed the opening of the trenches, the French still made the most of their time. The energetic engineer *Colonel* Haxo closed off the canals to the city and ordered French skirmishers to drive back the Spanish outposts, so that his engineers could better scout the fortress. After a brief exchange of musketry on the night of the 26th, the Spanish garrison seemingly gave up on all attempts at holding onto the outer fortifications and Haxo's men had free reign to formulate a plan of attack.[50] For his part, Suchet crafted a bold plan to gain a major advantage over the enemy and issued it to his officers on the 28th.

Suchet's plan called for the first parallel to be opened on the night of the 29th in a single major operation. Using the cover of darkness, 1,600 infantrymen crept up unnoticed to within 900 feet of Lérida's walls, where they began to chip away at the ground with the utmost possible silence, a feat only made possible by Suchet's meticulous preparations and

---

49   Suchet, *Memoirs of the War in Spain*, Vol.I, p.134.
50   Suchet, *Memoirs of the War in Spain*, Vol.I, p.136.

the absence of a glacis. Two elite companies lay down on the open ground between the work zone and the city, bayonets fixed and ready to intercept any sortie the Spanish might attempt to disrupt the workers, while a full battalion was kept in the rear as a reserve. Hearing the muffled sounds of digging, the Spanish defenders fired off several volleys of grapeshot and even threw a few fireballs. But the gunners were firing into the dark with nothing except for the faint sounds of shovels hitting the ground to guide their aim, and, as a result, the grapeshot had little effect, allowing the French to pull off their daring night operation with just two killed and two wounded.[51]

The sunrise of the next morning revealed the surprise to the astounded Spanish sentries, who saw before them that the first parallel had been nearly completed in a single night just 900 feet from the fortress walls. The defenders frantically unleashed a storm of grapeshot and musketry as compensation for their inertness the previous night, managing to shoot off *Général de Brigade* Buget's hat and shatter his telescope, but having little other effect.[52] The French had managed to save themselves considerable time and lives by gaining an early foothold near the city walls. The first parallel was completed the night of the next day to stretch along the entire northern face of Lérida all the way to the Segre. Its completion allowed Suchet to establish three batteries: four 8-inch mortars formed the first, with the aim of laying down counter-battery fire on the citadel; the second consisted of four 12-pounder cannon which targeted the right side of the Magdalen bastion, as to eliminate its supporting enfilade fire to the Carmen bastion; finally, six 16-pounder cannon were placed to target the left side of the Carmen bastion.[53]

Taking lessons from earlier sieges to heart, Suchet had established strict precautions to safeguard against all possible attempts by the garrison at disrupting the digging, and to bolster the confidence of the men involved. Work crews were rotated from centre companies of all of his 19 battalions to ease the fatigue of siege warfare, while trench guard duty was given to the elite companies. Most of the major trench work was conducted during the night, while daytime was used to perfect the works or conduct low-risk digging. Though heavy rains on 1 and 2 May badly flooded the trenches, requiring the construction of drains to divert the water, the French war machine proved to be relentless, slowly digging and pushing no less than three zig-zag trenches by flying saps towards the walls of Lérida as well as extending the first parallel to gradually encompass the citadel by 4 May.[54] The Spanish watched the French entrenchments creeping towards their walls with trepidation, but did little to contest them other than a sharp skirmish on 3 May, in which Harispe made an attempt to take the bridgehead. Harispe deployed two horse artillery howitzers to shell the city, only to elicit a massive barrage from the city arsenal. The French assault was turned back by the heavy artillery fire hardly before it began, at which point some of the Spanish defenders sallied out of the bridgehead to shoot across the river at the main French siege

---

51   Belmas, *Journaux des siéges*, Vol.III, p.97.
52   Belmas, *Journaux des siéges*, Vol.III, p.98.
53   Suchet, *Memoirs of the War in Spain*, Vol.I, p.140.
54   David Rumsey Map Collection, 12140.007: Plan de Lerida, Pris le 13 Mai 1810, <https://www.davidrumsey.com/luna/servlet/detail/RUMSEY~8~1~291000~90062501:Plan-de-Lerida-----le-13-Mai-1810->, accessed 6 December 2022.

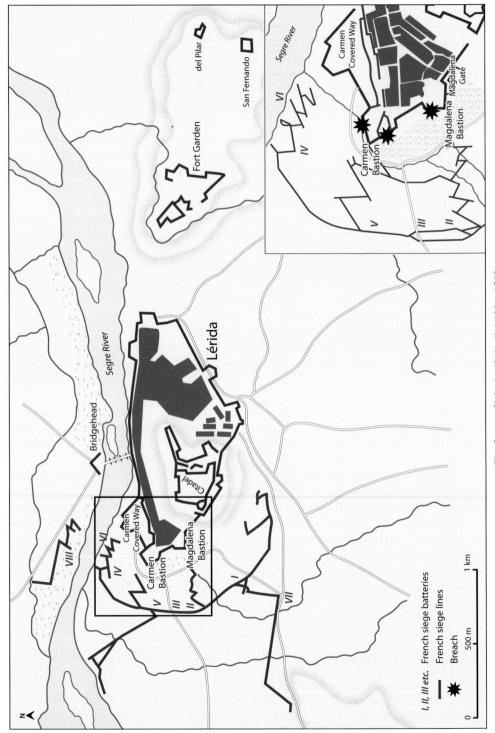

The Siege of Lérida, 13 April–14 May 1810.

line, only to be quickly driven back.[55] Later that night, a fourth battery of two 16-pounders and two 6-inch howitzers was positioned against the Carmen bastion.[56]

García Conde decided that more needed to be done. The four French siege batteries were a cause for much concern, and already the French made too many gains under Spanish complacency. At 5:00 p.m. on 4 May, García Conde ordered an intense bombardment on the French entrenchments by the guns of the citadel, followed by a sortie of between 500 to 600 men from the Carmen bastion and another column out of the Magdalena gate. Their target was the newly constructed Battery No. 4. The suppressive bombardment and the surprise advance by the Spanish had left little time for the French to put their outermost siegeworks in a state of defence. As a result, the sappers and two companies of trench guards fled to the first parallel, where they rallied by the grenadier company of the 121e Ligne, the most immediate reserve at hand.[57] For a moment the Spanish held the outermost trenches and the fourth battery emplacement, until a fierce counterattack by the grenadiers halted any further progress. The Spanish held their own in the fierce melee for the trenches, but they soon were overwhelmed and retreated, as by this time the French had recovered from the surprise and were advancing all along the line to retake their entrenchments. As the sortie party fled back to Lérida, the freshly arrived French reinforcements fired at their backs, causing the retreat to become further disordered. The Spanish column from the Magdalena gate had been repulsed before it managed to reach the parallel. The sortie had been a scare for the French and made good gains at the start, but accomplished little else other than to put Suchet on a heightened sense of alert, even failing to disable the cannons in Battery No. 4. The Spanish seized 300 tools, and the French took losses of eight killed, 11 wounded, and nine captured.

Although that his micromanagement of the trench defences had made possible a rapid response that evicted the Spanish before they could do any further damage, Suchet ordered further precautions be taken, and the next day, had further entrenchments dug to support Battery No. 4. Due to the continual harassing fire of Spanish sharpshooters who ventured out of the bridgehead to shoot at the French workers, an entrenchment was dug on the left bank of the Segre to screen the bridgehead and secure the bank, and two heavy cannon were added to Harispe's artillery battery to counter a Spanish battery posted on the Lérida bridge.[58]

The heavy artillery batteries of the first parallel were fully fortified and positioned by 7 May. The city of Lérida was shaken awake that morning when Suchet began his bombardment at 5:00 a.m. Concentrated fire on the Carmen and Magdalena bastions knocked out several cannons, but the Spanish were quick in responding with counter-battery fire from

55   Arteche y Moro, *Guerra de la Independencia*, Vol.VIII, p.324.
56   Suchet also put out bounties for spent cannonballs his soldiers retrieved and brought to the artillery depot, paying 25 centimes for a 6-pounder shot, with the amount going up as the calibre increased.
57   Belmas, *Journaux des siéges*, Vol.III, p.103. The grenadier company was led by *Capitaine* Bugeon. Belmas claims Bugeon to be Bugeaud, however, Bugeaud was an officer in the 116e.
58   Belmas, *Journaux des siéges*, Vol.III, p.106; David Rumsey Map Collection, 12140.007: Plan de Lerida, Pris le 13 Mai 1810, <https://www.davidrumsey.com/luna/servlet/detail/ RUMSEY~8~1~291000~90062501:Plan-de-Lerida-----le-13-Mai-1810->, accessed 6 December 2022. Belmas refers to this battery as No 7, Suchet calls it No 8. Though batteries No. 5 and No. 6 were yet to be created, their construction was likely finished before this one, hence the order.

the citadel. The French got the worst of it after several hours of trading shots. While the Spanish replaced their dismounted guns from their massive artillery arsenal, the French could not as easily haul fresh pieces to the batteries. Voltigeur Jacques-Abraham Graindor of the 2/116e Ligne was on guard duty at Mortar Battery No. 1, and testifies to the effectiveness of the Spanish artillery:

> [O]n May 6 [7], we began to beat in the breach at daybreak, but our battery was dismantled by the artillery of the ramparts. Our company of voltigeurs was on guard at this battery, more than fifty gunners were killed while manning their pieces as were several of our voltigeurs; our battery was too weak and the enemy played his artillery with such force that it was impossible to resist it. This delayed the capture of the city.[59]

The battery commander, *Capitaine* Brador, was killed, and the battery itself suffered notable damage when a Spanish shell scored a direct hit and exploded right in its midst.[60]

García Conde quickly organized a sortie against Battery No. 1 to finish it off. Three hundred Spaniards, some equipped with explosive fire-lances to destroy the mortars, sallied out that night. They managed to surprise the French sentries and captured the first line of trenches, but once again the French reserves – elements from the 5e Légère and the 114e Ligne, along with some Polish troops – arrived swiftly to restore the situation. The Spanish were compelled to flee, and the French went in hot pursuit only to be quickly halted by a devastating volley of grape shot from Lérida's guns.[61] Spanish losses were slight at eight killed and nine captured, thanks to the cover of the fortress artillery, while the French suffered unnecessary losses of a similar count to the very same guns.

The siege was seemingly at a stalemate, but the French quickly regained the initiative. A second parallel was constructed, more artillery pieces were brought up to upgrade existing batteries, damaged cannons were repaired, and three new batteries dubbed No. 5, No. 6, and No. 8 were created.[62] French sharpshooters picked off any Spanish artillerymen that attempted to man the guns of the bastion while these preparations were put into place. Howitzer and mortar batteries utilized their extended arcs of fire to lay down a suppressive fire on the citadel, screening the heavy siege guns which focused on battering the city walls. Spanish gunners maintained a steady bombardment, but with significantly less effect than before.

At 9:00 a.m. on the morning of the 12th, Suchet ordered a grand bombardment by all eight of his artillery batteries, which totalled 15 cannon, eight mortars, and 11 howitzers. The Spanish responded with 30 of their own cannon: 20 from the walls, four from the citadel, and six from the bridge.[63] This time, the French gained the upper hand. The careful preparations since the failed bombardment of 7 May paid off, for the Spanish cannon were quickly silenced. An ammunition case in the Louvigny bastion of the citadel was hit and

---

59   Graindor, *Mémoires de la Guerre d'Espagne*, p.37.
60   Suchet, *Memoirs of the War in Spain*, Vol.I, p.144.
61   Belmas, *Journaux des siéges*, Vol.III, p.108.
62   The revised batteries are presented in the map and appendix.
63   Arteche y Moro, *Guerra de la Independencia*, Vol.VIII, p.328.

exploded, further compounding the chaos in the city. Able to work unhindered, the French gunners maintained a relentless barrage for the entire day, with each cannon reported to have fired over one hundred shots. By evening, the sustained bombardment had created two large breaches in the Carmen bastion.

Meanwhile, the situation in Lérida was getting more and more dire by the day. Despite the breaches, García Conde, perhaps heavily influenced by the restless citizenry, resolved to contest the town, something he knew had cost the French dearly at Zaragoza. To that end he began to barricade and entrench the streets, and placed artillery at strategic points from where their cannonballs could plough down the entire length of a street. Several Swiss deserters informed Suchet of these preparations, leading him to give up all hope that the breaches would be enough to convince García Conde to surrender.[64] Fanatical house-to-house resistance was the heart of Spanish siege defences in the Peninsular War, and while the Spanish may have let the French get so close to the walls, it was only by ineptitude that the Spanish had failed to use the full strength of their massive garrison and armed citizenry to inflict more damage on the French siege works. Suchet knew that against Spanish numbers, the fighting in the streets was apt to be a bloodbath for his men. What would render the Siege of Lérida controversial was the callous brutality so often seen in siege warfare, which in this case, came not so much from the troops fighting in the breaches and streets, but from the top-down, from Suchet himself. It was from this point that Suchet began to formulate his *coup de main* plan, to turn the civilians of Lérida into a burden for García Conde. At first glance, the forts on the plateau themselves were questionable targets, being so far away from Suchet's intended breach point. According to his *Memoirs*, Suchet decided to capture the outlying works on the plateau to deny a possible escape route for the Spanish in the city, for he intended to drive them all into the citadel and them concentrate his fire there to force a quick surrender.[65] This elaborate and cruel plan was conveyed to all of the officers well before the final storming.

Général de Brigade Vergez was once again tasked with taking the redoubts of San Fernando and del Pilar, as well as the outlying hornwork of Fort Gardeny. Both Suchet and Vergez had apparently learned from their earlier failure, for this time the French assault parties were well equipped with ladders and axes. On the moonlit night of 12 May, three French assault columns started their simultaneous assault. Suchet presents the strengths of the French storming parties as such:[66]

- Column 1: Commanded by Vergez, 114e Ligne (one battalion), 121e Ligne (four elite companies), 100 pioneers.
- Column 2: Commanded by Buget, 114e (four elite companies), 121e (two elite companies), 'several' sappers.
- Column 3: Commanded by Plagniol, 3e Vistule (two elite companies) and 400 pioneers.

The Spanish had failed to properly reinforce the del Pilar redoubt since the first attack, and its garrison was rapidly overwhelmed and put to flight just as in the first assault. The del

---

64   Suchet, *Memoirs of the War in Spain*, Vol.I, p.147.
65   Suchet, *Memoirs of the War in Spain*, Vol.I, p.148.
66   Suchet, *Memoirs of the War in Spain*, Vol.I, p.148.

Pilar garrison was intercepted by Plagniol's column as they fled to the hornwork, which was quickly taken. The defenders of Fort Gardeny fell back to the main compound. The San Fernando redoubt put up a tougher resistance, though several French companies managed to lay down a suppressing fire on the defenders long enough for the other storming parties to scale the walls. Surrounded, the Spanish defenders made a desperate last stand, inflicting heavy losses on the French as they swarmed all over the walls. At the end of the chaotic night battle, only a Spanish lieutenant and 20 men remained standing to surrender to the French. Suchet lists French casualties in this action as around 100, while the Spanish lost around 240 men and five cannons.[67] Exhausted French soldiers in their trenches and nervous Spanish civilians alike slept warily amidst the thunder of the French siege guns, which had been ordered to fire throughout the night in preparation for the inevitable assault.

The next day, 13 May, Suchet passed orders to Habert to prepare for a general assault that evening. The three assault companies designated to lead the attack were assembled in the second parallel: *Colonel* Rouelle led the first column, a company each of carabiniers and voltigeurs from the 5e Légère and a detachment of sappers that would attack the breach on the left side of the Carmen bastion; the second was led by engineer *Capitaine* Vallentin, who also had a company of carabiniers from the 5e and a detachment of sappers that was to attack the right face; the third, under *Lieutenant* Romphleur, was made up of a voltigeur company and some miners that were to follow behind Rouelle's column.[68] Following the assault companies would be sappers, pioneers, and infantry of the 1er Vistule, 5e Légère, 115e Ligne, and 116e Ligne. At 7:00 p.m., a prearranged signal of four simultaneous cannon shots marked the start of the attack, and the infantry clambered out of the trenches to rush the breaches.

The assault columns managed to gain the breaches without great loss despite being under heavy fire, but, in the entrenchments and fortified houses in front of the main street, the Spanish defenders fought with desperation, supported by artillery from the citadel and bridge. Each house became a blockhouse from which Spanish defenders poured volleys at the oncoming French. Graindor recounts the assault:

> [S]even or eight bombs had been set off around the breach to keep the enemy away but he was not far away, he was shooting us with intense fire as we went up. The fort was firing all its artillery on this side and sending us terrible volleys of grapeshot but this did not prevent us from reaching the town. We found ourselves in front of a barracks, where there was a Swiss regiment [Regimiento de Traxler 5° de Suizos] that did us a lot of harm, it wanted to charge us with bayonets but our elite companies launched themselves at it with such force that it was almost destroyed.[69]

Colonel Rouelle was wounded in the side leading his men down the main street, and for some time the battle hung in balance as both sides traded intense close-range fire. The Spanish continued to defend the entrenchments in the streets, even as Romphleur's column managed to fight their way to the Magdalena gate and blew it open from the inside, allowing

---

67   Suchet, *Memoirs of the War in Spain*, Vol.I, p.150.
68   Belmas, *Journaux des siége*, Vol.III, pp.119-120.
69   Graindor, *Mémoires de la Guerre d'Espagne*, pp.37-38.

The storming of Lérida, by F. Campana, From Blanch, Adolfo, *Cataluña: Historia de la Guerra de la Independencia,* (Barcelona: Imprenta y Librería Politécnica de Tomás Gorchs, 1861), Vol. II. (Public Domain)

The assault on the Carmen bastion, viewed from Battery No. 4., by Paul Philippoteaux, From Thiers, Louis Adolphe, *Histoire du Consulat et de l'Empire,* (Paris: 1865), digitized by the British Library

in more French soldiers. *Capitaine* Thomas Bugeaud, commanding a grenadier company of the 116e Ligne, captures the chaotic and frenzied nature of the fight. He wrote:

> The walls were escalated, the works were entered, several barricades were broken, and our enemies perished in crowds under our blows. A gate leading to the quays delayed us a moment: then several of our brave men were killed by a point-blank discharge. At last the gate was broken; we entered in a mass, racing with one another. Every man wanted to be first to strike, nothing could stop us – bayonets, shot, and pikes could not daunt our ardour. I have the luck of penetrating the mass with my company; I am the first to reach a fortified post, and I cut off a lot of the enemy with whom we treated to the edge of the sword and the bayonet.[70]

The decisive factor of the battle turned out to be Vallentin's column. Vallentin had not in fact led his men into the breach, but taken them along the city wall to enter Lérida from behind the Carmen bastion, into the city quay. As a result, the Spanish defenders in the main street found themselves outflanked and were forced to retreat. Simultaneously, Harispe successfully attacked Perena's men in the bridgehead from the east bank of the Segre. The gunners on the bridge and the garrison of the bridgehead found their retreat into Lérida cut off and fled through the French lines to the nearby fortress of Mequinenza.

Once the French had gained a foothold in the northern part of the city, a general advance was ordered. Suchet personally led the reserves into Lérida, and *Colonel* Robert stormed the city across the Lérida bridge. The overwhelmed Spanish defenders fell back to the citadel as the confusion of night fell. Yet the siege was not over yet. Spanish civilians hiding in their homes were dragged out, then forced at bayonet point to flee to the citadel. Some were shot as they fled up the street, their confusion surmounted by the garrison shooting down from the citadel. Suchet had ordered his troops to block every gate out of the city, making escape impossible.[71] The pathway up to the citadel was crammed with a horde of panicked soldiers and civilians forced upwards by the French in the town. They poured into the citadel in such a rush that García Conde, who had only intended to give entry to soldiers, had no time to respond or even consider closing the gates.[72] By the time he raised the drawbridge, the citadel was bustling with hundreds of civilians. Those who failed to escape to the citadel hid in the ditch and covered way of the citadel or fled to the churches. Within the city, French soldiers ran amok, looting and pillaging. Graindor continues:

> After a strong resistance, which did us a lot of damage, the whole garrison withdrew to the fort, which did not stop firing during the night. The city was destroyed, everything was turned upside down, all the stores were knocked down, merchandise was found everywhere in the stairwells from the cellar to the attic. I decided to do as the

---

70   Letter to Mdelle. Antoinette de la Piconnerie, 4 June, 1810, from Thomas R. Bugeaud, *Memoirs of Marshal Bugeaud From His Private Correspondence and Original Documents 1784-1849* (London: Hurst and Blackett, 1884), Vol.I, p.70.

71   Suchet, *Memoirs of the War in Spain*, Vol.I, p.153.

72   Andreas Daniel Berthold von Schepeler, *Histoire de la révolution d'Espagne et de Portugal, ainsi que de la guerre qui en résulta* (Liège: J. Desoer, 1829), Vol.II, p.617.

Spanish Infantry 1809-1810: Fusilero of the Regimiento 2° de Saboya (L) and Cazador of the Regimiento de Traxler 5° de Suizo (R), by Yinuo Liu, photography by Blake Bridge. (Author's Collection)

others did, but we didn't trade in money, we chose light goods. I took a piece of black silk handkerchief, it was not very heavy but it was day [sic] that I had not found a penny yet. We looted during the night without having the order to do so.[73]

But the battle was not over, for the citadel continued to hold out and rain fire at the French forces, and to end the siege Suchet had one final, tragic, card to play.

Every French cannon, howitzer, and mortar was ordered to concentrate its fire upon the citadel, which was crammed with several thousand soldiers and civilians seeking refuge.

---

73   Graindor, *Mémoires de la Guerre d'Espagne 1808-1814*, p.38.

In the 1707 siege the citadel had held out several days after the town had been taken – such a situation would cost Suchet time and lives that he could ill-afford.[74] While the Spanish soldiers and officers could be expected to withstand a bombardment, the same could not be said for the elderly, women, children, and unarmed peasants whom Suchet had forced into the citadel. His hope was that the devastation wrought by an intense bombardment would terrify the civilians enough that they would pressure García Conde and his officers to end the siege.[75] Throughout the night and into the morning of the next day the Spanish endured the terrible bombardment, their torment finally ending when García Conde raised a white flag at noon. *Général de Brigade* Valée and *Colonel* Saint-Cyr Nugues were sent to negotiate and sign the surrender terms with García Conde, while *Colonel* Haxo did the same for the commander of Fort Gardeny, which had not been attacked in the siege. At 4:00 p.m. the garrison of Lérida filed out of the city and laid down their weapons. After a month of gruelling siege-work, Lérida had at last fallen.

The terms of capitulation called for the surrender of 7,291 Spanish soldiers, officers, and generals.[76] Also taken in the surrender were 10 flags and the city's 105 cannon, as well as vast quantities of munitions and provisions. Nearly 2,000 Spanish soldiers and civilians are estimated to have been killed in the siege. Of those, some 500 were casualties of the bombardment of the citadel alone. French losses in the siege were about 1,100 killed and wounded.[77] Thirty-three French officers who had been held prisoner in Lérida were also rescued. The garrison of the city was granted the full honours of war, though they gave up their weapons and were marched into captivity. The officers were permitted to retain their mounts and sidearms.[78] Explicit conditions were made on the part of Suchet that granted the civilian gunners and militia full amnesty, and that they were free to leave the city on parole. On the other hand, Suchet granted his army two hours of officially sanctioned looting which saw the city's houses thoroughly pillaged of all money and valuables.[79] *Colonel* Henriod of the 14e Ligne was named governor of Lérida and accordingly promoted to *Général de Brigade*. Chronic gout had made field service painful for Henriod, but he had lost none of his hard-bitten edge and would govern Lérida with an iron fist on one hand and self-enriching corruption in the other. It would be up to Henriod to enforce the 1,500,000 franc levy Suchet imposed on Lérida on the orders of Napoleon both as retribution for its resistance and as a means to fund his army.[80]

---

74   Oman, *Peninsular War*, Vol.III, p.306.

75   Suchet, *Memoirs of the War in Spain*, Vol.I, p.154.

76   Suchet, *Memoirs of the War in Spain*, Vol.I, p.361; see also summary of the capitulation in Arteche y Moro, *Guerra de la Independencia*, Vol.VIII, p.504. Of those surrendered, 475 were wounded in the city hospital.

77   Digby Smith, *The Greenhill Napoleonic Wars Data Book* (London: Greenhill Books, 1998), p.342.

78   Arteche y Moro, *Guerra de la Independencia*, Vol.VIII, p.337, states that many Spanish officers were paroled on the condition that they would not take up arms, though this clause was later excluded from the official report.

79   Graindor, *Mémoires de la Guerre d'Espagne 1808-1814*, p.38.

80   Order of General Suchet imposing a war tax upon Lerida, from Belmas, *Journaux des siéges*, Vol.III, p.165. Letter 16505 to the Prince de Neuchatel, 27 May., 1810, from Bonaparte, *Correspondence de Napoléon*, Vol. XX, p.439-40.

Line Infantry Voltigeur, by Pierre-Albert Leroux.
(Anne S.K. Brown Military Collection, Brown University Library)

For Suchet, the quick end to the siege brought his army out of a position in which they were the most vulnerable to guerrilla warfare. With only 13,000 men to take a fortress garrisoned by 8,000, Suchet sought a rapid and decisive end, knowing that he could not sustain a prolonged siege. Against Suchet's well-defended siege lines, García Conde never committed enough men from his large garrison to raise the chances of a successful sortie. According to a report by José Obispo, the dual defeats at Margalef and Lérida led to up to 8,000 desertions in the 1° Ejército.[81] Napoleon sent orders for Suchet to demolish the outer fortifications of Lérida, so that the city would only need five to six hundred men in the citadel to control the population.[82] Suchet declined to follow these instructions, for he was unwilling to further stir the ire of the population and saw Lérida as an excellent base of operations in Catalonia.[83] This time, Suchet was wise to not submit himself to Napoleon's will against his better judgement, for Lérida would prove to be a vital French asset in supporting the campaigns that were to come.

The Siege of Mequinenza[84]

On the morning of 15 May, the day after Lérida had surrendered, the 121e Ligne was dispatched to Mequinenza, where it began to screen the town from the left bank of the Segre. Situated at the juncture where the Segre flowed into the Ebro, Mequinenza and its fortifications were vital to controlling river traffic. Its capture would also be of symbolic importance, for it was also the final Spanish stronghold in Aragon.

Though Mequinenza's garrison had been inactive during the Siege of Lérida, such was the association between the two that Suchet's original orders were to besiege both at the same time.[85] However, the French had clearly underestimated Mequinenza's defensive capabilities. While it was not a large city like Lérida, nor possessed a large garrison or particularly formidable defensive works, Mequinenza's greatest defensive feature was the terrain on which it was situated. The elevated castle held a commanding view of the intersection of the Segre and Ebro rivers from a 500-foot-high plateau – too elevated for any siege guns to batter the castle from ground level.[86] This plateau was the southernmost tip of the Monnegre mountains, which extended along the right bank of the Segre River all the way from Fraga to the confluence of the Segre and Ebro. Three sides of the plateau were either too steep or were right up against the Ebro, so that the only available avenue of assault was the western face, where most of the castle's defensive works were concentrated. The castle itself was

---

81   Antonio Moliner Prada, *Tarragona (mayo-junio 1811): Una ciudad sitiada durante la Guerra del Francés* (Madrid: Doce Calles, 2011), p.35.

82   Letter 16505 to the Prince de Neuchatel, 27 May 1810, from Bonaparte, *Correspondence de Napoléon*, Vol. XX, pp.439-440.

83   Arteche y Moro, *Guerra de la Independencia*, Vol.VIII, p.338-9.

84   Unless otherwise cited, narrative background is summarised from: Arteche y Moro, *Guerra de la Independencia*, Vol.VIII, pp.339-342; Belmas, *Journaux des siéges*, Vol.III, pp.179-204; Suchet, *Memoirs of the War in Spain*, Vol.I, p.165-176.

85   Letter 16245 to the Prince de Neuchatel, 12 February 1810, from Bonaparte, *Correspondence de Napoléon*, Vol. XX, pp.241-242.

86   Oman, *Peninsular War*, Vol.III, p.309.

medieval but had been modernized. The town of Mequinenza was on the little corner of land between the Ebro and the steep slope of the plateau, which formed two narrow access points into the town, both of which were lightly fortified. The town and castle were garrisoned by 1,000 men and 50 guns under *Coronel* Manuel Carbón, who had fought in Blake's ill-fated 2º Ejército back in 1809. Though his men must have been demoralized by the fall of Lérida, Carbón rejected initial French offers for him to capitulate. After the fall of Lérida and O'Donnell's defeat at Margalef there was little hope of relief for Carbón and his men. Despite this, the Spanish resolved to put up a gallant defence, placing well-founded faith in their highly defensible position.

On the evening of 19 May, Suchet arrived before Mequinenza on the right bank of the Segre with the 114e Ligne and 2e Vistule. The next day the French advanced onto the plateau and drove in the Spanish outposts, and part of the 121e was brought across the river to the right bank and took up position behind a hill on the flat ground north of Mequinenza. After assessing the situation and tasking Musnier with overseeing the siege of Mequinenza, Suchet departed to secure Lérida and attend to governing Aragon. The French artillery departed for Mequinenza not long after the infantry; on 18 May, *Général de Brigade* Valée had received orders from Suchet to take part of the French siege train at Lérida to besiege Mequinenza. For the French, getting their siege train to Mequinenza was itself a challenge. The Spanish had destroyed the bridge over the Cinca River at Fraga, forcing the French to build a pontoon bridge. Its construction was delayed for 11 days due to the violent swelling of the river by up to 10 feet, and it was only with great difficulty and persistence that the siege train finally began to cross on 31 May.[87]

While this first hurdle was being overcome, Musnier began to consider how he would move his siege artillery, once it arrived, onto the plateau and directly in front of the castle from which they could breach its walls, for the whole fortress complex was situated too high up for a bombardment from ground level to be effective.[88] While most of the road along the ridgeline needed only minor repairs, the greatest difficulty arose at the steep decline which separated the Monnegre ridgeline and the plateau with Mequinenza Castle. The existing road which led straight down into the ridge and then back up the plateau and to the castle was too steep for the heavy guns to navigate – the guns would simply roll downhill and flatten anything in their path. Under Musnier's and Haxo's supervision, a new path was built down the ridge in a wide zig-zag pattern to diminish the acute downward slope. This path eventually joined the original path up the relatively gentle slope of the plateau. Some 200 Catalan peasants and an equal number of French infantry were employed as laborers, and at some points it became necessary to use gunpowder to blow through rocks.[89]

While this road was being dug, the French actively went on the offensive to hem in the garrison by seizing the banks of both rivers. Mequinenza became fully surrounded with the arrival of Montmarie on the right bank of the Ebro. Immediately after seeing off the remnants of Lazán's 2º Ejército from Aragon, Montmarie had received orders to assist in the siege of Mequinenza, and arrived on 28 May from Alcañiz with the 14e Ligne, forcing Spanish troops on the right bank of the Ebro to retreat. The engineer *Général de Brigade*

87   Belmas, *Journaux des siéges*, Vol.III, p.182.
88   Suchet, *Memoirs of the War in Spain*, Vol.I, p.167.
89   Suchet, *Memoirs of the War in Spain*, Vol.I, pp.167-168.

The Siege of Mequinenza, 15 May–8 June 1810.

Joseph Rogniat arrived two days later with a bevy of engineers and sappers as well as a convoy of tools and supplies to assist in the siege: a much needed reinforcement, for III Corps was in need of siege specialists.[90]

The Mequinenza garrison was concerned with the pace of French progress, and thus made a sortie of 800 men on 31 May preceded by a cannonade. Their sortie was spotted and lost the element of surprise: by the time the Spanish reached the French outposts, they were met with withering fire from 300 voltigeurs and driven back. In contrast, French gains only grew in the early days of June. By 1 June the siege train was at last on its way across the Cinca to Mequinenza. On the night of 2 June, the voltigeurs of the 114e overran a Spanish outpost behind a hillock about 200 yards in front of the fort. Haxo lost not a moment in bringing up 500 workers to begin construction of the first parallel.[91] Despite most of the digging being done in the cover of the night, the French work crews were kept pinned in their shallow trench by steady volleys of grapeshot from the castle, whose gunners aimed their guns to the sounds of pickaxes ringing against the rocky soil. The work party lost nine killed and 23 wounded, but the Spanish garrison failed to stop the completion of the trench.[92] That same night, the Poles of the Vistula Legion took a Spanish forward post outside of the western wall of the town and managed to establish a trench across the narrow strip of land between the hill and the Ebro. Montmarie posted sharpshooters on the right bank of the Ebro to harass the defenders in the town. The vice was tightening around Mequinenza. Knowing that the French were in need of boats to navigate the Ebro, Carbón ordered the 11 boats in the town to leave for Spanish-held Tortosa.[93] It was convenient in any case for them to do so, for the recent French gains had made Mequinenza's populace eager to flee. Packed with civilians and their belongings, these boats raced down the Ebro. Two ran aground and were taken by the French, but the other nine managed to get away safely.

On the night of 3 June, the first parallel on the plateau was extended and strengthened, and the foundations for the siege batteries were laid out. Against the town of Mequinenza itself, the French were unable to set up any artillery. The narrow valley in which they were situated offered a clear field of fire from a tower where the Spanish had mounted a cannon. Montmarie's sharpshooters harassed the defenders of this tower to great effect, eventually forcing the Spanish to abandon it and retreat to the castle. This opened up an opportunity to take the town, and on 4 June, *Général de Brigade* Rogniat ordered the 2e Vistule and a company of sappers to storm the town. The Poles to scale the walls and occupy the tower and outlying houses by 9:00 p.m., at which point the garrison conceded the town and withdrew up the plateau through the steep path leading up from the town to the castle. Musnier's men immediately set about securing the town; the Poles garrisoned the houses next to the path leading up to the castle to prevent any escape or sortie attempt, in response to which the garrison threw down shells and stones from above.[94]

Slowly but surely the French were closing in on the castle, pushing up zig-zag saps to create a second parallel. Three batteries had been hauled up – the first, four 8-inch mortars placed

90   Suchet, *Memoirs of the War in Spain*, Vol.I, p.169.
91   Belmas, *Journaux des siéges*, Vol.III, p.186.
92   Suchet, *Memoirs of the War in Spain*, Vol.I, p.170, claims that he lost 50 men.
93   Oman, *Peninsular War*, Vol.III, p.310.
94   Belmas, *Journaux des siéges*, Vol.III, p.190.

behind the first parallel to bombard the castle; the second, a battery of two 24-pounder guns and two 6-inch howitzers targeting the right face of the leftmost bastion; the third, four 24-pounders and two 16-pounders, targeting the rightmost bastion and the curtain wall.[95] Despite sporadic fire from the garrison, the saps inched to within 60 yards of the wall. On 5 June, 40 French grenadiers stormed the last Spanish outpost, dubbed the 'horse shoe' for its shape, and added this entrenchment to the siege works.[96]

Suchet arrived from Zaragoza on the 7th to oversee progress on the siege. He was fortunate in his timing, for the guns were nearly in position for the bombardment. At around 5:00 a.m. the next morning, 16 guns of the siege batteries opened fire on the bastion and wall in front of the castle. The Spanish put up a counter-battery fire and managed to knock out three guns, but by 9:00 a.m. a large section of the castle wall was destroyed.[97] With all of their artillery silenced, the garrison resorted to musketry, but it was little use against the furious bombardment. Knowing that his garrison would be slaughtered if the castle was stormed, *Coronel* Carbón hauled up a white flag at 10:00 a.m. and requested a truce, during which Suchet offered terms of surrender. Carbón had done what was expected of him as a fortress commander by conducting a valiant defence. *Capitaine* Remi-Pierre-Charles-Noêl Ponssin of the engineers wrote to his wife of the siege:

> Three nights in a row I marked out trenches under the most intense enemy musketry and grape shot. Unfortunate soldiers fell beside me, dead or wounded. I have not a scratch on me. The defenders surrendered this morning, after fifteen days of siege. They have handed us a heap of ruins. We cannot deny them that they defended themselves as very brave people.[98]

The capture of Mequinenza signified a landmark point in Suchet's career as well as Imperial fortunes in the Peninsular. Suchet's senior aide-de-camp, *Chef d'Escadron* Bernard Meinrad Meyer de Schauensée, was dispatched to France with news of the victories and 10 captured Spanish flags, Suchet's contribution to the collection of war trophies Napoleon's armies had amassed at Les Invalides.[99] The last Spanish stronghold in Aragon had fallen, leaving Suchet's occupation uncontested save for the dwindling guerrilla bands. There had been fewer and fewer guerrilla activities during the Siege of Mequinenza, in part due to Suchet's redirected attention to consolidating his holdings in Aragon. The partisans were slowly being expunged from Upper Aragon, for guerrilla bands were being defeated by gendarme units many times smaller than they were, and Habert was wreaking havoc on their bases in Catalonia.[100]

95   David Rumsey Map Collection, 12140.009: Plan de Mequinenza, Pris le 8 Juin 1810. <https://www. davidrumsey.com/luna/servlet/detail/RUMSEY~8~1~291002~90067364:Plan-de-Mequinenza%2C-Pris-le-8-Juin->, accessed 6 December 2022.

96   Suchet, *Memoirs of the War in Spain*, Vol.I, p.174.

97   Suchet, *Memoirs of the War in Spain*, Vol.I, p.176.

98   Letter of *Capitaine* Ponssin to Mdme. Ponssin, 9 June 1810, from De Neef, *Devils, Daggers, and Death*, p.206.

99   Report of Suchet to Prince Berthier, 8 June, 1810, from Belmas, *Journaux des siéges*, Vol.III, p.190.

100 Alexander, *Rod of Iron*, p.76; Oman, *Peninsular War*, Vol.III, p.310.

In contrast to the Siege of Lérida, where a large garrison and fortress had been brought to submission by a bombardment and conventional siege, Mequinenza posed an entirely new challenge where dislodging a small but geographically well-situated garrison had placed the focus of the siege on engineering efforts. Suchet capitalized on his gains by sending Montmarie with the 14e Ligne and 3e Vistule to make a foray into Valencia and seize Morella, which was taken on 13 June. Morella commanded the mountain pass from Valencia into Aragon, making it useful both as a forward base to threaten Valencia and as a buffer for Aragon. Realizing their error in failing to properly garrison the town, the Valencian government dispatched O'Donojú's division to recapture it on 25 June.[101] The Valencians pushed the French into the castle after several hours of hard fighting, but the attack failed when Montmarie sallied out with the garrison to break the Spanish encirclement.

Guerrilla Warfare During the Siege of Lérida

The guerrillas in Aragon had not been entirely idle while Suchet was away with his main army, though Suchet's operations in 1809 had greatly reduced their effectiveness. On 15 April, 38 gendarmes of the 10e Escadron hunted and engaged a large group of Spanish guerrillas and Swiss and Polish deserters led by Cantarer. Although too few to wipe out the 300-strong *partida*, the gendarmes inflicted heavy casualties and chased off the guerrillas.[102] Hoping to strike in Suchet's rear in the absence of the bulk of III Corps, the Marqués de Lazán led the remnants of the 2° Ejército from Valencia to seize Alcañiz in early May. The garrison under *Capitaine* Wikowski was forced to hole up in the citadel and send for aid when Lazán's men retook the city itself. When the garrison refused to surrender, Lazán was forced to commit to a siege. The Spanish lacked proper siege equipment and resorted to mining the castle walls. This became too great a danger to ignore, so a private of the 114e Ligne named Rolland snuck into the Spanish lines and rolled a howitzer shell into the mine, causing its premature collapse.[103] Things went from bad to worse for Lazán when *Général de Brigade* Montmarie arrived with a relief force of 2,000 men. Lazán's men were driven out of Alcañiz by the bayonet, then pursued by Montmarie's cavalry, losing 408 men.[104]

On 13 May, a convoy of 300 mules loaded with supplies headed to Zaragoza escorted by 315 infantrymen of the 14e Ligne and 32 gendarmes under the overall command of *Chef de Bataillon* Petit was ambushed by Villacampa's men at a pass near El Frasno. It was a textbook ambush, where the concealed Spanish suddenly opened fire at close range into the French convoy. Nearly surrounded, the French abandoned the mules and made a run for the nearby village of Paracuellos while under fire. About half of the escort managed to break out of the ambush, the remainder, including Petit, were killed or captured.[105] Villacampa's men

---

101   Suchet, *Memoirs of the War in Spain*, Vol.I, p.177.
102   Martin, *La gendarmerie française en Espagne et en Portugal*, p.331.
103   Maurice Jules Bertaux, *Historique du 114e régiment d'infanterie* (Niort: Imprimerie Th. Mercier, 1892), p.50. Rolland was awarded the *Legion d'Honneur* for this feat.
104   Alexander, *Rod of Iron*, p.76.
105   Suchet, *Memoirs of the War in Spain*, Vol.I, p.162; Petit was reportedly murdered before he could be exchanged.

also captured the elderly *afrancesado* mayor of El Frasno who had been with the convoy, and reportedly burned him alive. This ambuscade was the only major guerrilla success against Suchet during the Siege of Lérida. Immediately after the fall of Lérida Suchet took to destroying the guerrilla bands which he had feared would wreak havoc on his supply lines during the siege. Habert and his men were unleashed against Campoverde's 1º Ejercito and the guerrilla bases in Catalonia, while Chlopicki was able to drive Villacampa all the way to Cuenca, capturing 174 men.[106] A successful counter-guerrilla operation by gendarme *Chef d'Escadron* Halmont resulted in the capture of guerrilla leader Don Pedro and several of his lieutenants, who were executed.

The fall of Mequinenza meant that Suchet had finally destroyed all conventional opposition against him in Aragon. In that process his forces had also essentially decapitated the guerrilla movement in Aragon by either directly hunting them, or indirectly defeating them by taking their bases of operation. For many Aragonese the war began to seem like a lost cause, and the comforts of home tempted many to abandon the hard life of a guerrilla. With the surrounding Spanish bases captured and guerrillas suppressed within Aragon, the population became less and less willing to take up arms against the French.

---

106   Alexander, *Rod of Iron*, p.77.

5

The Siege of Tortosa

Preparations and Manoeuvres[1]

After the fall of Mequinenza, *Capitaine* Ponssin wrote 'The capture of Mequinenza opens the road to Tortosa and Valencia. We are going to leave this region, where we lacked everything, for one of the richest and most beautiful in Spain.'[2] Ponssin's excitement reflected that of the army, and the ambitions of French high command in subjugating all of Eastern Spain. Aragon was firmly in Suchet's hands, and with the capture of Lérida he now had a foothold in Lower Catalonia. Orders soon arrived from Paris dictating that he should now continue his campaign in Lower Catalonia and take the city of Tortosa. Dated 29 May, the order stated:

> The emperor supposes that you are now master of Mequinenza; in that case you will take immediate measures for getting possession of Tortosa also. The marshal duke of Tarentum will at the same time direct his forces on Tarragona. Take care in the meanwhile to collect all your artillery and to adopt every measure necessary for marching on Valencia and for storming that city; we must, however, in order to undertake that operation have Tortosa and Tarragona in our power.[3]

Tortosa, an old city of 10,000 people, occupied a key position along the main landward route between Valencia and Catalonia.[4] French grand strategy called for the isolation of the two pockets of resistance from each other, so as to render mutual support impossible, and taking Tortosa would seemingly accomplish that goal. However, the intermediary position of Tortosa between the two provinces also meant that any besieging army would be vulnerable to attacks from both O'Donnell's Catalonian forces and Caro's Valencians. Suchet knew that his field force would not be enough to take Tortosa and operate safely deep in enemy lines and accordingly, he was reassured by the news that *Maréchal* Etienne Jacques Macdonald, the Duc de Tarante, the newly-appointed commander of VII Corps, would

---

1   Unless cited otherwise, this section is summarized from Suchet, *Memoirs of the War in Spain*, Vol.I, p.179-234; Belmas, *Journaux des siéges*, Vol.III, p.407-417; Oman, *Peninsular War*, Vol.III, p.492-504.
2   Letter of *Capitaine* Ponssin, 9 June, 1810, from De Neef, *Devils, Daggers, and Death*, p.206
3   Suchet, *Memoirs of the War in Spain*, Vol.I, p.184.
4   Gates, *The Spanish Ulcer*, p.292.

support the operation by striking at the Catalonian stronghold of Tarragona and keeping O'Donnell occupied so that Suchet could operate against Tortosa unhindered.[5] Suchet would have to collaborate frequently with Macdonald, and this joint campaign would come with its own set of challenges.

Since his severe drubbing at Margalef, the indomitable Enrique O'Donnell had been hard at work in the summer months reorganizing the battered 1º Ejército. By the end of July he had consolidated his forces and amassed 22,000 men in five divisions to protect the borders of Catalonia. His position, with his main base of operations at Tarragona, was an excellent one: his forces enjoyed the support of the Royal Navy, and his central position enabled him to react quickly or strike at either Macdonald or Suchet. But against the combined overwhelming forces of III and VII Corps, O'Donnell stayed on the defensive – for now. Two of his divisions screened Macdonald, two others watched the Aragon border to guard against any attempt at taking Tortosa, and the fifth acted as a reserve for either front. The hotheaded and energetic O'Donnell found himself at odds with the Catalonian Junta over the relationship between conventional and irregular warfare. A professional soldier, O'Donnell espoused the virtues and effectiveness of Spain's regular armies, particularly his own 1º Ejército, and requested more men in the hopes that he could bring his army up to a formidable 50,000 men.[6] The Catalonian Junta disagreed – time and time again veteran French battalions had outmanoeuvred and outfought Spanish armies whether outnumbered or not. In their eyes, the better course of option was to focus on guerrilla warfare, launching deregulated bands of *miquelets* and *somantenes* to attack French 'soft targets', which was far less of a burden on the 1º Ejército's strained military budget.[7] That is not to say that O'Donnell did not appreciate the immense contributions irregular military groups had made to the Spanish war effort. Indeed, he even issued a proclamation for a general call to arms in Catalonia and French-occupied Aragon, writing:

> Let all the inhabitants of these townships who are in a state of taking them fly to arms. Choose brave and well-known patriots as leaders. Let all those from the township of Tarragona go to Falset and Tibisa; all those from Lleida and Tortosa to the banks of the Ebro to intercept their [French] communications. There can be nobody that will provide any aid to the perfidious enemy; for he will be treated as an enemy by his own brothers.[8]

Eventually the tireless O'Donnell had his way, correctly convincing the Junta that guerrillas alone could not achieve decisive results against the French. He was permitted to form the *miquelets* into 'legions' to supplement his army, though these troops were to serve only for two years and be granted a month's leave each year.

Anticipating that Macdonald would also work on the timeline prescribed by Napoleon, Suchet began the necessary preparations for a campaign against Tortosa by first carefully laying out the groundwork for a siege operation. Musnier was again left in charge

---

5   Suchet, *Memoirs of the War in Spain*, Vol.I, p.184.
6   Oman, *Peninsular War*, Vol.III, p.313.
7   Oman, *Peninsular War*, Vol.III, p.313.
8   Arteche y Moro, *Guerra de la Independencia*, Vol.IX, p.252.

Enrique O'Donnell, by J. Serra, From Blanch, Adolfo, *Cataluña: Historia de la Guerra de la Independencia*, (Barcelona: Imprenta y Librería Politécnica de Tomás Gorchs, 1861), Vol. II. (Public Domain)

of governing Aragon, though this time Suchet implemented a unit rotation, so that Buget was now assigned to Upper Aragon and Vergez to Lower Aragon. The more land Suchet conquered, the more troops it required to hold, so 3,500 men were detailed to guard French lines of communications along the Ebro. Another 8,400 men were left in Aragon for security duties, leaving Suchet with a field force of just 12,000 men. The newly-captured fortresses of Lérida and Mequinenza were put to use as bases of operation for the coming campaign. Valée was tasked with assembling a siege train at Mequinenza of 52 guns with 700 rounds for each, while grain stores were established at Lérida by requisitioning portions of the local harvest. The major advantage Suchet possessed was that both his target city and his supply bases of Mequinenza and Lérida were along the Ebro River, allowing him to make greater use of boats to directly transport supplies. Though it was estimated that the boats could do in three days what a thousand pack animals could not do in a month, the boats alone could not do the work, for the heavy artillery could only be transported to Tortosa on the Ebro by boat when fall rains brought the water level back up to a viable height for heavily-laden ships to sail, necessitating roadwork to facilitate transportation of men and supplies by land.[9] On 21 June, Pâris' brigade began to secure the old ruined road which ran from Mequinenza to Tortosa, while Rogniat led four companies of sappers and some 1,000 infantrymen in the gruelling task of rendering the road useable for artillery and wagons under an unbearable summer sun in a hostile and rugged landscape.[10]

The siege of Tortosa would bear resemblance to the siege of Lérida, not the least because both cities were wholly anchored on one side of the Ebro. As he had done in the Lérida campaign, Suchet designated separate routes of march for his divisions so that they would approach the city from opposite banks and occupy strategic positions to isolate Tortosa. The situation was still too tenuous to fully consolidate the French army at Tortosa, as it was necessary to watch for both Caro and O'Donnell. Laval's 1st Division of 6,000, followed by a small mixed column under Boussart, was ordered to march from Alcañiz and take a direct overland route to arrive in front of Tortosa on the right (west) bank of the Ebro, while Habert's 3rd Division would march south from Bellpuig and position itself on the left bank of the Ebro at Garcia, to be ready on short notice to march to Tortosa. Three miles out of Tortosa on 4 July, Laval's division encountered a detachment of Swiss infantry which they chased back to the gates of Tortosa.[11] But the French would hardly get a moment of rest, for the Tortosa garrison was determined to stop the French before their siege lines could be fully established. That same day, 2,000 men of the garrison led by Governor Manuel Velasco poured out of the tête-de-pont under the cover of the fortress guns and threw back Laval's advance posts, nearly overrunning them.[12] During this sortie, the 14-year old Francisco Agustin Arandi joined the sortie party and made himself a city hero by shooting dead a French officer.[13] Nonetheless, the French seized the ferry crossing at Amposta, which left

9   Belmas, *Journaux des siéges*, Vol.III, p.414.
10   Suchet, *Memoirs of the War in Spain*, Vol.I, p.187.
11   Brandt, *In the Legions of Napoleon*, p.122. Daniel Fernandez y Domingo, *Anales ó Historia de Tortosa* (Barcelona: Establecimiento Tipográfico de Jaime Jepus: 1867), p.191. Brandt describes the Spanish outpost Laval encountered as the Guardias Valonas, however, they were most likely Swiss infantry.
12   Arteche y Moro, *Guerra de la Independencia*, Vol.IX, p.256; Brandt, *In the Legions of Napoleon*, p.122-123.
13   Fernandez y Domingo, *Anales ó Historia de Tortosa*, p.191.

only the pontoon bridge at Tortosa as a viable means of communication between Valencia and Catalonia. The French attempted to sabotage this last crossing by setting some barges on fire and drifting them downstream, but the scheme failed. As Habert and Laval conducted their concentric manoeuvres, Pâris' brigade advanced to Mora, 30 miles north of Tortosa, where Suchet established his headquarters on 6 July. Various towns were occupied along the routes between the separated French units to maintain a secure line of communications, and pontoon bridges were erected at Mora and further downstream at Xerta to link the French forces on opposite banks. Between 6-8 July, Laval's men began to dig entrenchments, which were vigorously contested by sorties from the garrison.

III Corps was well into making its preliminary preparations for the siege when, much to his horror, Suchet was informed on 9 July that Macdonald was still at Girona and had yet to move against Tarragona. Macdonald was running far behind the prescribed Imperial time-line by delaying his offensive manoeuvres to consolidate his own precarious situation. The food stores in Barcelona, his base of operations, were running dangerously low. Catalonia could barely supply its population with enough food in peacetime conditions and relied on Aragon for food imports; now impossible until a reliable line of communication could be established between the two provinces.[14] The only way to bring in food was through the overland route from France: the British Mediterranean fleet controlled the seas, while the overland route from Aragon to Barcelona ran through the Catalan mountains, where Spanish guerrillas and regular units alike were sheltering. But each convoy in the winding passes of the Pyrenees required a full division as an escort, and through the summer months Macdonald arranged for no less than three massive convoys to fill his food stores. Macdonald thoroughly despised his new assignment, and for good reason.[15] He was isolated from any other French force, and the mountainous regions were hotbeds of guerrilla warfare. Macdonald's inability to support Suchet threw a massive wrench into the siege operations, none the least because it freed up the 1º Ejército. Suchet was extremely distressed, for 'From that moment the position of general Suchet before Tortosa, was no longer the same; he even regretted that he had been tempted to invest it, but as he felt persuaded that a retreat might be attended with fatal consequences, he determined to maintain himself where he was…'[16]

O'Donnell was not one to sit back and wait for Suchet and Macdonald to get into position. The union between III and VII Corps was to be prevented by all means, and the energetic O'Donnell knew that he needed to delay, if not prevent, the junction of the two French corps. Suchet's worst fears were realized when one of O'Donnell's divisions nearly overwhelmed the voltigeur company of the 2/116e, which had established a forward position at Tivissa, on 10 July. Though attacked from all sides, the voltigeurs escaped to Mora with heavy losses after desperate fighting. The Spanish advanced on the pontoon bridge at Mora the next day, which was held by two battalions of the 116e Ligne, and supported by 96 Polish lancers under Klicki.[17] Graindor writes, 'the enemy was ten against one, they were everywhere, they occupied all the defiles of the hill. We were only two weak battalions without

14   Oman, *Peninsular War*, Vol.III, p.311.
15   Oman, *Peninsular War*, Vol.III, p.312.
16   Suchet, *Memoirs of the War in Spain*, Vol.I, p.194.
17   Graindor, *Mémoires de la Guerre d'Espagne 1808-1814*, p.41-42. The primary eyewitness of the engagements at Tivissa and Mora, Jacques-Abraham Graindor, refers to the entire incident as the

artillery or cartridge boxes and, our own [ammunition] depleted, we had to resort to our bayonets.'[18] It was a desperate fight for survival by the 116e Ligne; acting-colonel *chef de bataillon* Ausmane was hit leading his men, and the regiment suffered about 300 casualties. Charges by Klicki's lancers kept the Spanish at bay, as did a manoeuvre by *chef de bataillon* Bujot, who conducted three companies to hide in a ravine and remove the white shako covers worn by the 116e Ligne, before redeploying them on the main road. The distinction in headgear gave all the combatants the impression that Bujot's men were of a different unit: 'The enemy believed that we had reinforcements and we also believed it, we started to take courage, the enemy started to bend, we made splendid charges with our bayonets. The Spaniards, after having overrun us all day, abandoned the battlefield and we spent the night among the dead and wounded.'[19]

The following day, Pâris arrived with reinforcements and Habert threatened the Spanish flank a few days later. On the 12th, 1,500 men of the garrison launched another and took the French outposts at the villages of Jesus and Las Roquetas by surprise. Their progress was short lived when a Franco-Polish counterattack drove the Spanish back, inflicting about 100 casualties. These scares prodded Suchet to enlarge the bridge at Xerta to better allow his troops to respond to threats on either bank of the Ebro. But even additional reinforcements could not prevent the Spanish from delivering a large food convoy into the city on the 14th, and all throughout July the Spanish garrison energetically bombarded the French skirmished with their posts.[20]

On 30 July, O'Donnell made a feint towards Mora with 10,000 men, attacking Habert at Tivissa while personally sneaking 2,500 troops – two infantry regiments and the cavalry Regimiento de Santiago – to Tortosa to bolster the garrison there. The arrival of these reinforcements rejuvenated the spirits of the people. On 3 August, O'Donnell harangued his troops and the citizenry in what one can imagine as a grandiose and chauvinistic speech, to which the garrison responded that they would 'vanquish or die.'[21] Then, at 4:00 p.m., O'Donnell unleashed 800 infantrymen of the augmented garrison and 60 cavalrymen of the Regimiento de Santiago across the Tortosa bridge and out of the bridgehead. They were formed into three columns, the right comprised of the 3/Regimiento de Soria under *Coronel* José María Torrijos, the center was made up of the Legión Cataluña under *Teniente Coronel* José Fabregues, and on the right was *Coronel* Edmundo O'Ronan with 100 Spanish marines and sappers.[22] The Spanish withheld their fire, sprinting to the French lines with bayonets lowered, shouting 'Viva Fernando VII!'.[23] This bold attack drove back Laval's forward posts, but there was sufficient advance warning for the French to hurry out of their camp and form a line of battle. Spearheaded by their cavalry, the Spanish attacked with renewed energy in

---

'Battle of Tivissa'. Based on contextual evidence, the author believes that the battle Graindor details as the 'Battle of Tivissa' was in fact the engagement at Mora.

18 Graindor, *Mémoires de la Guerre d'Espagne 1808-1814*, p.42.
19 Graindor, *Mémoires de la Guerre d'Espagne 1808-1814*, p.42.
20 Fernandez y Domingo, *Anales ó Historia de Tortosa*, p.197.
21 Brandt, *In the Legions of Napoleon*, p.148.
22 Diversos-Colecciones, 78, N.62: Diario del sitio de la plaza de Tortosa durante el mes de Agosto.
23 Fernandez y Domingo, *Anales ó Historia de Tortosa*, p.200.

the presence of O'Donnell and his reinforcements, making steady progress in some places and destroying the French siege works. Von Brandt writes of the action:

> They [Spanish cavalry] turned our defences and charged right into the village of Jesus, our headquarters. Here they sabred some of our cavalry and killed one of the sentries posted at the general's door. Fired on by the duty company, they broke up and fled in different directions and very few of them seem to have made it back to Tortosa. If they had not lost their heads, they might have destroyed the artillery park, which was poorly guarded, and then come back and taken us in the rear… For the infantry there was some short but bloody hand-to-hand fighting which we soon won. The *Miquelets*, above all, were fighting like madmen and almost impaled themselves on our bayonets in attempting to get at our officers. I caught sight of one of them, a huge swarthy-looking man drunk on patriotism or something else, coming straight at me. He was about to make a lunge at me when one of my sergeants killed him.[24]

Chlopicki, waving his cane in the midst of the firing line, rallied his men and outflanked the Spanish centre column, compelling them to retreat back to the bridgehead, a process which was aided by the arrival of Laval at the head of a column of grenadiers. Torrijos had over-extended himself in his enthusiastic attack, and a large part of his column was cut off and captured.[25, 26] Both sides suffered around 200 casualties.[27]

Though substantially less active than O'Donnell's Catalonian army, the 2° Ejército of Valencia did make some attempts to contribute to the summer campaign. In early August, *Mariscal de Campo* Luis de Alejandro Bassecourt led his division to retake Morella, which Suchet had seized in June, and draw away Suchet's attention. Bassecourt attempted to surround Morella and cut off the French, but Montmarie's brigade arrived and drove the Valencians back. On 6 August, French scouts apprehended a *coronel* of the Regimiento de Granada near Lérida. Upon searching him they discovered a letter detailing the movements of *Teniente General* José Caro's 2° Ejército. 20,000 soldiers, half regulars and half *somatenes*, were moving towards Tortosa. Though badly outnumbered by the two Spanish armies, Suchet occupied a central position in the mountainous Ebro valley, and as long as he kept O'Donnell and Caro separated he could defeat them in detail. No aid could be expected in time from Macdonald, who was still moving his supply convoys to Barcelona,

---

24   Brandt, *In the Legions of Napoleon*, p.126.
25   Diversos-Colecciones, 78, N.62: Diario del sitio de la plaza de Tortosa durante el mes de Agosto.
26   Suchet, *Memoirs of the War in Spain*, Vol.I, p.198; Brandt, *In the Legions of Napoleon*, p.126. Suchet credits Laval with pushing back the Spanish assault, but Brandt states that the action had already been decided in Chlopicki's favor by the time Laval arrived.
27   Suchet, *Memoirs of the War in Spain*, Vol.I, p.199; Arteche y Moro, *Guerra de la Independencia*, Vol.XI, p.265. Arteche y Moro claims that a battalion flag or eagle standard of the 116e Ligne was taken in the sortie. It is not mentioned anywhere else, and if such an event did occur, the flag was likely retrieved after the siege. Suchet claims to have captured 220 prisoners in the retreat, but Arteche y Moro disputes this, though he concedes Spanish losses of 112 killed and wounded. Diversos-Colecciones, 78, N.62: Diario del sitio de la plaza de Tortosa durante el mes de Agosto. Official Spanish records place casualties at 26 killed, 80 wounded, and 187 captured.

but Suchet had confidence in his tight-knit veteran force. Leaving a small force under Pâris to guard Mora and watch for further incursions from Catalonia, Suchet repositioned Habert to Xerta, and personally rode to Laval's division, accompanied by Harispe and some reserve troops. By the 14th, Suchet had assembled 11 battalions of infantry and 800 cavalry, some 6,000 men, with which to battle the 2° Ejército, though this came at the cost of having to temporarily abandon the blockade of Tortosa. Suchet's advance guard of a squadron of 4e Hussards drove back the Valencian advance guard, alerting Caro, who was encamped at Cervera del Maestre. The Valencians took up a defensive position, but the timid Caro pulled his troops back after learning that Suchet was advancing in force.[28] Though he suffered a heart attack on 16 August, Suchet pressed on, eager to defeat the 2° Ejército for good, and for a moment it seemed as if the battle he so confidently sought would be his when the Spanish stopped their retreat and formed up in two lines.[29] However, just as the French were getting into a battle line themselves, Caro ordered a retreat, and his army withdrew in good order, denying the French battle once more.[30]

Perhaps on the surface Caro's actions may equate in terms of brilliance with the Roman Consul Quintus Fabius Maximus Verrucosus' famed withdrawal strategy against Hannibal. Caro's strategy of threatening Suchet but denying battle forced Suchet to constantly respond to the Valencian threat at the expense of the forces blockading Tortosa. Though Caro had over a three-to-one numerical superiority, his line infantry was of poor quality and the militia that made up half of his force were generally worthless in a straight fight against professional soldiers, so Caro's retreat was in some ways sensible.[31] However, Caro had conducted his retreat in fear of the French rather than with any justifiable strategy.[32] His disgusted subordinates, including his own brother, *Brigadier* Juan Caro y Sureda, staged a coup, forcing Caro to resign his position as commander of the 2° Ejército to be replaced by Bassecourt.[33] Caro then fled to Mallorca, fearing that the populace over which he had ruled with an iron fist would lynch him once they learned of his cowardice and eviction from power.

Suchet returned to Mora on the 20th to learn from one of Macdonald's aides-de-camp that Macdonald was finally advancing. Leaving *Général de Division* Baraguey d'Hilliers in charge of Northern Catalonia in his absence, Macdonald had skirmished heavily with the 1° Ejército and forced his way into the plains before Tarragona on the 13th with a field force of 16,000 in three divisions – all of his 50,000 men that were available for field duty, for such was the war in Spain that the rest were needed to hold Upper Catalonia and Barcelona, or were sick or wounded. French forces reconnoitred the area, driving in the Spanish outposts, until they were met with a determined fire from O'Donnell's troops and a British frigate. Macdonald was without his siege train, for it was not yet ready, and the land around Tarragona was found to be desolate of any forage. Unable to sustain pressure on Tarragona, Macdonald instead opted to join up with Suchet at Lérida to create a more feasible plan of operations, and marched for Valls on the 25th. Seeing the French retreat, O'Donnell sent

---

28   Arteche y Moro, *Guerra de la Independencia*, Vol.IX, p.267.
29   Fuertes, *La ocupación francesa de Zaragoza*, p.22.
30   Suchet, *Memoirs of the War in Spain*, Vol.I, p.201.
31   Oman, *Peninsular War*, Vol.III, p.494.
32   Oman, *Peninsular War*, Vol.III, p.494.
33   Alexander, *Rod of Iron*, p.85.

orders to his subordinates to harry the enemy's march, never giving Macdonald a moment of rest. Having received advance notice of Macdonald's movements Suchet was already at Lérida when Macdonald arrived there on 29 August. The two commanders concurred that it would be best to focus all efforts on Tortosa. Suchet would conduct the siege itself and defend against the Valencian army, while Macdonald would protect the lines of communication and prevent O'Donnell from interfering. Suchet grudgingly permitted Macdonald to dive into the grain stores at Lérida. Macdonald lent Suchet his Neapolitan division of 2,500 inexperienced and second-rate troops who were stationed at posts along the Ebro to guard the siege convoys.

Issues of supply continued to pose a problem for the French. Food was a problem, for the Catalonian plains lacked forage and what little had been there had been taken by O'Donnell's army, thus, it became necessary to transport food all the way from Zaragoza. The land between Mequinenza and Tortosa was unforgiving, its roads poor, while the Ebro had yet to rise to a level where the barges could navigate comfortably, though a surprise flood allowed for 26 siege guns to be transported to Xerta in early September.[34] The guerrillas continued to be active in the few regions they still held sway over in Aragon, and were ever-present in Catalonia, harassing Suchet's operations: Graindor writes, 'In this country all the peasants were insurgents, they shot at us from the tops of the mountains and then came down and murdered soldiers between columns; several villages were set on fire [whose] inhabitants had murdered soldiers.'[35] When the water level of the Ebro began to rise high enough in mid-September for the convoys boats to sail, guerrillas targeted these vital transports. On 15 September, a Neapolitan battalion guarding the riverbanks was ambushed by thousands of Catalonian irregulars.[36] Despite their excellent defensive position, the Neapolitans surrendered en masse.

At around this time the most famous of the Spanish guerrillas, Francisco Espoz Ilundian, better known as Mina, entered Aragon. He was the uncle of Javier Mina, and had rallied his nephew's group after its defeat and the capture of its leader. In July and August his group of around 3,000 was destroying convoys of several hundred men, and even defeated an 800-strong Polish battalion. Napoleon was furious, and organized a massive pursuit. Seven French mobile columns under *Généraux de Division* Honoré Charles Reille and Jean Baptiste Drouet d'Erlon were unleashed against Mina, who fled towards the weakly-held Navarre-Aragon border. Mina attacked Suchet's tiny gendarme outposts, but the tough military policemen repulsed each attack. The pursuit slackened, for Reille was unwilling to push Mina further into the lightly-defended Aragonese heartland, while d'Erlon was needed for Masséna's invasion of Portugal.[37] Mina took the opportunity to slip away into Castille and regroup his forces.

In the southern mountains around Teruel, Villacampa's band was running rampant, capturing the garrison at Calamocha. His attempt to move further into Aragon was repulsed by Vergez on 17 July. The chastened Villacampa withdrew back to Teruel and usurped command of José Palafox's 1,000-strong *partida*, which had moved south after raiding Borja

34   Suchet, *Memoirs of the War in Spain*, Vol.I, p.207.
35   Graindor, *Mémoires de la Guerre d'Espagne 1808-1814*, p.39.
36   Oman, *Peninsular War*, Vol.III, p.503.
37   Alexander, *Rod of Iron*, p.84.

A guerrilla attack on a French convoy, by Paul Philippoteaux, From Louis Adolphe Thiers, *Histoire du Consulat et de l'Empire* (Paris: Paulin, 1865), digitized by the British Library

Francisco Espoz y Mina, by Francesco Boggi. (Rijksmuseum)

and Tarazona. Villacampa's augmented force destroyed a 200-man tax collection force under *Capitaine* Canteloube, then struck a convoy herding 8,000 sheep on 7 September. *Colonel* Plicque's outnumbered escort of elements of the 114e Ligne and 4e Hussards only managed to escape with losses after abandoning the sheep. Villacampa moved on northwards towards Montalban, collecting recruits as he pushed deeper into Aragon. Suchet could not let Villacampa run wild behind his supply lines, and dispatched Habert to Alcañiz with the 5e Légère to join with Plicque and Klicki to confront Villacampa. The guerrilla leader managed to evade the pursuit and disappear into the mountains, though the missing sheep were reportedly recovered.[38]

August saw the Sarto *partida* chased into Aragon from Navarre. These guerrillas raided the barracks of the 10e Escadron des Gendarmes at Exea on the night of 8 August. The guerrillas managed to break into the barracks and kidnap a few gendarmes and civilians before they were driven off in a furious room-to-room knife fight. On 13 August, the gendarmes of the 13e Escadron at Berdún were also beset by the Sarto *partida*, but managed to hold them off and drove them off with a bayonet charge. The guerrillas retreated to Anso, where they were attacked on the 20th by Renouvier's men from Jaca; Sarto was killed and his *partida* ceased to exist.[39] Such small raids by the guerrillas never ceased on French fortified posts, but the guerrillas were almost always repulsed by the garrisons. On 28 September, the Pesoduro *partida* attacked the Exea garrison, but this time it was prepared. The gendarmes checked the guerrillas, then *Chef d'Escadron* Luce ordered a ferocious counterattack by 50 foot gendarmes from the front and 40 mounted troopers to cut off the guerrilla line of retreat. Pesoduro was wounded and his band routed with heavy losses.[40]

The entire summer had been spent in meticulous preparation for the siege of Tortosa. The supply lines had been somewhat stabilized, and the threat of relief armies temporarily staved off, though neither O'Donnell nor the 2° Ejército had been dealt a decisive blow. The siege train was yet to be brought into position, but already Suchet was tightening the noose around Tortosa. At Ulldecona Suchet placed a Corps d'Observation, comprised of part of Montmarie's brigade and Boussart's column, under Musnier to guard against Valencian attempts to break the blockade, while Pâris took over command at Zaragoza. Habert was sent back to Tivissa to watch against O'Donnell. On 6 September, Harispe was given command of the 1st Division, which had been blockading Tortosa. The division's commander, Anne Gilbert de Laval, was out of action fighting a fever for 20 days, but the man who had led his division to many victories could not win the battle for his life, and died on 16 September. He had been a key member of Suchet's cadre of reliable generals and had fought alongside III Corps since the beginning of the war, dying too early to see its finest hour yet, but living long enough to see the reversal of fortunes in what had begun as an unhappy campaign for Aragon. Harispe was rightly deemed a suitable successor and officially given command of the 1st Division and promoted to *Général de Division* on 12 October; Harispe's prior role as chief of staff was filled by the capable Saint-Cyr Nugues.[41]

---

38   Suchet, *Memoirs of the War in Spain*, Vol.I, p.213.
39   Martin, *La gendarmerie française en Espagne et en Portugal*, p.338. Angered by their defeat, the guerrillas massacred the prisoners taken at Exea, including the wife of trooper Robida.
40   Martin, *La gendarmerie française en Espagne et en Portugal*, p.340.
41   Suchet, *Memoirs of the War in Spain*, Vol.I, p.209.

Yet the Spanish would not let the French take Tortosa so easily, and once again, O'Donnell would attempt to seize the initiative, for a new plan was in the works in his active mind. He could not risk bringing his army against either III Corps or VII Corps. Though the 1° Ejército was one of the better armies Spain fielded in the Peninsular War, it was still outmatched by the French armies, particularly their excellent cavalry. Yet Spanish field armies possessed more than just guerrillas as assets to help even the odds with their French adversaries. Less frequently employed was the uncontested supremacy of their own naval forces and that of their British allies. A bold plan was concocted to strike at the heart of French-occupied Catalonia by way of amphibious and landward assault to lure Macdonald back north, at which point O'Donnell would rapidly reposition his army against Suchet. Two divisions under Obispo and Eroles would keep Macdonald separated from his base of Barcelona. In the meantime, O'Donnell and Campoverde would lead a division of 6,000 infantry and 400 cavalry up north by land, while the amphibious portion of the plan would be undertaken by a force of 500 men. These men were embarked from Tarragona and sailed north under the utmost secrecy, on transports and feluccas escorted by HMS *Cambrian* and the Spanish frigate *Diana* under the overall command of the highly capable and gallant Charles William Doyle, the British commissioner in Catalonia, who had been actively aiding in the defence of that province.[42] O'Donnell likewise conducted his march in total secrecy – he needed to strike before d'Hilliers became aware of the Spanish and concentrated his scattered forces. The need to guard large areas of land against guerrillas had left French occupation forces stretched thin.

O'Donnell's large force slipped past the French patrols and garrisons around Barcelona, and on 13 September reached the town of Vidreres, 15 miles south of Girona. The area between Girona and the Mediterranean was held by an understrength brigade of mostly Rheinbund battalions under *Général de Brigade* François Xavier Schwarz, totalling some 1,500 men scattered in various garrison posts. O'Donnell attacked the next day, driving back Schwarz's outposts. The French general sent desperate orders for his men to regroup and prepare to fall back on Girona, but it was too late. By nightfall, Schwarz and 700 men had been forced to surrender at La Bisbal. Everywhere else, smaller French and allied garrisons were being mopped up by O'Donnell's other columns to complete the annihilation of Schwarz's brigade. O'Donnell embarked his prisoners, numbering over 1,000, onto the ships and ordered Campoverde to lead the division northwards into the mountains to continue the fight. The brilliant operation reaped a personal reward – the Cádiz regency proclaimed him Conde de La Bisbal.[43] A less-desired reward for O'Donnell's courage was a wound in the right foot, which had turned out to be much more serious than first thought, forcing him to recuperate before engaging in active service again.[44] Suchet offered to send O'Donnell one of his personal surgeons alongside a request for a certain *Lieutenant* Deschatz of the 5e Légère to be exchanged. O'Donnell reportedly politely declined the offer, but did release Deschatz on parole.

Macdonald did not learn of the destruction of one of his brigades until two weeks later, for the heavy guerrilla presence in Catalonia forced messengers from Upper Catalonia to detour

---

42   Oman, *Peninsular War*, Vol.III, p.497.
43   Arteche y Moro, *Guerra de la Independencia*, Vol.XI, p.276.
44   Smith, *The Greenhill Napoleonic Wars Data Book*, p.345.

all the way into France to reach Zaragoza! Seeing through O'Donnell's plan and realizing that the Spanish raiding force was beyond his grasp, Macdonald did not immediately return to Catalonia as O'Donnell had hoped he would, thus denying O'Donnell his strategic goal for several weeks. But the situation was worsening in Upper Catalonia: Campoverde's division was making havoc from the mountains, and Barcelona had been cut off. The supplies Macdonald had so carefully stockpiled were already running low, and several convoys had been lost to the rise in guerrilla activities. An attempt to subdue Campoverde failed miserably when an Italian brigade was repulsed as it attempted to attack his defensive position. On 28 October, Macdonald wrote to Suchet of his intentions to return to Barcelona and provide escort for a vital convoy from France, departing with his army on 4 November.[45]

Suchet resolved to continue the blockade of Tortosa on his own until Macdonald could once again reinforce him, yet the situation in the passing weeks of the autumn made the siege seem ever distant, for the Spanish redoubled their efforts to end the French conquests with a major assault across multiple fronts. The guerrilla struggle only intensified when the Cádiz Regency organised a junta of several prominent nobles and bishops in Castille to help raise a revolt in Aragon, and to that end, sent *Comandante General* José María de Caravajal to work with Villacampa. Caravajal ordered Villacampa to join him at Teruel, where he was amassing an army with the ample arms and funds provided to him to prosecute a campaign against Suchet.[46] Meanwhile, the Valencians were making another attempt at breaking the blockade of Tortosa under their new leader: Bassecourt and his 7,500 regulars had assembled Vinaroz, 30 miles south of Tortosa. Mina had regrouped his forces after the August pursuit and was moving through Aragon to reach Navarre. Only O'Donnell was unable to participate in the renewed Spanish autumn offensive – his wound had become infected with gangrene, and Spanish doctors sent him to recover at Mallorca for his own sake. He was temporarily replaced by the reluctant *Teniente General* Miguel Iranzo, whom Oman describes as 'a very poor substitute for the hard-fighting Spanish-Irish general.'[47] Even without the threat of O'Donnell's 1º Ejército of Catalonia, the events of the fall would delay Suchet's operations for months, and even threatened to stop his invasion of Catalonia.

On his way to Navarre, Mina decided to strike against a small French garrison at the ancient Roman city of Tarazona. Two messengers were sent with surrender terms, but the garrison commander promptly executed them – the 140-man garrison would fight to the last man. Outraged, Mina ordered an attack on 9 October, no quarter was to be given. As the garrison commander had coldly calculated, his men fought with desperation, and after several hours of hard fighting, Mina's guerrillas were nowhere closer to taking the town's strongpoints. The guerrillas were forced into a humiliating retreat when they learned that a column of 1,100 men under *Général de Brigade* Claude Marie Joseph Pannetier was en route to relieve Tarazona.[48] On 11 October, Pannetier caught up with Mina. The Spanish cavalry stood no chance against their French counterparts and the subsequent combat saw the guerrillas slaughtered, and Mina shot in the leg.[49] His band was beaten and dispersed,

---

45   Suchet, *Memoirs of the War in Spain*, Vol.I, p.214.
46   Alexander, *Rod of Iron*, p.86.
47   Oman, *Peninsular War*, Vol.III, p.501.
48   Alexander, *Rod of Iron*, p.84.
49   Tone, *The Fatal Knot*, p.106.

with up to 50% casualties. Mina would work tirelessly to replenish his force, but for now he was out of the action.

Suchet sent Chlopicki with 4,000 men to destroy Caravajal and Villacampa before they could inflict any serious damage. Caravajal dithered for a day before deciding to retreat from the fast-moving Chlopicki; the French reached Teruel on 30 October, only a few hours behind the retreating Spanish.[50] The next day, the Spanish artillery train at the end of the march column was captured by the French cavalry. Chlopicki took six guns, as many caissons, 100 artillerymen, and 78 horses and mules, but he lacked the men to both escort his prize to Zaragoza and pursue Caravajal. He opted to end the pursuit and bring home the meagre winnings; within a few days Villacampa and Caravajal were back to raising troops for a mass insurrection in Aragon. The disappointed Suchet sent Chlopicki back to finish the job. The French marched back to Teruel on 10 November and found that Villacampa and Caravajal had raised nearly 8,000 men, but split into two equal formations in positions separated by several hours, a potential opportunity for the French to defeat each group separately. Chlopicki advanced against Villacampa at Fuensanta on 11 November. Villacampa opted to stand and fight, for Caravajal was only two hours away and would surely march to the sound of the guns.[51] The difficult terrain negated Chlopicki's powerful cavalry which would normally have broken through Villacampa's line with ease: this battle would have to be fought by the bayonet. Chlopicki formed his men in two attack lines – the first was composed of two battalions of the 121e and the elite companies of the 1er Vistule under *Colonel* Klicki, the second was made up of the fusilier companies of the 2e Vistule under *Colonel* Kozinowski. The rest of Chlopicki's force stayed in reserve. Villacampa's men stood up to the Franco-Polish assault, firing from their defensive positions down the steep slope. But Caravajal did nothing while this battle raged on. *Colonel* Millet of the 121e had his horse shot from under him, then, as he continued to lead his men, was knocked down by a spent bullet, but jumped back up again to join the fight. Under such exemplary and dangerous leadership did the French and Poles ascend the heights. Villacampa withdrew in good order when the French closed in on his men and turned his flank. The two-hour engagement ended with 143 casualties for the French, while Spanish casualties are estimated to be slightly higher. Though the guerrillas had still lost in a straight fight, the margin of victory was diminishing for the French. It was an eerie sign of things to come for the French – the guerrillas were getting more experienced and organized.

Leaving Klicki with 1,800 men at Calamocha, Chlopicki headed back to Tortosa. Caravajal proved to be just as much of an enemy to the *partidas* as the French, for he took the bulk of Villacampa's men to form new battalions, which weakened Villacampa's *partida* so much that it was out of action for the rest of November. Villacampa would face another defeat on 18 December when Klicki, guarding the Jiloca area, was informed of a Spanish concentration around Ojos-Negros and a cavalry vanguard at Blancas. The talented Klicki gave Villacampa the slip by a night-time force march undetected through the Spanish lines, and ambushed the cavalry detachment at Blancas with a battalion each from the 1er Vistule and the 121e Ligne and some lancers and cuirassiers, capturing 150 men.[52] This was one

---

50   Suchet, *Memoirs of the War in Spain*, Vol.I, p.221.
51   Alexander, *Rod of Iron*, p.87.
52   Suchet, *Memoirs of the War in Spain*, Vol.I, p.276.

defeat too much for Villacampa, who fell back to the Albarracín hills and ceased to play any further role in the Tortosa campaign.

The efforts of Suchet's flank detachments enabled his supply lines – the veins of his army – to keep flowing, though they were not entirely out of danger. Various attempts were made by the Spanish to ambush the grain and munition flotillas Suchet sent down the Ebro, with mixed results, occasionally managing to destroy a boat or two. Most notably, on 3 November, a convoy of 17 barges was caught in a sudden current and swept ahead of the escort infantry walking along the riverbanks.[53] Six-hundred guerrillas lying in wait attacked the barges, of which two ran aground and were burnt before the escort and elements of the Mequinenza garrison caught up and dispersed the guerrillas after a heated firefight. Macdonald's absence left elements of the 1° Ejército free to focus on Suchet. *Brigadier* Pedro García Navarro, the former governor of Tortosa, led a brigade to Falset, from where his men continued to raid the convoys and the east bank of the Ebro in early November; these raids and a sudden drop in the river level severely compounded Suchet's efforts to assemble his siege train. The situation was becoming so bad that *Généraux* Abbé and Habert were sent to deal with Navarro and guard the banks of the Ebro. Habert discovered one of Navarro's camps on 12 November, and took it in a surprise attack with 1,500 men. Suchet ordered for more pressure to be put on Navarro, and another expedition was organized, this time against Navarro's main body at Falset. The attack was planned as a three-pronged pincer movement to completely encircle and wipe out Navarro's force. Habert would attack from the centre, Abbé was to flank the Spanish left, and a tertiary force under *Chef de Bataillon* Avon would attack the Spanish right.[54] The attack was carried out on 19 November, but Habert's centre force ended up advancing ahead of the flanking column and stormed the camp before the pincers could close the trap. Navarro tried to restore the situation by personally leading his reserves into combat, but it was to no avail, and he and 300 men were captured by the end of the fight.[55]

The Valencian front was off to a surprisingly auspicious start for the Spanish when on 5 November the 114e Ligne was ambushed at La Jana by part of Bassecourt's army, losing over 100 men, while Bassecourt launched several naval raids to drive the French from their positions at Ebro delta.[56] On the 25th of that month Bassecourt finally launched his much-delayed offensive from the coastal fortress of Peñiscola with a grand total of 8,000 infantry and 800 cavalry. A flotilla of 27 gunboats bombarded French coastal positions at Rapita on 26 November, and Bassecourt advanced his army to attack Ulldecona, where Musnier's force of around 2,500 was encamped. Bassecourt split his force into three columns – the first under *Brigadier* Porta was to advance to Alcanar and attack Musnier's left, while Bassecourt and the Conde de Romré would lead the centre column towards Vinaros, then further split their force to create another column that would flank Musnier's right by taking the Serra de Godall heights.[57] The last column led by *Colonel* Melchor Alvarez was to march all the way from the town of Traiguera to Les Ventalles, cutting off Musnier's line of retreat to Tortosa.

53   Suchet, *Memoirs of the War in Spain*, Vol.I, p.232.
54   Suchet, *Memoirs of the War in Spain*, Vol.I, p.227.
55   Oman, *Peninsular War*, Vol.III, p.504.
56   Alexander, *Rod of Iron*, p.86.
57   Arteche y Moro, *Guerra de la Independencia*, Vol.IX, p.304.

If Bassecourt's elaborate plan saw fruition, Musnier would be completely surrounded in the Ulldecona valley. However, this overly-complex night march was asking too much from the inexperienced Valencians, who could barely be trusted to hold a firing line. Almost from the onset the operation faced difficulties. Porta's inexperienced column suffered delays, which forced Bassecourt to make several stops. French scouting parties brought news of Bassecourt's movements to Musnier, who immediately ordered his men out of the barracks and to prepare for battle, before, suddenly, Spanish cavalry and guerrillas attacked an encampment of the 14e Ligne on the outskirts of Ulldecona. Bassecourt had sent his cavalry and some guerrillas ahead of his main force and they managed to gain the element of surprise in the darkness, but the disciplined French infantry were quick to rally and a few volleys were sufficient enough to check the fragile Spanish cavalry, who were dispersed by a charge of the 4e Hussards. The French were shocked then, when daybreak revealed that Bassecourt's men had managed to get into their flanking positions on the heights around Ulldecona and occupy the small medieval castle on the outskirts of the town.

Musnier realized the peril of his position and ordered counterattacks all along the line. *Colonel* Esteve led a battalion of the 14e Ligne and some hussars in driving the Valencians out of the castle. Upon witnessing the repulse of the Spanish left, the force at Les Ventalles in the rear of the French withdrew. Bassecourt's main force also retreated to Cenia after seeing their attack beginning to fall apart, but Montmarie and Boussart would not let them escape unpunished. The 13e Cuirassiers quickly caught up to the Spanish along the coastal road to Peñiscola and turned their retreat into a rout. The ill-trained Valencians scattered for the hills, and the disgraced Bassecourt fled to the safety of Peñiscola. The Valencians lost 800 killed or wounded and 1,500 captured in their humiliating defeat.[58]

Despite his forces being overstretched across garrisons and field forces, Suchet and his talented lieutenants managed to deal with the uncoordinated Spanish attacks individually and successfully protected both their supply lines and Aragon. By the end of November, all of the munitions and artillery had arrived at Xerta from Mequinenza, then been taken to Tortosa for a grand total of 52 heavy guns, 30,000 shells and cannonballs, and 90,000 pounds of powder.[59] More good news followed for Suchet. Macdonald had finished escorting the convoy and seeing to the situation in Catalonia, and on 13 December he arrived at Mora with 15,000 men to protect Suchet's siege operation against the 1° Ejército.

Much to the credit of the Spanish, their determination and unrelenting effort had delayed what was supposed to be a summer siege into December. The raid on La Bisbal was among the best performances of the Spanish army in the Peninsular War. The operations around Tortosa demonstrated how closely tied the fates of Spanish conventional and irregular operations were. Though the partisans under the skilful leadership of Villacampa and Mina had enjoyed moderate successes, the defeat of the 2° Ejército and the lassitude of the 1° Ejército after O'Donnell's departure had made the Spanish strategic goal of breaking French siege efforts impossible in the fall. Guerrillas were needed to tie down French troops and raid supply lines, while only with a sizeable regular army could the Spanish defeat Suchet in

58   Suchet, *Memoirs of the War in Spain*, Vol.I, p.230.
59   Oman, *Peninsular War*, Vol.IV, p.229.

battle, once his field force had been bled out for garrisons. Neither scenario materialized, and the fate of Tortosa was sealed.

For the French, the preparations for besieging Tortosa represented just one example of how difficult cooperation was between independent corps commanders in the Peninsular War. Plagued by supply problems, communication difficulties, incessant partisan warfare, and petty rivalries (although thankfully Macdonald and Suchet did not have to contend with the latter problem), French commanders often struggled or failed to bring their units together to achieve a single goal. That the French were able to triumph against the difficulties and determined resistance is a testament to the capabilities of Suchet and his generals. Put on the defensive against the myriad of Spanish assaults, Suchet was shifting around troops to plug incursions and offensives while retaining his holdings in Aragon. Though they struggled to score a decisive win against the increasingly powerful guerrillas, Suchet and his subordinates showed themselves more than adept at countering Spanish conventional forces, and adequate enough against the guerrillas.

The Siege of Tortosa[60]

Until this point French efforts in the campaign against Tortosa had been concentrated entirely on supply management, counter-guerrilla operations, and warding off the armies of Catalonia and Valencia – all necessary precautions before fully investing the objective. For several months III Corps had only maintained a blockade of the city from the west bank, but with the surrounding area secure siege operations could be initiated. The strategic success of French forces in the summer and fall of 1810 meant that there was little hope of relief for Tortosa. The Valencian army was nearly worthless and needed just 7,000 men under Musnier at Ulldecona to screen it. Macdonald could keep the 1° Ejército in check with his 15,000 men, leaving Suchet free to batter the walls of Tortosa without worry.

The city of Tortosa was a similar proposition to that of Lérida – enclosed by a bastioned curtain wall and protected on one side by a river, with only a bridgehead on the other bank, connected to the city on the left bank by a pontoon bridge. Tortosa had also been besieged in 1708 by the Duc d'Orleans, who further fortified the city after its capture. The city walls rose onto a rocky plateau on the western side, on which were three bastions and a redoubt. Separated from the bastioned section of the plateau by a ravine was Fort Orleans. The south was fairly flat, dominated by the Capuchin plains. Towards the northern end of the city was the Castell de la Suda, the main citadel of the city. Further north on an outlying plateau was the sizable Fort Tenaxas, which covered the northern suburbs of the city. Houses inside the city had been reinforced during the blockade in preparation for the siege. The garrison numbered some 7,179 men including 600 gunners manning 182 cannon, supported by civilian artillerymen and militia.[61]

---

60   Unless otherwise cited, siege operations summarized from Suchet, *Memoirs of the War in Spain*, Vol.I, p.235-263; Belmas, *Journaux des siéges*, Vol.III, pp.419-445; Arteche y Moro, *Guerra de la Independencia*, Vol.IX, pp.315-348; Oman, *Peninsular War*, Vol.IV, pp.230-340.
61   Lipscombe, *The Peninsular War Atlas*, p.184

As formidable as the Tortosa fortifications were, there were several undeniable problems faced by the garrison. The artillery park was short of spare gun carriages in case the fortress artillery was dismounted or damaged, as would inevitably happen in the heated artillery duels of siege warfare. The city treasury also lacked funds to sustain an effective defence – a meagre 50-60,000 reales had been scrounged from the city elites, but it was not enough to address the severe supply problems and the pay of the garrison was left in arrears.[62] The French blockade had taken a toll since it first began in July, for troops were now limited to half-rations, and even at that rate there was only enough bread for 20 days and soup for 40.[63] The greatest weakness in Tortosa was its Governor, *Brigadier* Miguel de Lili Idiáquez, Conde de Alacha. He had overseen the Spanish retreat at the Battle of Tudela in 1808 with great valour and determination, so was naturally ranked as a skilled commander. But by December of 1810, Alacha was old, suffering from war wounds and rheumatism, and worse, had become indecisive and fickle. Most of the burden of command fell on the shoulders of his second-in-command, *Brigadier* Isidoro de Uriarte, as the former governor Manuel Velasco had fallen ill.

Suchet's forces spent the first weeks of December getting into position and making the final preparations for the siege. Quickly realizing the need for a nearby crossing point to connect both French camps across the Ebro, Suchet assigned Valée to construct three pontoon bridges on various points along the Ebro, which were completed on the 15th. These bridges allowed the gabions, entrenching tools, and supplies that had accumulated on the right bank to be easily brought over to the left, where the main siege operation would be conducted. Spanish forces on the Coll de l'Alba heights west of Tortosa were dislodged by Habert on the night of 16 December and driven back into the city. Abbé took command of the left bank with the 114e, 115e, and 3e Vistule in his charge, while Habert screened the west of the city. Harispe's 2nd Division was deployed on the southern face of the city. The rough terrain features offered the French enough natural cover that they were able to push their camps closer to the city and tighten the siege lines.[64] While the siege was beginning to get underway, Macdonald had been forced to pull out of his position once more. The barren Catalonian landscape proved inhospitable for his troops for lack of food. Macdonald had been posted at Perello to guard against attacks from the north, but was running low on supplies so he had moved his troops to Ginestar, 20 miles north of Tortosa, from where he could still reinforce Suchet in a day's march. In his absence, Macdonald granted Suchet use of *Général de Division* Bernard-Georges-François Frère's 6,000-strong division and the 24e Dragons. This division was posted along the Tarragona-Amposta road to protect Suchet's rear lines.[65]

French engineers determined on the 18th that the best place to concentrate a breaching point was against the southernmost demi-bastion of San Pedro. Being the last bastion in the city wall and right against the river, there was little enfilade fire covering the western face of the bastion. That bastion and the adjacent Temple demi-lunette would become the focal points of the siege. Both were well protected by outer works consisting of a glacis, a

62   Arteche y Moro, *Guerra de la Independencia*, Vol.IX, p.318.
63   Arteche y Moro, *Guerra de la Independencia*, Vol.IX, p.317.
64   Belmas, *Journaux des siéges*, Vol.III, p.418.
65   Oman, *Peninsular War*, Vol.IV, p.241.

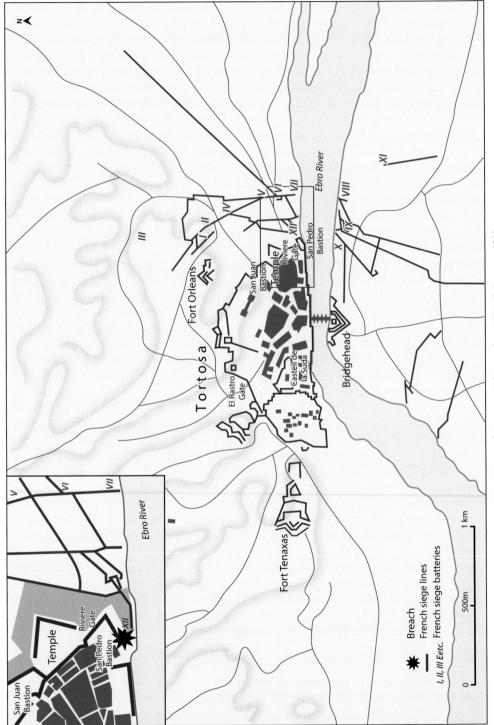

The Siege of Tortosa, 16 December, 1810–2 January 1811.

jagged covered way that formed a crownwork, a palisade/abatis, and a ditch. The covered way extended into a large and open place d'armes next to the Ebro, a potential position for an entrenchment and artillery position within it against the San Pedro bastion, if it could be taken. The soil on the riverbank was also soft and ideal for digging entrenchments. However, the entire plain of operations on the southern end of the city was dominated by the plateau with Fort Orleans, and it became vital to screen the fort in order to protect the main siege lines from enfilade fire.[66] Any attack on Fort Orleans could also serve as a distraction from the main effort against the San Pedro demi-bastion. On the 19th the first trenches were dug in front of Fort Orleans by 500 workers protected by 400 men of elite companies. The rocky plateau proved difficult to dig in, however, and the constant fire of the defenders caused several casualties for the engineers in their shallow trench. Under such conditions, the first parallel against Fort Orleans would not be finished until 22 December.

The Spanish sentries sluggishly changed their posts on the morning of the 21st, but the presumed monotony of guard duty was broken by a horrifying surprise – a first parallel 600 yards long had been dug in the night, just 160 yards from the San Pedro ditch. The previous night had been dark and filled with the howling of the wind and the defenders had kept a lax watch. Rogniat immediately saw the opportunity and soon 2,300 French infantrymen and engineers were toiling away to finish the first parallel against Tortosa. At the same time, two straight communication trenches were dug to secure a line to the camps and a nearby ravine that offered cover.[67] The men on the right bank had also taken advantage of the weather and dug a first parallel opposite the bridgehead. This sudden coup greatly expedited the siege effort by allowing the besiegers to begin the siege from a forward position without having had to advance and work there under fire from the city, much as Suchet had done while besieging Lérida. However, this also had the double effect of energizing the Spanish defenders into bolstering their defences – even Alacha himself assisted in creating roofing for the artillery, while civilians worked to barricade the streets.[68]

The struggle at the walls of Tortosa had escalated with the sudden French progress on the night of the 20th. Spanish artillery fired everywhere in an attempt to harass the French diggers, but the soil on the Capuchin plains was soft, allowing the French to dig themselves in deep. On the western plateau, part of the trenches was destroyed under a heavy bombardment from Fort Orleans, but by 22 December the first parallel had been finished, and that front was in any case meant to be a diversion. The French saps zig-zagged closer to the walls, reaching within 80 yards of the covered way of the San Pedro bastion the next night, during which the defenders hurled incendiaries and canister shot from the covered way in an attempt to stymie the besiegers. This was partially successful and forced the French workers to retreat four times, but four times they came back to finish the job.[69] From that point, work began on the night of the 23rd on a second parallel to connect the two saps. It was dug at an oblique, as to avoid the fire of Fort Orleans whose defenders put up a strong opposition. Rogniat recounted 'The fire was very intense; the enemy made sorties on almost all points, which dispersed the workers from the attack on Orleans, where, for this reason,

66   Arteche y Moro, *Guerra de la Independencia*, Vol.IX, p.315.
67   Suchet, *Memoirs of the War in Spain*, Vol.I, p.242.
68   Arteche y Moro, *Guerra de la Independencia*, Vol.IX, p.322.
69   Arteche y Moro, *Guerra de la Independencia*, Vol.IX, p.322.

almost nothing was done.'[70] The second parallel was finished the next night, just 60 yards from the San Pedro demi-bastion and 106 yards from the Temple demi-lunette. The right bank had also seen progress, with the construction of a second parallel and a redoubt to anchor the left end of that trench. The Spanish defenders never ceased their fire on the French, but it did little to stop the methodical digging.

Enough progress had been made that Valée decided to order the positioning of the artillery for the next step of the siege. Batteries 1-3 were to be placed in front of Fort Orleans, 4-7 would be positioned along the main line of trenches to target the San Pedro bastion and the city itself, and 8-10 were to perform the same purpose, but from the other bank of the Ebro with the added task of blasting the quays and the pontoon bridge. The batteries were composed as follows:

- Battery 1: four 24-pounders
- Battery 2: two 24-pounders, two 16-pounders, and two 6-inch howitzers
- Battery 3: four 10-inch mortars
- Battery 4: two 12-pounders, two 6-inch howitzers
- Battery 5: four 24-pounders
- Battery 6: four 16-pounders
- Battery 7: two 8-inch howitzers
- Battery 8: four 8-inch mortars
- Battery 9: three 24-pounders, two 6-inch howitzers
- Battery 10: six 12-pounders, two 6-inch mortars[71]

The placement of the batteries took several days and the sites came under heavy artillery fire, particularly those on the Orleans plateau where the ground was rocky and tough to fortify. The French managed to construct a second parallel against Fort Orleans, which they lined with sharpshooters to maintain a suppressive fire on the Spanish gunners and provide some succour for the sappers.

Christmas held little respite from the miserable conditions for the soldiers sitting in the trenches or guarding the fortress walls. French saps zig-zagged their way from the second parallel to reach the glacis of the San Pedro bastion.[72] The intense Spanish artillery fire failed to stymie the attackers, for the 1,500 shots fired by the fortress guns daily inflicted an average of just 20-30 casualties.[73] To counter the concerning progression of events, Uriarte proposed night time sorties by small strike teams of 300 men, whose primary objective would be to utilize the element of surprise to overwhelm forward posts and do as much damage as possible before quickly retreating to the fortress before greater casualties could be incurred.[74] At 11:00 p.m. that night, a heavy bombardment preceded a sortie from the San Pedro bastion against the second parallel which was repulsed by the trench guards of the

70   Joseph Rogniat, *Relation des Sièges de Saragosse et de Tortose* (Paris: Chez Magimel, Libraire Pour l'Arte Militaire: 1814), p.56.
71   Fernandez y Domingo, *Anales ó Historia de Tortosa*, p.219.
72   Oman, *Peninsular War*, Vol.IV, p.234.
73   Rogniat, *Relation des Sièges de Saragosse et de Tortose*, p.56.
74   Uriarte's diary, cited in Arteche y Moro, *Guerra de la Independencia*, Vol.IX, p.324.

44e Ligne, at which the Spanish renewed the bombardment with greater intensity. Not two hours later another sortie was made, which became bogged down in the narrow trenches and was repulsed as well. This time, the French took advantage of the Spanish retreat to push their saps even further to within 25 yards of the place d'armes. Both sides would not be long in waiting for the next sortie; the Spanish defenders continued to put up a desperate resistance and placed 25 grenade specialists at the place d'armes to throw their payload at the saps – when even this failed to stop the French, they sallied out from the covered way on the night of the 26th.[75] *Sergent* Clause of the sappers, a holder of the Légion d'Honneur, held back the Spanish in the narrow trench at the cost of his life, buying enough time for the trench guards to arrive and drive the garrison back. The Spanish were chased up the glacis and the impetus of the pursuit carried the French into the place d'armes, which they promptly occupied and entrenched until a sap could be dug to connect it to the main siege lines. This sudden coup saved the French time and lives that would have been lost crawling by saps up to the place d'armes. All this had been accomplished in merely seven days of work and hot action, and the French had yet to even fire a single one of their artillery pieces, a near-unheard of feat for the siege standards of the time. The rapid Spanish raids caused some damage and casualties as Uriarte had expected, though their successive nature placed the French on high alert for the next one, and the designated force of 300 men was too small to make a significant impact.

Determined to stymie the French siege works, Uriarte ordered another sortie on the 28th. His previous strategy of small night-time raids would not be enough – only a large-scale assault had a chance at stopping Suchet's juggernaut army. Six-hundred guerrillas led by Miláns del Bosch were to debouch from the El Rastro gate and sprint alongside the city walls to attack the entrenchments in front of Fort Orleans. Another group of 600, divided into three columns, followed by 300 sappers, would assault the trenches that lay just yards from the San Pedro Bastion and the place d'armes.[76] The Spanish preceded their attack with a relentless bombardment to soften up the French lines, during which *Capitaine* Ponssin was killed by a shot to the head. A simultaneous barrage by the garrison's mortars at 4:00 pm signalled the start of the sortie. Del Bosch's attack was a dismal failure, for the moment they entered the French entrenchments Habert arrived with the elite companies of the 5e Légère and 116e Ligne. The Spanish fired at the oncoming French, but were soon forced into a melee, in which *Capitaine* Bugeaud was noted to have distinguished himself at the head of his grenadier company of the 116e.[77] The outnumbered guerrillas quickly retreated. On the other side of the battlefield, the Spanish did not need to travel far to reach their target. Portable ramps crashed down over the ditch and onto the covered way to form gangways over which the sortie party poured out.[78] The French were caught in a state of confusion, and the Spanish retook the covered way and the place d'armes by the bayonet. A group of sappers led by engineer *Lieutenant* Jaquard made a desperate attempt to hold back the attackers, but were quickly overwhelmed and killed to the last man. The Spanish reached the second parallel, destroying siege works and burning gabions as they went until Abbé led forward

75   Arteche y Moro, *Guerra de la Independencia*, Vol.IX, p.324.
76   Arteche y Moro, *Guerra de la Independencia*, Vol.IX, p.327.
77   Suchet, *Memoirs of the War in Spain*, Vol.I, p.251.
78   Arteche y Moro, *Guerra de la Independencia*, Vol.IX, p.328.

Sortie by the Tortosa Garrison, by Paul Philippoteaux, From Thiers, Louis Adolphe, *Histoire du Consulat et de l'Empire*, (Paris: 1865), digitized by the British Library

the 44e Ligne in a counterattack and stopped the sortie, then drove them back to the covered way, though the French were unable to retake the place d'armes. The Spanish had made the most of the short time in which they occupied the trenches and had caused significant damage, particularly with regard to the entrenchments at the place d'armes and the second parallel. Nonetheless, the French recovered with astounding speed, for they spent the rest of the 28th and the 29th on re-securing the place d'armes and repairing the damage done to the trenches, as well as beginning a third parallel extending across the glacis face of the Temple demi-lunette into the place d'armes in front of the San Pedro bastion.

Just a day after the Spanish had launched their sortie, the French were ready to begin their bombardment. As the sun rose on 29 December the 45 guns of the breaching batteries opened fire. Within hours the guns in the San Juan bastion, Temple demi-lune and the San Pedro Bastion were all but silenced (the bombardment left just a single working gun between the three, in the San Juan bastion), the pontoon bridge left heavily damaged with five boats sunk, Fort Orleans likewise damaged, and a breach blown into the curtain wall next to the Riviere Gate behind the demi-lune.[79] The mortar batteries rained shells into the streets, and the terrible bombardment forced the civilians out of the San Pedro neighbourhood and into the inner city. The artillery of the citadel and the bridgehead attempted a counter-battery fire on the French batteries on the right, but the French guns were too well entrenched for the long-range fire to have much effect.

That night brought further progress for the besiegers as they fortified the place d'armes against the San Pedro bastion and completed the third parallel. The next day brought no end to the bombardment, with fewer and fewer Spanish guns being able to respond. The guns in Fort Orleans had been silenced and the ramparts of the Temple demi-lune reduced to rubble. For the French, work began on an 11th battery on the right bank, to be comprised of two 10-inch mortars to lay down fire on the citadel.[80] During the night of the 30th, the French attempted to dig a passage into the ditch between the place d'armes and the San Pedro bastion so that the miners could attack the bastion itself. The counterscarp of the place d'armes had not been bricked up and was purely earthen – it was thought to be a simple enough task to dig a path into the ditch, but the Spanish defenders resolved to stop the French at all costs. Two cannon laid down an effective enfilade fire, while grenades and flaming fascines were thrown at the French; such was the intensity of the Spanish defence that all attempts that day at forcing the ditch were given up. The French instead decided to focus on consolidating their gains and further fortifying the covered way with gabions and trenches. Mortar and howitzer shells arced through the night sky and crashed down into the city, setting several fires. By now the defenders' artillery was all but destroyed and they were denied the ability to return fire for at least the satisfaction of retribution.

In response to the rapidly deteriorating situation, Alacha called a meeting at Uriarte's house and prominent civil officials and ranking military officers were summoned to decide the best plan of action to defend the city. The Minister of Finance estimated that there was only enough bread left for 16 days, and soup for 20 – and that was on the continued policy of

---

79   Belmas, *Journaux des siéges*, Vol.III, p.435.
80   David Rumsey Map Collection, 12140.010: Plan de Tortose, Pris le 2 Janvier 1811.< https://www.
      davidrumsey.com/luna/servlet/detail/RUMSEY~8~1~291003~90067363:Plan-de-Tortose%2C-Prise-
      le-2-Janvier>, accessed 28 December 2022.

half-rations.[81] A 20-day truce was suggested, and if no relief army came in that time, Tortosa would surrender; it was hardly likely, however, that Suchet would agree to such terms when he had the city in the palm of his hand. Others hoped that Tortosa would become a second Zaragoza, where the citizenry and garrison would fight tooth and nail for every house.

By 31 December, the men at the bridgehead had been evacuated by boat for it was feared that they would be cut off entirely if the pontoon bridge took any more damage. The guns in the bridgehead were rolled into the Ebro or spiked, and the French were quick to seize the abandoned position. The unopposed French artillery continued to rain destruction on the crumbling fortifications of Tortosa: the right face of the San Pedro bastion was utterly wrecked in the bombardment, presenting an opportunity for the French to advance against it once more. Gabions, sandbags, and tin sheet roofing were used as cover for the miners, who descended into the ditch and managed to dig all the way to the scarp, thanks to the suppressive fire of the artillery which had silenced the two Spanish cannon that had stopped the French siege efforts the day before.[82] At the same time a twelfth battery of four 24-pounder guns was constructed on the covered way within point-blank range of the right face of the San Pedro bastion![83] A sap managed to reach the place d'armes of the crownwork between the covered ways of the Temple lunette and San Pedro bastion, which was subsequently fortified as a debouching point for storming parties against the breach in the main curtain wall next to the Riviere Gate just across the ditch.

As the French tightened their grip around Tortosa, the Spanish were frantically searching for a way to relieve the city. The Catalonian Junta had been scraping together a relief expedition, begging the Cádiz Regency for supplies and attempting to cooperate with Valencia and the *partidas* of Villacampa and Caravajal. Campoverde and Iranzo each took a division to assess the situation; the former took up position at the fort at Coll de Balaguer to observe Frère, the latter occupied Montblanc.[84] Iranzo ambushed a French foraging party of 650 on 1 January near Lérida, but this action failed to divert Suchet's attention. The failed Spanish autumn offensive had blunted the strength of the guerrillas and the regular Spanish armies alike, leaving them helpless to get past Suchet and Macdonald's detachments. The looming danger of Macdonald's army kept both Spanish divisions pinned, and nothing could be done to stop the French from battering away at Tortosa.

The only other incident against the French occurred too distant from the siege to have any impact. A minor action was fought on 25 December at Palamos, near Girona, when Captain Thomas Rogers of the 74-gun HMS *Kent* led a squadron to raid a French convoy of eight merchant vessels and a few small escort vessels which were anchored at the harbour. Under the cover of a naval bombardment, Captain Fane of HMS *Cambrian*, who had escorted O'Donnell's force at La Bisbal, led ashore 350 sailors, 250 marines and two light guns, with which he destroyed the three heavy guns guarding the harbour, the supplies, and the ships. The French garrison had initially retreated away from the overwhelming assault, allowing the British to complete their objectives with scant loss. However, they immediately took to the offensive after the arrival of reinforcements and seeing that the British rear-guard was

81   Arteche y Moro, *Guerra de la Independencia*, Vol.IX, p.331.
82   Belmas, *Journaux des siéges*, Vol.III, p.438.
83   David Rumsey Map Collection, 12140.010: Plan de Tortose, Pris le 2 Janvier 1811.
84   Oman, *Peninsular War*, Vol.IV, p.241.

disordered in its withdrawal. A mission accomplished began to fall apart into a disaster when the British troops began to retreat not to the beach where they could embark under the protection of the fleet, but through the town of Palamos. As the British fell back through the town to their embarkation point, the French garrison took up positions behind the walls and in the houses of the town and shot up the retreat, throwing it into confusion and leading to a number of men being left behind.[85] While the raid accomplished its objectives, it had come at the cost of a full third of the landing party – 33 killed, 89 wounded, and 87 missing or captured, including Captain Fane, who had heroically remained on the beach to direct his men.

The situation inside Tortosa was rapidly deteriorating. Alacha summoned a council meeting, yet he himself failed to show up. He had withdrawn himself to the citadel after transferring his responsibilities to Uriarte, though explicitly mentioning that he was still in command. The conclusions at the council meeting were no less heartening than their leader's resignation to defeat. Each sector commander piled bad news onto bad news regarding the state of affairs – there were not enough artillerymen left standing to man what guns were still serviceable, no work was being done to repair the damage to the walls because the civilian workers had fled, the French had widened the breaches enough to be practicable, and hundreds of soldiers were deserting to hide in the town.[86] The city militia had all but dispersed to their homes. There would be no fanatical defence of the streets as at Zaragoza or Girona. The Catalonian Junta had been hard at work in attempting to scramble together a rescue, but those in Tortosa were unaware of said efforts or their lack of success.[87] Several plans were tossed around: the garrison could better fortify the breaches and defend it when the inevitable storming came; the garrison should attempt to break out of the city entirely, or abandon the residential areas to fall back to the higher northern part of the city, which the civilian leaders naturally objected to vehemently. For all the debates and discussions of carrying on the fight, the truth weighed heavily in the minds of the council–there was no word or hope of a relief army, and every day the French were fast closing in. The breaching battery would be completed soon, and then there would be no more chances left to surrender. It was decided that the best course of option would be to propose a truce to Suchet and avoid a storming of the city. Word was sent to Alacha about the decision and the proposal was approved.

On the morning of 1 January 1811, a white flag was raised in the city, to which the French batteries fell silent. A small delegation led by *Coronel* Luis Veyán entered the French camp with terms of surrender from the Conde de Alacha. The offer was for a 15-day truce to be established, and if a relief army did not arrive in that time, Tortosa would be given to the French, and the garrison permitted to march to Tarragona with all arms, baggage, and the full honours of war. Suchet immediately saw through the one-sided deal, and presented a counter-offer. Though the Spanish offer was out of the question, Suchet was naturally delighted that the garrison had already asked for a truce. The Spanish delegation returned to Tortosa with *Colonel* Saint Cyr Nugues in tow, who Suchet had tasked with presenting his terms to the governor and the council directly. Suchet's terms were that the officers

---

85   William James, *The Naval History of Great Britain* (London: Macmillan and Co., 1902), Vol.V, p.129.

86   Arteche y Moro, *Guerra de la Independencia*, Vol.IX, p.337-8.

87   Wimpfen's report, from Suchet, *Memoirs of the War in Spain*, Vol.I, p.370.

would be permitted to retain their swords and baggage into French captivity, alongside the entire garrison. A rejection of his terms would warrant a final assault. Uriarte placed Nugues in a house instead of taking him to the castle, unwilling to show the Frenchman the desperate plight of the civilians who had sought refuge in the castle.[88] Alacha descended from his hideout in the castle to meet with Nugues, but Nugues proved to be absolutely unrelenting in his negotiation: there would be no surrender on anything but the terms Suchet offered. Alacha and the councilors with him could not accept the terms, and bluffed to Nugues that the Spanish still held a number of means by which they could make life difficult for the French. With negotiations going nowhere, Nugues returned empty-handed to the French camp.

The French continued the siege with redoubled efforts, now knowing that the city was losing the will to fight. The existing breach was widened and mines positioned to blow up the walls. Uriarte desperately readied his men at the breach, lining the area with sharp-shooters and stationing reserve units, but morale had plummeted in the garrison, and Uriarte doubted his men could withstand the onslaught. With the fortifications crumbling against the relentless bombardment, Alacha raised three white flags on 2 January. Suchet permitted a negotiation to take place, but refused to cease fire in order to further mount pressure on the Spanish negotiators. Additionally, he was tired of Alacha's games – the last time he had tried to surrender he had rejected Suchet's terms, and Suchet was concerned that the Spanish would use the ceasefire to repair the breach.[89] Messengers scrambled back and forth from Tortosa to the French lines. Suchet demanded that one of the Spanish strong-points be surrendered to him first before he would order the bombardment to end; that way he could be assured of the garrison's surrender. He knew he held all the cards, especially after the governor had discreetly conveyed to Suchet that he 'could place no dependence on the willingness of the garrison to abide by the course he might determine': in other words, Alacha was losing control of the garrison.[90] From the fickle and wavering responses he had been getting, Suchet discerned that the governor had little fight left in him, and immediately sought to exploit this.[91] If he could convince just this one man to surrender, then the entire garrison might surrender along with him.

Escorted by a company of grenadiers from the 116e Ligne, Suchet himself marched into Tortosa under a flag of truce, and addressed the governor in his castle. He reiterated his offer of capitulation, and proclaimed boldly that if his offer in accordance with the 'laws of war' was rejected, the only alternative was death to the entire garrison, for his gunners were by their pieces and storming parties had filled the trenches – only at his command could the fury of III Corps be calmed.[92] Alacha was dumbfounded and intimidated by this display of extreme bravado, and quickly agreed to a surrender without even consulting his council, which had previously advocated a continuation of resistance; Uriarte even sought to continue the siege by abandoning the outer wall and withdrawing to the citadel. Suchet had prepared for this moment – Abbé and 600 grenadiers rushed in before the dazed garrison lining the

---

88   Arteche y Moro, *Guerra de la Independencia*, Vol.IX, p.341.
89   Oman, *Peninsular War*, Vol.IV, p.237.
90   Suchet, *Memoirs of the War in Spain*, Vol.I, p.258.
91   Oman, *Peninsular War*, Vol.IV, p.238.
92   Suchet, *Memoirs of the War in Spain*, Vol.I, p.259.

fortress walls and rapidly secured the key fortifications of the city. The siege was over, and the garrison laid down their arms, though some over-eager storming parties looted part of the city. The French had suffered around 400 casualties, while the Spanish had lost 1,400 killed and wounded, plus another 3,974 captured.[93] The rest of the original garrison of 7,179 had deserted. It had taken the French just 17 days to besiege and capture Tortosa, although that would have been impossible without the six months dedicated to blockading the city and eliminating surrounding opposition to secure the supply lines.

Tortosa had fallen with such rapidity that the Catalonian Junta had had no time to organize a proper relief effort. *Mariscal de Campo* Luis Wimpfen wrote:

> It was naturally expected, considering its strong garrison… that it would maintain a protracted defence, so as to afford us the means of coming to its assistance…the town of Tortosa, disappointing our expectations, surrendered to the enemy on the 2nd of January, a few days only after the siege had been regularly commenced.[94]

Certainly, the inconsistent leadership displayed by Alacha, especially in the final moments of the siege, played a role in the fall of Tortosa by creating an air of despondency and incompetence, which further lowered the morale of the garrison despite the best efforts of men such as Uriarte. It is also possible that Suchet had agents within the city, and these fifth columnists helped subvert morale and resistance efforts.[95] Likewise, the populace had turned to human instincts of self-preservation and abandoned the defences rather than display the exceptional civilian resistance of Zaragoza and Girona that the garrison's leaders had hoped to emulate. Not only did Alacha shut himself in his castle on the grounds of age and illness while refusing to relinquish full command but he was also said to have interfered with and countermanded orders, and, in the dramatic last moments of the siege, succumbed to Suchet's force of personality and surrendered.[96] Iranzo and the Catalan Junta were outraged at the surrender, especially because the garrison still had ample provisions. They condemned Alacha to death for cowardice and treason; ironically Alacha was saved from this fate by his captivity in France, so the Junta went as far as to execute him in effigy![97] The leadership of the Spanish armed forces in Catalonia had fared no better. *Mariscal de Campo* Marqués de Campoverde harboured ambitions to attain supreme command over the 1° Ejército, and to that end began to disseminate the idea that Catalonia's salvation lay with him.[98] Campoverde was fortunate to have the support of the able and popular Father Antonio Coris, who organized a series of demonstrations in Campoverde's favour, to which Campoverde 'humbly acquiesed' to the demands of the mob. Despite the request

---

93   Suchet, *Memoirs of the War in Spain*, Vol.I, p.260, reported the capture of 9,451 men, confirmed by one of the Spanish officers in the city, Juan Prats. That figure is highly unlikely and only suffices if Suchet's far-fetched estimate of the original garrison size at 11,000 is to be believed. Oman, *Peninsular War*, Vol.IV, p.239, puts the Spanish losses at 1,400 killed and wounded, and 3,974 captured; the rest were lost to desertion.
94   Wimpfen's report from Suchet, *Memoirs of the War in Spain*, Vol.I, p.370.
95   Arteche y Moro, *Guerra de la Independencia*, Vol.IX, p.348.
96   Oman, *Peninsular War*, Vol.IV, p.239.
97   Prada, *Tarragona*, p.91.
98   Prada, *Tarragona*, p.93.

of the Catalonian Junta, Iranzo declined to crack down on the increasingly rowdy agitators. Attempts were made to reach a compromise by giving Campoverde military command and Iranzo civil authority, but this led to a riot, so the Junta caved into the pressure. The people had their way, and on 6 January, Campoverde got his desired promotion to *Capitán General* of the 1º Ejército, and began his despotic tenure by arresting his opponents, reducing the power of the Junta and other public bodies.[99]

More than anything, however, the siege attested to the skill and determination of III Corps and its commanders in that they were able to so rapidly overcome the fortress defences through professionalism honed at Zaragoza, Lérida, and Mequinenza. Suchet had acted with speed and decisiveness to end the siege before a relief attempt could be made, though the likelihood of success for any such attempt is questionable given Suchet's reinforcement by Frère's division. Campoverde and Iranzo were too weak to do anything against both Macdonald and Frère's formidable forces, which hovered in close support of Suchet for the duration of the siege. Thus, the fate of Tortosa had been decided in the summer and autumn of 1810 when the outcome hung in the balance – little could be done to save the city once the French had secured their position.

Coll de Balaguer and Counterinsurgency Operations

Suchet naturally followed up on his seizure of Tortosa, by targeting other nearby forts, as he had done with Mequinenza after Lérida. In a way this was the siege version of a battlefield pursuit. Fort San Felipe occupied the mountain pass of Coll de Balaguer, through which ran the coastal road from Tortosa to Tarragona. It was a small fort, and Suchet hoped to avoid a full siege by simply taking it by storm or through other means. Habert was ordered to capture the fort, and set out from Perello on the night of 8 January with the 14e and 115e Ligne, as well as some supporting artillery. Upon arriving in front of the fort the next morning, Habert lost no time in setting up a battery of four howitzers and preparing for a general assault. After the completion of his display of force, Habert offered the garrison the option to capitulate before the impending assault; the garrison sent a counter-offer saying that they would surrender if no help came within four days.[100] Habert refused, and opened his attack with a barrage of shells from the howitzers, followed by a wave of skirmishers which drove in the Spanish outposts. The main infantry assault stormed the walls with ladders and quickly routed the garrison, which had been disoriented by the brief bombardment and failed to put up an effective resistance.

The attack on Fort San Felipe closed out with a minor episode. The next morning, a group of 15 Spanish soldiers led by a captain landed on the shore and made their way to Fort San Felipe bearing instructions for the garrison, unaware that the fort had fallen the previous day. The Spanish were simply allowed to enter the fort, upon which they found surrounded

---

99   Prada, *Tarragona*, p.96. Campoverde humbly claimed that he had been offered the role of *Capitán General* by Juan Caro, who himself had declined it, and publicly denied that he had sought the position out of personal ambition.

100   Suchet, *Memoirs of the War in Spain*, Vol.I, p.266.

by Frenchmen and were taken prisoner.[101] A pair of British gunboats which
had escorted the Spanish were driven off
by the fort's artillery.

The fall of Totosa also allowed Suchet
to bring the bulk of his forces against
the guerrillas once again. At the same
time Spanish forces were recovering
from earlier setbacks and gearing up
for another fight; Bassecourt ordered
Juan Martín and his 2,000 infantry and
500 cavalry away from their successful
operations in Castille to bolster Spanish
efforts against Aragon. Juan Martín
was to join Villacampa's band in the
Albarracín hills to create a single force
of 7,000, a formidable showing in light of
the severe drubbings dealt to the guerrillas in the Tortosa campaign. Suchet
was thrilled at the concentration, for it
gave him the chance of bagging a large
partisan force in a single blow.[102] A
pincer-style operation was planned, with
Pâris and Abbé tasked with crushing the
guerrillas between them. Each general

Juan Martín Díez, by J. Donon, from Victoriano Ameller,
Los mártires de la libertad Española. (Public Domain)

led a brigade of four battalions and some cavalry; Abbé left Morella for Teruel, while Pâris
left Zaragoza to reach Molina on 29 January. Villacampa and Juan Martín were aware of the
French advance but struggled to find an escape route. The line of retreat southwest, deeper
into the Sistema Ibérico mountains, was blocked at Cuenca by *Général de Division* Armand
Lebrun de la Houssaye's dragoons of the Armée du Centre. The partisan commanders
decided to chance a retreat north, reaching Molina the same day Abbé arrived at Teruel.[103]
But the Spanish ended up right in Pâris' line of march, clashing with the cuirassiers of the
advance guard on 30 January. Villacampa decided to give battle the next day at Checa as
he had before at Fuensanta, given that he outnumbered Paris by two to one odds and held a
good position in the mountains. Disregarding the odds, Pâris threw his main body of men
across the snowy hills, screened by a cloud of skirmishers. There was good reason for this,
for during the night, Pâris had sent a detachment to outflank Villacampa's position, and
now he sprung the trap. The Spanish defence caved in with small resistance, and the guerrillas scattered. The French took 68 casualties, and captured 60 guerrillas; Spanish killed
and wounded likely exceeded that of the French.

---

101 Suchet, *Memoirs of the War in Spain,* Vol.I, p.207.
102 Alexander, *Rod of Iron*, p.88.
103 Alexander, *Rod of Iron*, p.88.

Pâris continued the pursuit, and rendezvoused with Abbé at the village of Frías on 4 February before splitting up, the former going north to Guadalaxara and the latter continuing to Cuenca.[104] Villacampa and Juan Martín retreated north to the Guadalajara region, where *Général de Brigade* Joseph Léopold Sigisbert Hugo, the father of the future writer Victor Hugo, commanded several garrisons. With Pâris hot on their heels and Hugo holding the north, the noose was tightening around the guerrillas. Pâris' troops destroyed guerrilla munition factories which they discovered in the mountains, while Abbé drove back Caravajal to Valencia. Yet Hugo was completely unaware of the Pâris-Abbé operation, and instead had committed 1,700 men on a wild-goose chase for Juan Martín, who had spread rumours that he was concentrating at Sigüenza, northeast of Guadalajara, with 8,000 men, when in reality he was running for his life over 60 miles away.[105] The French had been given the slip and the guerrillas escaped through the gap left by Hugo to fight another day. The immense effort put into the nearly two-week long operation had only netted 100 prisoners and destroyed a few guerrilla arms factories and hideouts, once again exemplifying the difficulties faced in offensive operations against the *partidas*.

Suchet changed strategies after the indecisive Abbé-Pâris operation, from an offensive one to purely defensive. The right bank of the Ebro was to be heavily garrisoned by six regiments of infantry and one of cavalry to completely deny the guerrillas any chance of gaining a foothold in Aragon.[106] This was largely feasible due to the fall of Tortosa and the freeing up of thousands of troops from the field force for defensive operations in territories controlled by Suchet. Suchet's defensive strategy proved to be highly effective and Juan Martín and Villacampa were unable to dislodge large concentrations of veteran French troops. Montmarie's brigade beat back Juan Martín on 9 March at Cobeta, but declined to pursue in accordance with Suchet's defence-only plan.[107] While this strategy was purely responsive to whatever the guerrillas did, it worked perfectly with the goals of holding territory in Aragon and consolidating French rule over the local area – a far cry from the days when III Corps troops would occupy Spanish towns only to abandon them and their newly-appointed *afrancesado* officials to the guerrillas a few days later. The guerrillas could only dash themselves at the heavily guarded regions, where French influence began to thrive. The unfortunate side effect of the new strategy was that it simply pushed the guerrillas into other areas, and Hugo bore the brunt of the burden. Even as Hugo's outposts were being overrun, Suchet refused to lend help, and it was only thanks to La Houssaye that Hugo was saved from more defeats.

At the start of February, a Polish unit was ambushed near Belchite by the Benedicto *partida*, with only two men out of 50 managing to escape. Perhaps in light of recent successes, their commander had neglected standard watch procedures, allowing a group of guerrillas to get a jump on them. Suchet was outraged and made public his displeasure in his orders of the day for 12 February, warning all officers to never let their guard down.[108] But all in all, counterinsurgency efforts in Upper Aragon fared quite well. Unlike Lower Aragon, where

---

104 Suchet, *Memoirs of the War in Spain*, Vol.I, p.278.
105 Alexander, *Rod of Iron*, p.90.
106 Alexander, *Rod of Iron*, p.90. This was later reduced to five regiments.
107 Alexander, *Rod of Iron*, p.91.
108 Suchet, *Memoirs of the War in Spain*, Vol.I, p.286.

large bands such as those of Villacampa and Juan Martín held a presence, backed by the 2º Ejército, Upper Aragon had no large guerrilla formations that provided a solid foundation for resistance. A powerful column led by Harispe, supported by local garrisons, broke and scattered the *partidas* of Solano and Baella.[109] Suchet's government continued to secure their taxable territories in the absence of organized guerrilla bands.

French successes all across the board in Aragon encouraged Suchet to commit some of his troops once more to Navarre in January of 1811 to shore up Reille's rapidly deteriorating situation there, where Mina was contesting French rule. The arrival in Navarre of a brigade under Harispe consisting of three battalions, a unit of Spanish gendarmes, and some cavalry resulted in a successful operation where Reille and Harispe worked in tandem to manoeuvre and entrap Mina, forcing him to scatter his guerrillas.[110] His mission complete, Harispe returned to Aragon on 22 February as Suchet was beginning to set the stage for his next, and most ambitious campaign yet, taking the stronghold of Tarragona.

---

109 Martin, *La gendarmerie française en Espagne et en Portugal*, p.350.
110 Alexander, *Rod of Iron*, p.91.

6

A Baton Crowned in Blood

The Siege of Tarragona[1]

The capture of Lérida, Mequinenza, and most recently, Tortosa, gave Suchet a powerful foothold into Catalonia. Next on the imperial hitlist was the coastal fortress city of Tarragona, the base of operations and the last bastion of the 1° Ejército. To prepare for the Tarragona operation, III Corps was greatly augmented at the expense of Macdonald's Armée de Catalogne. Napoleon had personally ordered several units from the latter to be transferred to Suchet's command for the coming operation. These were the 7e, 16e, and 42e Ligne, the 1er Légère, *Général de Brigade* Luigi Gaspare Peyri's Italian Division, *Général de Division* Claude-Antoine Compère's Neapolitan Division, and the 24e Dragons.[2] As such, Suchet's command went from 26,000 to 43,000, undergoing an appropriate change in name as well befitting its augmentation, from III Corps to the Armée d'Aragon. It was no mean feat to be commanding twice the number of troops in just two years since Suchet began in 1809. In turn, Macdonald's unsuccessful army was reduced from 40,000 to 25,000 men and, correspondingly, its zone of control was reduced to Barcelona and Upper Catalonia. No longer was it required to screen Suchet's operations.

Tarragona also held a special distinction for Suchet. The size of the lands Suchet administered, and the army he was leading, was becoming far too large to befit the responsibilities of a *général de division*, and Napoleon deemed it time to dangle some baubles ahead of this promising and successful general in a war where such adjectives were ever-more scarce. On 9 March, Napoleon wrote to Berthier

> [T]o write a particular letter to General Suchet to show him my satisfaction with the good conduct he has maintained in the campaign which has just taken place; that I expect a lot from his zeal to push forward the siege of Tarragona. When that city is taken, he will have truly conquered Catalonia. It is necessary that the officer

---

1   Details of French siege operations summarized from Suchet, *Memoirs of the War in Spain*, Vol.II, p.21-105; Belmas, *Journaux des siéges*, Vol.III, p.471-627.
2   Claude-Antoine Compère is not to be confused with his older brother and fellow general Louis-Fursy-Henri Compère, who was also in the service of the Kingdom of Naples for some time.

that you will send to him tell him in person that it is in Tarragona that he will find his baton of a Marshal of France.[3]

The promise of the coveted baton of the *Maréchal d'Empire* and entry into the imperial elite motivated Suchet to persecute his campaign to take Tarragona with the same zeal and ruthless efficiency that Napoleon so highly praised.

However, with great power must also come great responsibility, and while the transfer of nearly three divisions worth of troops to Suchet's direct command enabled him to even dream of launching an operation against Tarragona, they now were suddenly many more mouths to feed. His territorial acquisitions in Lower Catalonia, a province without much agriculture, did not help either. For lesser commanders it would have been a logistical nightmare, but, for Suchet, this was the moment where all his work in governing Aragon paid off. Due to low levels of insurgent activity, Suchet was able to collect 2.5 million kilograms of wheat at his supply bases of Mora and Lérida. Having already increased his demands for wheat by 40 percent, Suchet felt a little guilty about further starving the Aragonese by taking their livestock, and so procured most of his sheep and oxen from France or by raiding Castille and Valencia.[4] Establishing the freshly captured Tortosa as his point of departure, Suchet amassed there a formidable arsenal of siege guns and munitions.

Suchet could not depart immediately, however. While Macdonald left Suchet with the designated units, such was the situation in Catalonia that Macdonald needed a massive escort of 7,000 infantry and 700 cavalry under Harispe to safely get back to Barcelona. Macdonald left Lérida on 30 March, and sloughed his way through the Catalonian countryside, losing some 600 men to the guerrillas and Sarsfield's division, which harassed the flanks and rearguard of the column. After safely depositing Macdonald in Barcelona, Harispe's column made its way back to join Suchet on 9 April – all of that just to escort one man!

Suchet was acutely aware of the various threats facing Aragon. The Tortosa campaign had seen the Armée d'Aragon only tighten its grip on Aragon despite the numerous guerrilla raids, but the situation in Navarre was another story. Though Harispe had left Navarre back in February thinking that Mina had been beaten, the French had yet to learn the way of the *partida*, which simply reorganized and rebounded after scattering. By March, any gains the French in Navarre were completely overtaken by a massive resurgence in guerrilla activity. In early April, Mina crossed into Aragon from Sangüesa with two infantry battalions (1,500 men) and 200 cavalry to strike at the weakly defended Cincovillas region, which was being held by just the gendarmes of the 9e Escadron at Sos and the 10e at Exea. To counter Mina, Suchet dispatched a column of 500 Poles to Exea, and the gendarmes attempted to effect a concentration at Sos, but Mina outmanoeuvred the French and caught the 150-man 10e Escadron out in the open on the road to Sos at Castilliscar on 8 April, wiping out the 10e Escadron with his lancers.[5] Mina then fell back to Navarre with his prisoners, while leaving a battalion in Cincovillas. This sudden blow shook Suchet into action. After the defeat at Castilliscar, Suchet sent another column under Chlopicki with 800 elite company infan-

3   Napoleon to Berthier 9 March 1811, entry 17444 in Bonaparte, *Correspondence de Napoléon 1er*, Vol. XXI, p.537.
4   Suchet, *Memoirs of the War in Spain*, Vol.II, p.11.
5   Martin, *La gendarmerie française en Espagne et en Portugal*, p.351.

trymen and 200 hussars to reinforce the Poles at Exea. Chlopicki retook Cincovillas and secured the region. On 4 April a Valencian force of 1,500 sent to raid Morella was intercepted at a mountain pass by *Colonel* Dupeyroux and 1,000 men of the 115e Ligne. The Valencians were attacked from the front and outflanked by the voltigeur companies, who marched over the steep heights to surprise the enemy rear, forcing their retreat. The Benedicto *partida* was destroyed as well by the 115e Ligne in April.[6] Another raid was attempted on Ulldecona by a mixed force of Spanish cavalry and infantry, but this too was easily repulsed by elements of the 13e Cuirassiers and the 4e Hussards led by *Chef d'Escadron* Rubichon.[7]

Suchet's next response to Mina's victory at Castilliscar was less impressive, for he then began to bicker with Reille. Suchet wanted Reille to garrison Sangüesa, but Reille refused, stating that he did not have enough troops to spare and that Suchet should take responsibility for Sangüesa since it was more of a problem for him, despite it being in Reille's jurisdiction. Incredibly, neither commander gave in and Sangüesa remained without a garrison and free for Mina to utilize as a base of operations.[8]

The threat of homegrown Aragonese guerrillas had been extinguished due to effective administration and counter-guerrilla operations, but as Castilliscar showed, the guerrilla threat continued to be posed by outside *partidas*. These heavily militarized and mobile brigades were much more difficult to deal with than a band of angry peasants under the local friar that could easily be suppressed with traditional counter-guerrilla policies. The moment his army left for Tarragona, Aragon would be beset from Navarre, Castille, and Valencia by Spanish incursions. So concerned was Suchet with defending his holdings that he decided to commit 22,000 men – over half of the Armée d'Aragon – to occupational duties in Aragon and parts of Lower Catalonia and Navarre, a feat only capable thanks to the substantial reinforcements from the Armée de Catalogne. His original deployment of this powerful garrison in March, which had heavily focused on the right bank of the Ebro, was changed after Castilliscar, namely, by transferring more units to Cincovillas, which was now held by Chlopicki with a battalion of the 14e Ligne, two of the 2e Vistule, and 200 hussars, some 3,000 men with the object of watching Mina.[9] Compère's Neapolitans, along with a company of the 5e Légère, formed the garrisons at Zaragoza and Calatayud. To guard Daroca, Molina, and the Jiloca River, Pâris commanded two battalions each of the 44e Ligne and 3e Vistule, 300 hussars, and four guns, some 4,300 men. At Teruel Abbé had a brigade of eight battalions of the 121e and 114e Ligne, 300 cuirassiers, and two guns, some 4,500 men. These two brigades would play more than a purely defensive role, for they were to act as secondary field force that would guard Suchet's lines of communication from any attacks from Valencia, while also being available on hand to reinforce Suchet's main field force when need be.[10] *Colonel* Dupeyroux of the 115e Ligne was posted with his regiment and some Poles, some 2,550 men, in Alcañiz, Morella, and Rapita to protect the Ebro

6   Alexander, *Rod of Iron*, p.92.
7   Suchet, *Memoirs of the War in Spain*, Vol.I, p.280.
8   Alexander, *Rod of Iron*, p.94.
9   Suchet, *Memoirs of the War in Spain*, Vol.II, p.8-10. Suchet details the March deployment of his garrison units in his memoirs, but does not detail their actual deployment during the Tarragona operation besides giving Chlopicki's force details.
10   Suchet, *Memoirs of the War in Spain*, Vol.II, p.9; Alexander, *Rod of Iron*, p.96.

supply line from Valencian incursions. As for more direct support of Suchet's planned operation, a garrison of 2,200 held Lérida and one of Suchet's supply routes to Tarragona, while another 2,200 were used to hold the Ebro-Mora-Tortosa supply line.[11] Adding to Suchet's locally-recruited counterinsurgency forces was the creation in March of four companies of Aragonese Fusiliers, numbering under 200 men.[12]

After dedicating over half of his army to garrison duty, Suchet fielded the infantry divisions of Habert, Harispe, and Frère and Boussart's (much reduced) cavalry division for a total of some 29 battalions and 10 squadrons – a little under 20,000 men, including the substantial artillery and engineer component.[13] That Suchet could only spare a field force of that size for a taxing siege against an enemy which he would not outnumber by much is a testament to the effectiveness of the Spanish guerrillas. But his heavy garrisoning of Aragon and Lower Catalonia by veteran French and Polish troops would truly pay dividends in the weeks to come.

However, just as Suchet meticulously preparing for the advance on Tarragona, he received disturbing news that the fortress city of Figueras in Catalonia had been seized in a daring raid by several thousand Catalan militia and guerrillas, which had managed to gain entry into the city and overwhelm its complacent garrison. Both Macdonald and *Général de Division* David-Maurice-Joseph Mathieu de La Redorte, the Governor of Barcelona, urgently requested that Suchet dispatch the units from the Armée de Catalogne under his command to assist.[14] Pleas of 'All is lost in upper Catalonia unless General Suchet sends the troops that have passed under his command to our succour,' and 'The consequences of this disastrous event, with the circumstances of which I am not acquainted, are incalculable. All the forces of the enemy are proceeding towards Figueras,' threatened to unhinge the campaign for Tarragona and gave Suchet a few moments of hard thinking. In the end however, Suchet refused to be deterred from his mission.[15] His reasons were as follows:[16]

- Firstly, any reinforcements sent to Figueras would take weeks to get there, and the whole diversion would probably force Suchet to delay besieging Tarragona by a month, a month in which his soldiers would sit idle and consume valuable supplies, while the Spanish further readied Tarragona's defences.
- Secondly, if a substantial portion of the 1º Ejército was conducting operations against Macdonald, then there would be no better time for Suchet to strike at Tarragona, which would be depleted of troops.
- Thirdly, Suchet correctly surmised that Macdonald could handle the situation on his own, and that Tarragona was the more important of the two cities. He also presumed that Napoleon, enraged at a massive upset at Figueras, would send reinforcements from

---

11   Detailed deployment is given in Appendix X.
12   Ricardo Pardo Camacho , 'La Guerra de la Independencia en la Provincia de Castellón: Dos Castellonenses', Aular Militar (2009), <https://www.aulamilitar.com/D08_14_1813.pdf>, accessed 18 August 2022. Companies were recruited from Daroca, Calatayud, Alcañiz, and Teruel.
13   Suchet, *Memoirs of the War in Spain*, Vol.II, p.21.
14   Suchet, *Memoirs of the War in Spain*, Vol.II, p.14.
15   Letters of Macdonald and Maurice Mathieu, from Suchet, *Memoirs of the War in Spain*, Vol.II, p.13.
16   Suchet, *Memoirs of the War in Spain*, Vol.II, p.15-17.

France to Upper Catalonia, which was much easier to do than Suchet sending troops from Aragon.
- Fourthly, sending troops to Figueras would essentially entail losing the blaze of offensive initiative that the new Armée d'Aragon had been running in its string of successes, and fall back on reacting to Spanish initiatives. Rather than let Figueras become a diversion for the French, Suchet turned the tables by ignoring Figueras and continuing the Tarragona operation, making Tarragona a diversion from Spanish efforts in Figueras. He calculated that Campoverde's 1° Ejército would be forced to redirect its attention from Figueras to the more important Tarragona. Thus, by attacking Tarragona he would be indirectly helping Macdonald.

The taking of Tarragona, after all, was supposed to be the defining moment of Suchet's career, and he would not let anything get in the way of his marshal's baton. As it turned out, Suchet's calculations were completely correct, for when d'Hilliers' men blockaded Figueras, Campoverde attempted a relief expedition, which was defeated. Then followed news that Suchet was before the gates of Tarragona, forcing Campoverde to choose between Figueras and the 1° Ejército's base of operations. He naturally picked the latter, abandoning Figueras to its fate – as Suchet had predicted. Upon gaining a full grasp on the situation, Napoleon would praise Suchet's deduction and strategic thinking as 'soldier-like.'[17]

With the necessary preparations made to hold down Aragon and Lower Catalonia, Suchet began directing his field force to Tarragona. Suchet set out with Harispe's division and the Italian Division from Lérida on 28 April, followed shortly by Frère's division and a convoy bearing 570,000 pounds of flour. For the purposes of the siege, the Italian division was combined with *Général de Brigade* Jean-Baptiste Salme's brigade to form a composite division under the overall command of Harispe. Boussart's cavalry was split to form the rearguard and advance guard. Between 29 and 30 April, Harispe's and Frère's divisions arrived at Montblanc, where the French dropped off 400 men of the 1er Légère and 14e Ligne to garrison the place to secure the lines of communications between Suchet's siege lines at Tarragona and Lérida. Habert meanwhile, was traveling out of Tortosa and to Tarragona with his division and the siege train by way of the Royal Road, where it was continually harassed by Codrington's naval squadron, much delaying its progress. But because the main Catalan field army had been lured to Figueras, the French faced little opposition on their way. On 2 May, Suchet's main force reached Reus, which he designated as his base of operations for the siege. The following day saw Suchet's vanguard under Salme drive in Spanish outposts along the Francoli River, while the rest of the army took up positions around the city, and within a week his entire force had assembled to begin the siege.

Tarragona had its origins as Tarraco, the first Roman city in Spain, and the traces of this bygone era were still very prominent when the siege began. Two Roman aqueducts, which were still in use ran into the city, one from the northwest plateau known as Monte Olivo, the other from the northern hills.[18] Large portions of the ancient city walls had survived,

---

17   Suchet, *Memoirs of the War in Spain*, Vol.II, p.17.
18   David Rumsey Map Collection, 12140.012: Plan de Tarragone. <https://www.davidrumsey.com/luna/servlet/detail/RUMSEY~8~1~291005~90067361:Plan-de-Tarragone->, accessed 6 December 2022.

though those of the western side of the city had been destroyed in the War of the Spanish Succession and later rebuilt.[19] After a scare in 1808 when the French nearly took the city, Tarragona's fortifications had been repaired and modernized, especially under O'Donnell's direction. In all, some 30 million reales and countless hours of labour had been dedicated to preparing the city defences.[20] The city of Tarragona itself was built on a large plateau which sloped gently to the west and southwest, but dropped steeply on all other sides. The entire complex resembled a parallelogram. Built directly on the plateau was the historic upper city, which had been the main city for the ancient peoples. In addition to the main city wall, the northeast face of the upper city was ringed by five lunettes linked by a covered way. This line of fortifications, forming an outer wall, ran from the northernmost corner of the main walls of the upper city, all the way to the Mediterranean. while the lower city occupied the flatter lands along the coast. The upper and lower city were divided by a line of bastions and curtain walls which faced down into the lower city, forming an inner line of defence for the upper city in case the more easily accessible lower portion was overrun. The zone around the inner wall was kept free of houses or cover to offer the defenders an unobstructed field of fire.

The lower city was walled by a formidable line of bastions and lunettes, and behind that first line of defence was the detached Fuerte Real (Fort Royal). Outside of Tarragona proper were several key features. Some 1,200-1,400 yards west of the city was the mouth of the Francoli River, guarded by Fort Francoli. An elongated traverse ran along the coastline from Fort Francoli back to the main city walls to protect the harbour. About 600 yards northwest of the city was the large aforementioned plateau of Monte Olivo, which had a fort named Fort Olivo on its southernmost tip, closest to the city. The Roman-era Ferreres Aqueduct ran along the eastern face of Fort Olivo. North and east of the city was a series of valleys and rugged hills, guarded by a redoubt and a larger outlying fort dubbed Fort Loreto. While the heights may have looked to be favourable artillery positions, the ground was rocky and thus poor for digging conventional parallels and saps, and difficult to move the heavy siege guns onto.[21] Likewise, the northeast face of the upper city was elevated and would be difficult to besiege. The entire southern face of the city was bordered by the Mediterranean, and the French possessed no naval assets to make any advantage of that. In contrast, Catalans would enjoy the support of the Anglo-Spanish Mediterranean fleet, which could provide fire support, facilitate troop and supply transportation by sea, and launch amphibious assaults. For any besieger, the best option for a siege was to begin from the west, which was dominated by mostly flat farmland nestled between the Francoli River and the Olivo plateau, and attack the lower city.

As formidable as Tarragona's walls were, totalling well over a dozen bastions and lunettes and countless other supporting works, all was not to perfection in the defences. *Mariscal de Campo* Juan Senen de Contreras, who later took command of the garrison, writes that the city:

---

19   Juan Senen De Contreras, *Relation of the Siege of Tarragona and the Storming and Capture of That City by the French in June, 1811* (London: J. Booth, 1813), p.5.
20   Prada, *Tarragona*, p.114.
21   Belmas, *Journaux des siéges*, Vol.III, p.484.

[C]ould not support a regular siege, on account of the unnumbered defects in its weak fortifications, most of the works not being yet finished, or having attained no consistency, without fosses or covered ways, and without gates to communicate with each other, or make strong sorties on the enemy to drive him from his works…[22]

Facing Suchet's army of 20,000 was the 7,000-strong Tarragona garrison under the leadership of the acting governor Juan Caro. 4,500 of the garrison were from Courten's division, for Tarragona's nominal garrison of a half-dozen or less battalions would have barely sufficed to just hold the upper city, so it was quite fortunate for the Catalonian cause that Courten's regulars were present. Doyle estimates that the garrison numbered 6,000 men, and 8,200 with the militia.[23] Even then though, the garrison found itself thinly stretched along the long walls and forts of Tarragona. Fort Olivo alone required a garrison of 1,000 men. The garrison possessed roughly 350 pieces of artillery of various types and calibres, but only 500 artillerymen, so 200 sailors and an equal number of militiamen supplemented the gunners. A squadron of 120 cavalrymen was formed using the officer's horses.[24] Campoverde had taken the best of the 1° Ejército to Figueras, though this was not a particularly bad thing, for such a powerful force was better off in the field than cooped up inside the city. Governor Caro and his men resolved to do their best to hamper French siege operations as much as possible until sufficient reinforcements arrived. As the French closed in, Caro expelled large numbers of foreigners from the city for fear of sedition, though he had just as much to fear from *afrancesados* within his ranks.[25] The city's population had ballooned from 11,465 people at the start of 1808 to 26,128 at the start of 1811, especially due to refugees fleeing from the fall of Lérida and Tortosa.[26] Supporting this inflated population had been a massive burden on the city, and the streets were unsanitary, with various diseases running rampant. Tarragona's financial situation was in shambles however, and the Junta was badly in want of funds to pay their soldiers and purchase supplies. Many of the wealthy shirked their tax payments, and so starved was the population of specie that many had to pay their tax quotas with food.[27]

One of Suchet's first moves in the siege was to block off the aqueducts for his own use and deny the flow of water to the garrison, though the defenders never ran out of freshwater during the siege, for they simply obtained it from the mouth of the Francoli.[28] The inability to fully encircle the city due to the Mediterranean Sea meant that Suchet could not rely upon the dwindling of enemy supplies to supplement his siege efforts, for a continuous stream

---

22   Contreras, *Relation of the Siege of Tarragona*, p.15.
23   Adam G. Quigley, *Antes morir que rendirse: Testimonios británicos en el asedio de Tarragona 1811* (2019, Kindle e-book), p.21; Prada, *Tarragona*, p.111. Sources conflict on the initial strength of the Tarragona garrison. One Spanish general, de Salas, claimed that Tarragona had 6,660 men, of which 2,520 were militia.
24   Quigley, *Antes morir que rendirse*, p.21.
25   Quigley, *Antes morir que rendirse*, p.22.
26   Prada, *Tarragona*, p.130.
27   Prada, *Tarragona*, p.126; see also *ibid.*, pp.119-129 for an explanation of the financial situation of the 1° Ejército.
28   Contreras, *Relation of the Siege of Tarragona*, p.8.

of supply ships would keep the defenders well provisioned. That was the first of two major assets of the garrison which Suchet needed to neutralize before beginning the siege.

Fortunately for Suchet, at that moment, the bulk of Captain Edward Codrington's Royal Navy squadron was at Rosas supporting the operations of Campoverde around Figueras. As such, there were only three British warships around Tarragona: HMS *Cambrian*, *Sparrowhawk*, and *Termagant*. Also accompanying them was a sizable fleet of British and Spanish gunboats which were invaluable for their ability to sail in the shallower waters close to the shore. In bombarding the French, the larger British vessels ran the risk of running aground, as some captains found out in a few close scrapes. The fleet could easily bombard Suchet's siege lines, as well as open up the possibility of having to deal with sorties not only from Tarragona, but from the sea as well. Suchet wrote:

> If Tarragona had not been a sea port, and our land army had been able to blockade it completely, these daily conflicts would have afforded us the advantage of gradually exhausting the garrison, and depressing its spirit...but the case was totally different: the port was kept in continual bustle by the English and Spanish Ships. A convoy arrived from Valencia bringing ammunition, money, provisions...[29]

Throughout the entire siege, the Spanish would maximize their benefits from this major asset, which allowed them to ferry troops and generals in and out of the city with ease to bolster the garrison or coordinate relief efforts.

The second problem Suchet faced was Fort Olivo. Its elevated position of 200 feet above ground level gave it a clear field of fire over the western plains of the city where Suchet would be focusing most of his siege efforts, and it was absolutely necessary to capture the fort in order to attack the lower city. Fort Olivo's defences were quite formidable on the surface; after outlying entrenchments on two hillocks was a 400 yard long corrugated glacis, followed by the customary ditch and a layered defence of bastions and hornworks, with the main wall being made of solid rock.[30] Behind the main wall, Fort Olivo had a smaller fort independent of the main fort, while the latter was equipped with a mini-hornwork to act as a sort of a final redoubt. But despite its formidable structure, the defences were quite inadequate and offered its garrison of 1,200 men and 47 cannon poor cover. According to one eyewitness, Lieutenant C.J. Zehnpfennig of de Meuron's Swiss regiment in British service, who would later arrive at the siege as an aide de camp for the British officer Colonel E.R. Green, 'we found Fort Olivo in a dilapidated state, especially the Cavalier merlons, which were the thickness of a single sandbag that barely provided protection to the defenders, during the time we were there more than 20 men were wounded and killed near the door by cannonballs.'[31] Another observer noted that the quality and energy committed to the defence of Tarragona proper was not equalled in defending the crucial Fort Olivo.

On 4 May the French began their blockade of the city by driving in the Spanish outposts. Habert's division occupied the right bank of the Francoli, while Frère put his troops on the

---

29   Suchet, *Memoirs of the War in Spain*, Vol.II, p.43.
30   Nick Lipscombe, *Wellington's Eastern Front: The Campaign on the East Coast of Spain 1810-1814* (Barnsley: Pen and Sword Military 2016), p.26.
31   Quigley, *Antes morir que rendirse*, pp.53-54.

Admiral Sir Edward Codrington, by Thomas Lawrence.
(Anne S.K. Brown Military Collection, Brown University Library)

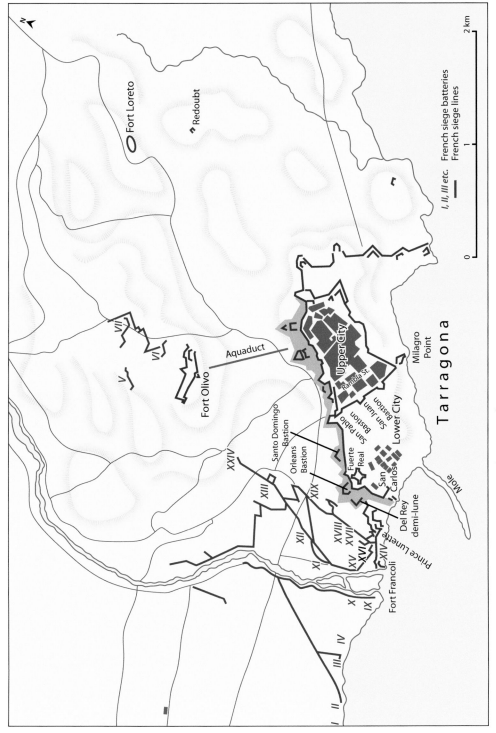

The Siege of Tarragona, 4 May–28 June 1811.

left and used the 3/1er Légère to establish communications with Habert across the river. Harispe sent Salme's brigade to gain a foothold on the plateau against Fort Olivo. The French were met with heavy artillery fire from the fort and a stubborn defence by the Spanish outposts, losing nearly 200 men, but managed to establish themselves on the plateau. The two Italian brigades of Peyri's division occupied the roads to Valls and Barcelona and swiftly captured Fort Loreto and the supporting redoubt in the northern hills.

Suchet's arrival was immediately met with determined resistance. While unable to launch major sorties for a want of troops, the Spanish defenders fired their artillery continuously to maintain pressure on the French – the bombardment was at times so intense that the soldiers could barely cook their soup.[32] The Anglo-Allied squadron also contributed, targeting the French siege train which was lumbering along the coastal road from Tortosa and slowing their arrival. Despite orders to re-join Codrington's squadron at Rosas, Captain Charles Bullen of the HMS *Cambrian* decided to remain at Tarragona and sent a request for Codrington to return to Tarragona. So did Caro to his superior, Campoverde. In response to the naval bombardment, Suchet ordered artillery positions to be constructed along the road to limit the area of operations of the Mediterranean Fleet. Throughout 5 and 6 May the Spanish launched several sorties from the city and Fort Olivo. Under the cover of the fort artillery, they energetically sallied out against the 7e and 16e Ligne of Salme's brigade screening the fort. Suchet conceded that 'The Spaniards displayed extraordinary enthusiasm… though always repulsed they indicted upon us serious losses… from fifty to sixty wounded were daily carried to the hospital.'[33] The early sorties would be the beginning signs of an active and dogged effort by the garrison to defend Tarragona, and the two French line regiments of Salme's brigade would bear the brunt of the attacks on and from Fort Olivo.

The small sorties and bombardments failed to make a dent in Suchet's well-practiced siege operation. After some delay in their arrival, the massive arsenal of 66 siege guns, 700 rounds, 100,000 bags of earth, 12,000 entrenching tools, 8,000 gabions, and countless fascines, ladders, and other siege equipment were being assembled at the artillery park at La Canonja, on the right bank of the Francoli under Habert's supervision.[34] Great care also went into immediately establishing a hospital for the wounded at Reus. Suchet set up his headquarters in Constanti, in the midst of his siege camp, and dispatched small parties to create fortified posts to establish French control over the surrounding countryside and safeguard the passage of convoys. Suchet's patrols engaged in something that bordered on a *chevauchee*. One eyewitness wrote:

> The first operations of the enemy to begin the siege of this Plaza were to sow terror in the population in the area, driving away and dispersing the inhabitants of the small towns with gunshots, looting, committing all sorts of the usual iniquities… seizing all kinds of food, livestock, and other articles conducive to their comfort and the work they were going to undertake: to that end they demolished countless houses, taking the wood from their construction and even the tiles; they forced

---

32   Suchet, *Memoirs of the War in Spain*, Vol.II, p.24.
33   Suchet, *Memoirs of the War in Spain*, Vol.II, p.49.
34   Suchet, *Memoirs of the War in Spain*, Vol.II, p.25.

many people as prisoners to work as sappers in the front line where some became victims of our fire.[35]

After scouting the city's defences, Suchet's engineering officers presented their findings to the general. A conference was held to determine the direction of the siege, and it was decided that the focus of French efforts would be an attack on the lower city of Tarragona by way of the western plains, for there the ground was soft and easy to dig.

Suchet's precautions in guarding his lines of communication bore fruit, for on 6 May 2,000 Catalan *miquelets* from Manresa attacked the garrison at Montblanc in force, but were repulsed. It was clear that from the start Suchet had created an efficient system of mutual support between the divisional camps as well as the garrisons securing his lines of communications. A field force of four battalions and 200 cavalry under Frère was sent to drive off the lingering *miquelets* and resupply the Montblanc garrison. The *miquelets'* attempt to disrupt Suchet's rear lines was followed by news that d'Hilliers had checked Campoverde's attempt to relieve Figueras. This was good news for Macdonald, but it meant that Campoverde would most probably head back to Tarragona in an attempt to relieve his base of operations. As Suchet anticipated, Campoverde made full priority of Tarragona upon hearing on 5 May that it was under threat, taking his pick of 4,000 men from the divisions of *Mariscal de Campo* Joaquín Ibañez, Baron de Eroles, and *Brigadier* Pedro Sarsfield y Waters to rush to join the defence, even before Caro's official request for assistance arrived! On 8 May, some 60 feluccas, escorted by Codrington's HMS *Blake* and a Spanish frigate, *Diana*, arrived off of Mataró to embark Campoverde and his men for Tarragona.[36] Such was the haste of the embarkation that soldiers were randomly placed onto the boats, with the intention of sorting them back out to their official companies once they reached Tarragona. Codrington wrote, 'The truth is that, if I had not done it that way, the soldiers would still be there on the beach…'[37] In the meantime, Sarsfield and Eroles remained with the main field army to continue active operations.

Suchet had consumed several days in securing his rear lines, digging in, readying the siege train, and repelling Spanish attacks, and so it was only on the night of 7 May that he went on the offensive. To secure the coastline and drive off the British squadron, Suchet ordered Rogniat to construct a large redoubt on the right bank of the Francoli under the cover of night. Daylight revealed the construction, and the Anglo-Allied squadron bombarded the redoubt, but they failed to stop the construction.[38] Suchet offered his soldiers five sous for each enemy cannonball they brought him, and French soldiers scrambled about to scavenge for these, at very high risk to themselves.[39] Over the following days the French began work on three coastal batteries left of the redoubt along the shore, and dug a long communication trench which traversed the entire field between the upstream bridge of the Francoli and the

---

35   From Prada, *Tarragona*, p.128. It is said that the people of Reus were levied 800 Reales a day to pay for the meals of Suchet and his staff.

36   Edward Codrington, *Memoir of the Life of Admiral Sir Edward Codrington* (London: Longmans, Green, and Co., 1873), Vol.I, p.210.

37   Codrington, *Memoir of the Life of Admiral Sir Edward Codrington*, Vol.I, p.210.

38   Quigley, *Antes morir que rendirse*, p.27. During this operation the HMS *Cambrian* nearly ran aground.

39   Emmanuel Maffre-Baugé, *Superbe et Généraux Jean Maffre* (Fayard, 1982), p.88.

redoubt to connect the two. A defensive trench was dug to span the length of the Francoli until it intersected with the communication trench short of the stone bridge.

With the threat of the Anglo-Spanish squadron diminished for the immediate moment, Suchet focused on his other major obstacle: Fort Olivo. On the night of the 13th Suchet directed an attack to be made against the hillocks 300 yards in front of Fort Olivo to use them as a potential staging ground against the fort itself. Eight elite companies from the 7e and 16e Ligne and the Italian 2° Leggera and 4° di Linea took the two trenches with little resistance, and 400 workers to followed up to fortify the trenches before daybreak put them in full view of the fort's artillery. This was a prudent measure, for the Spanish attempted to dislodge the French from the hillock with a hail of artillery fire. After seeing that their artillery had done little damage against the portable gabions the French had put up, the Spanish organized a three-pronged attack to retake the entrenchments. The columns – numbering 5-600 men in all – marched out as if on parade, officers at the head and colours flying boldly. The Spanish advanced under withering French fire to the exhortations of the officers. The Spanish retreated with losses of around 40, though one of the officers managed to plant a flag close to the entrenchments before he was shot down.[40] The taking and retention of this position was quite useful for the French, for the two entrenchments would act as a first parallel against Fort Olivo, without having to have been dug under fire.

That same day saw further French progress on the other side of the battlefield, where the coastal redoubt Rogniat had been working on was completed and armed with a battery of two 24-pounders (Battery No. 1), while the three supporting coastal batteries were likewise outfitted:

- Battery No. 2: Two 12-inch mortars
- Battery No. 3: Two 24-pounders
- Battery No. 4: Two 10-inch mortars

The French siege guns in their entrenched batteries were a match for Codrington's squadron, and the British did not take too lightly to this pricking of their pride, for no longer did Britannia rule the waves around the shores of Tarragona. The Anglo-Spanish squadron sought to reassert its advantage and at noon of 14 May organized a two-pronged assault on the redoubt. One force made a landing while the ships suppressed the fire of the redoubt, and another force attacked out of Tarragona, in all 1,500 infantry, 150 cavalry, and two howitzers, but the redoubt garrison hunkered down and fought off all of the uncoordinated attempts to gain the place. Voltigeur Graindor later wrote of the engagement and the terrifying effectiveness of the British fleet:

> Our voltigeur companies marched to help this redoubt but the English squadron, being brought very close to the shore, sent us terrible broadsides; the cannonballs fell in our companies like hail and take away arms and legs and cause terrible carnage. The bombs and shells still burst among us, in less than half an hour we lost only 20 voltigeurs who died in Reus a few days later from their wounds. But in

---

40   Belmas, *Journaux des siéges*, Vol.III, p.490.

spite of all those floating citadels which hurl death into our ranks, the enemy from the city could not destroy our works and withdrew...[41]

When Habert arrived with reinforcements, the Spanish retreated under the cover of the naval bombardment. The French lost over 150 men, the Spanish 218.[42] On the other end of the battlefield, an outpost of Italians was besieged at the village of Callar by 600 *somantes*, until some dragoons drove them off. The garrison of Tarragona simultaneously made a sortie on the Barcelona road, but they too, were repulsed by Palombini's troops. The situation was growing a little too tense for the comfort of the Catalonian Junta, which decided on 14 May to relocate to the mountain base of Montserrat. A few people needed to remain behind, and at first, there were no volunteers.[43] Baudilio Brunels stepped forwards and offered to stay, on the condition that his family be evacuated – hardly reassuring. In the end, Brunel and three others were left behind to help manage the defence and put the city on a war footing.

The arrival of Campoverde on 10 and 29 May with reinforcements gave the garrison enough men to fully man the city defences and undertake more powerful offensive operations. Campoverde's force consisted of the regiments 2° de Saboya (two battalions), Voluntarios de Girona (one battalion), Iliberia (three battalions), and Santa Fé (two battalions).[44] In addition to providing fire support, the British ships helped transport a large quantity of supplies into the city, namely, the immediate delivery of 1,500 muskets, while 4,500 more muskets, 3,000 bayonets, 800,000 rounds, 80,000 flints, 9,000 coats, and 5,000 shoes remained offshore until it could be decided how best to utilize them.[45] Still, the garrison lacked enough trained artillerymen to man Tarragona's 350 cannons, so Doyle and Codrington set sail for Valencia on HMS *Blake* on the 16th to see if they could get any more reinforcements or supplies from there. While the *Blake* was at the Valencian fortress of Peñiscola, Doyle sent a letter to Carlos O'Donnell, writing 'I am on my way to you, and to Alicante to order gunners and whatever ammunition you can afford. Also to ask you, if possible, to lend 2,000 men to the Tarragona garrison to allow the same number of veteran soldiers, currently in the garrison, to join *Brigadier* Sarsfield.'[46] If Sarsfield could inflict a large enough defeat on Suchet, it just might force him to give up the siege. To sweeten the deal, Doyle wrote the following letter:

> Now my dear general, if you send these 2000 men, I will give you in exchange 2000 carbines, 2000 sets of gear, 2000 pairs of shoes and 2000 field coats, which will allow you to prepare and equip new recruits to replace the troops you send to Tarragona. All these things I have on board in this ship and I hope to be in front of Murviedro tomorrow at dawn...[47]

41   Graindor, *Mémoires de la Guerre d'Espagne 1808-1814*, p.51.
42   Oman, *Peninsular War*, Vol.IV, p.502.
43   Prada, *Tarragona*, p.116.
44   Oman, *Peninsular War*, Vol.IV, p.642.
45   Quigley, *Antes morir que rendirse*, p.45.
46   Quigley, *Antes morir que rendirse*, p.49.
47   Quigley, *Antes morir que rendirse*, p.50.

That was a deal, if there ever was one! O'Donnell eagerly agreed to send 2,300 infantrymen from two of his best regiments and 211 artillerymen, which would arrive at Tarragona on 22 May.

Back in Tarragona, the heavily augmented garrison launched a sortie of 2,000 men against an isolated trench manned by the 116e Ligne before Fort Francoli at 3:00 a.m. on 18 May.[48] The Spanish struck with the element of surprise on their side, and as the 116e Ligne advanced out of the trench against one Spanish column, another column appeared behind the 116e and captured the trench so that the French were sandwiched between two foes. A moment of disorder reigned when *Colonel* Rouelle attempted to get his regiment to turn about face, but his orders went unheard; fortunately, the battalion and company officers managed to direct the 116e to attack in the direction they had just come from. Graindor recounts 'we left one enemy column to charge the other

Charles William Doyle, by H. Meyer, (Miriam and Ira D. Wallach Division of Art, Prints and Photographs, New York Public Library)

which was blocking out retreat, it was ambushed in our trenches and fired several volleys at point-blank range. We jumped into the trench against their bayonets, they gave way.'[49] But the 116e remained surrounded and in a crossfire; during the heated firefight Rouelle was shot and wounded as he was organizing a counterattack, as were both *chefs de bataillon* present. *Chef de Bataillon* Augustin Alexandre organized the survivors in a counterattack, shouting 'Regiment, at my command; drummers, the charge!'[50] Alexandre's men were joined by a steady stream of reinforcements from Habert's division (the 117e Ligne, 5e Légère, and some cavalry) and the 1er Légère of Frére's division. The Spanish retreated, with both sides having suffering several hundred casualties.[51]

---

48   Suchet, *Memoirs of the War in Spain*, Vol.II, p.42; Contreras, *Relation of the Siege of Tarragona*, p.9. Suchet claims that the garrison sent out six thousand men, however this number is improbable considering the overall size of the garrison and Suchet's tendency for exaggeration. Contreras does not give the size of the sortie.

49   Graindor, *Mémoires de la Guerre d'Espagne 1808-1814*, p.52.

50   Graindor, *Mémoires de la Guerre d'Espagne 1808-1814*, p.52.

51   Suchet, *Memoirs of the War in Spain*, Vol.II, p.43, gives the casualty count as 200 for the Spanish, and concedes the loss of 150 men. Spanish losses were undoubtedly higher, for Prada, *Tarragona*, p.116, reports 196 wounded and an unknown number killed. Graindor, *Mémoires de la Guerre d'Espagne 1808-1814*, p.53, claims that the 116e lost nearly 300 men.

The Spanish defenders were unfazed by the constant stalemates, and resolved to never spare the French a moment of rest. The defenders of Tarragona were also greatly bolstered by civilian volunteers. civilian volunteers, and it goes without saying that they contributed heavily to the defense, be it keeping up a continuous output of military supplies or manning the defences themselves. Many women, one of whom was said to have fought at both the sieges of Girona and Tortosa and now was in Fort Olivo, contributed much to the defences by recovering dead and wounded while under fire, sewing sandbags to help repair the battered walls, and worked the undermanned fortress guns.[52] Some directly joined the combat, such as Rosa Venes, who partook in the sortie on the 18th and killed a French officer, earning her a promotion to Subteniente.[53] Many, including noblewomen, lost their lives in the duration of the siege. Troops and townsfolk alike clamoured for an incessant bombardment of French positions, to the despair of Spanish artillery officers, who feared that the enthusiasm of the garrison would deplete the munition stores![54] The resolute spirit of the defenders made Spanish generals and British officers only more eager to do their part in assembling reinforcements and supplies. Colonel E.R. Green, a British military officer posted with the 1° Ejército, even asked Secretary of State for War Lord Liverpool for 1,000 British infantry, plus engineer officers and artillerymen.[55] For Suchet, who had been forced to reduce his men to half-rations, it looked as if Tarragona would fight him in the spirit of Zaragoza – this would be no easy victory.

On 20 May the Spanish launched a sortie supported by field artillery against Salme's entrenchments in front of Fort Olivo. The 7e and 16e Ligne met the sortie with a counterattack, supported by the 1er Légère, pushing the Spanish back. That sortie was not the end of the day's events however. Sarsfield was reported to have advanced with 1,200 men from Valls to the town of Alcover, just 10 miles north of Tarragona. Sarsfield made camp on top of a steep hill overlooking Alcover called Mount Calvary, where he lit beacon fires to signal his presence to Tarragona.[56] A Spanish column of 800 sallied out to the Barcelona road against the redoubt in the northern hills that the Italians had taken in the early days of the siege, in order to try and establish communications with Sarsfield. This attempt was likewise repulsed when a unit of the 4° di Linea held the redoubt despite heavy losses and forced the Spanish to retire back to the city. At the same time, Suchet ordered 150 men of the Reus garrison to advance to a defensive position to screen the road to Alcover, while a task force of a battalion each of the 14e Ligne and 1er Vistule, 150 cuirassiers, and the 1/1er Vistule Lancers was placed under the command of Boussart and dispatched to prevent Sarsfield from establishing himself close to the French siege lines.[57] Upon arriving before Sarsfield's

52   Quigley, *Antes morir que rendirse*, p.55.
53   Salvador-J. Rovira i Gómez, *Tarragona a la Guerra del Francès* (Tarragona: Universitat Rovira i Virgili, 2019), p.65.
54   Rovira i Gómez, *Tarragona a la Guerra del Francès*, p.64.
55   Quigley, *Antes morir que rendirse*, p.54.
56   Oman, *Peninsular War*, Vol.IV, p.520.
57   Guy C. Dempsey, *Napoleon's Mercenaries: Foreign Units in the French Army Under the Consulate and Empire, 1799 to 1814* (Barnsley: Frontline Books, 2016), p.125. The lancers were the remnants of the 1st Company of the 1/1er Lanciers de la Vistule, which had served in III Corps since 1808 under *Colonel* Klicki. They may have been too few to be listed in orders of battle, but served on the French right flank at María and later as Suchet's bodyguard unit.

position, Boussart found the terrain to be unsuited for employing his elite cavalrymen; instead, he ordered the position to be stormed by his infantry and led the attack on foot. The French made it to the top of the hill under heavy fire and dislodged Sarsfield's force at the cost of 11 killed and 80 wounded. Sarsfield retreated further north, and decided to target Montblanc, which he bombarded with his howitzers. The *miquelets* succeeded in occupying the town, but *Chef de Bataillon* Année's garrison refused to surrender. Frère and Palombini were not long in arriving with reinforcements, and Sarsfield beat a retreat. Nonetheless, Suchet decided to abandon Montblanc for good, deeming the constant attacks on the position to be a diversion of manpower and redistributed the Montblanc garrison back to its parent units.[58]

Suchet was informed by his engineers that it would be at least 10 days before preparations for a siege against the lower town could be finalized, so he decided to use that time to concentrate on Fort Olivo, the taking of which was in any case necessary for the siege.[59] On the night of 21 May, a sap was crept forward out of the left end of the first parallel until a suitable location for a breaching battery was reached. Work began on the second parallel on 23 May, but the ground was rocky and difficult, and the constant fire of the defenders was accentuated by the spray of deadly rock fragments. It took a week of digging and hauling until four batteries were nearly in position. The first battery (Battery No. 5) of three 8-inch mortars was located behind the west half of the first parallel, and the second the second (No.7) consisting of three 16-pounders for counter battery fire, was in the left half. The main breaching battery (No. 6) of four 24-pounders, dubbed 'The Battery of the King of Rome,' was to be just 130 yards from the fort and a small fourth battery (No. 8) of two 6-inch howitzers would fire from a level area on the eastern slope of the plateau to enfilade Fort Olivo.[60] The heavy guns of the breaching battery had to be maneuvered to the battery positions *en bricole*, while the cannons of Fort Olivo fired grapeshot into the dark, but they were finally hauled into place on the night of 27 May. In a last-ditch effort to stop the breaching battery, the garrison made a sortie. Salme observed the oncoming Spanish and called up his reserves of the 7e Ligne, crying 'Brave 7e, forward!'[61] Just then, he was killed instantly by a shot to the head. Enraged by the loss of their commander, the men of the 7e Ligne beat back the sortie and pursued the Spanish all the way to Fort Olivo. The much-admired *Général de Brigade* Jean-Baptiste Salme was buried under the Ferreres aqueduct which was near his encampment, while his heart was embalmed with the intention of entombing it in Fort Olivo once it was taken. It was later decided that a more fitting place to intern the heart was the Torre del Escipions, where the famous Scipio brothers were reportedly buried.[62] Command of his brigade was transferred to *Général de Brigade* Florentin Ficatier.[63]

58   Suchet, *Memoirs of the War in Spain*, Vol.II, p.46.
59   Arteche y Moro, *Guerra de la Independencia*, Vol.X, p.242. Arteche y Moro argues that Suchet had blundered by failing to realize that the taking of Fort Olivo was crucial to the siege, and not starting his siege efforts there.
60   Contreras, *Relation of the Siege of Tarragona*, p.11.
61   Suchet, *Memoirs of the War in Spain*, Vol.II, p.49.
62   As it turned out, the tower did not contain the remains of the Scipios. The funerary tower was likely a mausoleum for a different Roman family.
63   Suchet, *Memoirs of the War in Spain*, Vol.II, p.58.

On the morning of 28 May, the French siege guns opened a devastating fire onto Fort Olivo. The garrison returned fire and scored several hits, but one by one the Spanish guns were dismounted and the walls damaged. The 24-pounders of the forward battery battered the walls until a small breach was created on the rightmost angle of the fortification. Despite heavy losses, the garrison hunkered down and endured the bombardment, though, much to the disgust of the soldiers, the fort's commander had recieved suspicious orders that required his presence in Tarragona, safely away from the bombardment.[64] For all the derision the walls of Fort Olivo received from the British observers, they fulfilled their purpose that day, for Rogniat determined that more damage needed to be dealt onto the fort before an assault could be launched and urged Suchet to postpone the assault schedule for that evening. To this, Suchet agreed.[65] During the night, the garrison of the fort did their best to repair the damage before the bombardment was renewed at dawn of the 29th.

The French made preparations were made for an assault on the night of the 29th, to be conducted under the direction of Ficatier. The 7e and 16e were permitted the dubious honour of leading the attack on the breach as the forlorn hope, given that they had suffered hundreds of casualties from Fort Olivo's artillery while besieging the fort for over three weeks. The attack columns were assembled in the evening, and Suchet conducted a review of the troops before going to a nearby hill with Harispe, *Général de Brigade* Giuseppe Federico Palombini, and Saint Cyr Nugues to observe the storming. The French plan of attack was an elaborate one which incorporated Suchet's other divisions. On a prearranged signal, Habert's division and Peyri's Italians yelled loudly, their drummers beat the charge, and hordes of skirmishers were deployed to harass the outer works of the city all along the line in a diversionary attack. The defenders of Tarragona replied with their artillery, but it was difficult for either side to hit anything in the dark and this succeeded only in creating magnificent flashes of light and a racket of shots and explosions.

The Spanish were unsuspecting of an assault that night, for, contrary to what the French expected, the bombardment of the 28th and 29th had failed to do critical damage to Fort Olivo, nor had it disabled much of the fort's artillery. Skirmishers of the 1er Légère sniped at the garrison of Fort Olivo from the westward slope, while another group of the 1er Légère, guided by a Spanish sergeant who had deserted from the Regimiento de Almería, stealthily weaved their way around the left of the fort under the cover of the artillery duel to gain the rear gate. When a sentry challenged the shadowy figures for the password, the sergeant replied that they were of the Regimiento de Almería, and the group was let through. As it turned out, the garrison of Fort Olivo, made up of the three battalions of the Regimiento de Iliberia and some artillerymen, was to be relieved that night by two battalions of the Regimiento de Almería as part of a process whereby the garrison of Fort Olivo was changed once every eight days. As the French light infantrymen hid and watched, 1,200 men began marching through the rear entrance of the fort! It was just at that moment, at 9:00 p.m., that the signal for the attack was given. But when the French attacked, Fort Olivo would be manned by not only the regular garrison, but the relief force as well.

64   Quigley, *Antes morir que rendirse*, p.68.
65   Camillo Vacani, *Storia delle campagne e degli assedj degl'Italiani in Ispagna dal MDCCCVIII al MDCCCXIII* (Milan: P.Pagnoni, 1845), Vol.III, p.129.

The first French assault column of 300 elite troops of the 7e Ligne led by *Chef de Bataillon* Miocque, equipped with 30 ladders, went for the breach, while a similar force from the 16e Ligne under *Chef de Bataillon* Reval, preceded by 30 sappers under *Capitaine* Papigny of the engineers, looped around the right of the fort to attack the ditch and gain one of the rear gates. Miocque's column ran into instant trouble when, upon closer observation, the 'breach' was found to be wholly impracticable – the artillery had done little damage against the solid rock wall. Seeking another way in, Miocque and his party descended into the ditch to try and scale the wall, but their ladders proved to be five feet short of the 20-foot-tall walls. The French attempted to scale the wall nonetheless, by having the soldier at the top of the ladder act as a human extension, but it was a slow going, and the alerted Spanish defenders began to shoot down the climbers.

Meanwhile, back at the rear gate, *Sergent* Delhandry and some 30 voltigeurs decided to chance it and dashed amidst the men of the Regimiento de Almería streaming through the rear gate of the fort.[66] Seizing the advantage of the darkness and gunfire, the French light infantrymen pressed themselves against the Spanish reinforcements and attempted to force a passage into the fort. The arrival of the relieving garrison and the attempted shift change in the midst of the flurry of activity and gunfire around Tarragona created enough confusion in the darkness that the relief force did not annihilate this tiny band, which was also helped by the fact that by this point a number of Spanish units wore uniforms similar to the French.[67] Once the infiltrators had managed to get inside the fort, chaos ensued as they began slashing and stabbing at random with briquets and bayonets into the crowded mass. Panic broke out amidst the garrison – were they being attacked by their own men? Those on the ramparts were unable to fire for fear of hitting their comrades. The French sappers heading Reval's column, which had looped around Fort Olivo, rushed forwards, but the Spanish managed to close and lock the rear gate just before they could fall prey to the terrifying axes of the sappers. The French beat at the gate without success, and a few who attempted to free-climb the wall were shot down.

The confusion within the fort gave Minoque's beleaguered force just the break they needed to revaluate the situation and come up with a different strategy. During the bombardment, *Capitano* Camillo Vacani, an Italian engineer, had noticed that the Ferreres aqueduct ran out of the glacis of Fort Olivo, across the ditch, and through the main wall.[68] It was blocked off by a palisade that had been partly shattered from the fire of the siege guns. Vacani directed the Italian sappers to chop down the ruined palisade with their axes, and in short time Minoque's storming party, joined by two of Suchet's aide de camps, Meyer and Deschallard, had traversed the two-yard-wide aqueduct and clambered over the main wall. By this time the garrison in that sector had fled or was distracted, so Vacani and his men were able to make their way into the fort with ease. At the rear of the fortress, Reval ordered several ladders to be brought up and the sappers and grenadiers overwhelmed the defenders in that section and open the gate for the rest of the column to follow.[69] Caught in the middle

---

66   Quigley, *Antes morir que rendirse*, p.69.
67   Prada, *Tarragona*, p.156.
68   Vacani, *Storia delle campagne*, Vol.III, p.133.
69   Suchet, *Memoirs of the War in Spain*, Vol.II, p.55.

of a shift change, the defenders were unable to effectively hold the points of focus of the assault and now the French were pouring into the fort.

Observing the success of the forlorn hopes, *Colonel* Mesclop led forward 500 Italians of the 2° Leggera and 4°, 5°, and 6° di Linea. The French and Italians managed to storm the internal crownwork on the right and silence its guns, but the western fort section held out as the defenders rallied and conducted a magnificent defence, in spite of being attacked from the front and rear. It was fortunate for the garrison that the French attack had occurred in the midst of a shift change, thus there were nearly double the number of defenders there normally would have been. Both sides fought bitterly for every foot of ground in a chaotic night melee, and the French gave no quarter in their frenzied attack. Crowds of men speared each other by the bayonet or broke bones with the swing of the musket. *Coronel* Gómez, commanding the Fort Olivo garrison, was stabbed no less than ten times in the chaos.[70] It was only at around 1:00 a.m. that the terrible fight drew to a close as the exhausted Spanish defenders retreated, leaving the French in possession of the fort.[71]

The events surrounding the storming of Fort Olivo are clouded with uncertainty, particularly as to which French unit stormed the rear of the fort – was it a few men of the 1er Légère as Suchet claims, or were they Reval's men? And what about the strange story of the Spanish sergeant? According to Lieutenant Zehnpfennig, Suchet was possibly aware of the change in garrison and thus concocted a scheme to get a party of French soldiers, a few of whom were disguised as Spaniards, to covertly join the incoming Regimiento de Almería to gain entry into the fort.[72] Neither Vacani nor Suchet makes mention of a plan involving disguises and deserters, though Roviro i Gómez writes that because of Campoverde's populist policies, military affairs were made public, including the scheduled garrison change, so it is within the realm of possibility that Suchet knew of the planned garrison change.[73] However the author finds it doubtful that Suchet had prior knowledge about the garrison change, for he would never have sent his assault parties in if he knew that the garrison of Fort Olivo was at twice its normal strength that night. Given how events played out that night, such a plan seems to have been high-risk and left too much to chance.

Truth be told, it was not an assault that should have succeeded, given the poor luck that resulted in twice as many defenders being there, and the lack of effect the French artillery had in creating a breach. But with initiative, courage, and the confusion of the night, the French and Italians had managed to take the fort. Some 3,000 Spaniards fought in Fort Olivo that night, of those, 300-400 were killed and 970 captured, many of the latter being wounded. In addition, vast quantities of munitions stored in the fort were taken, to be put to use against their former owners.[74] French losses were similarly heavy, between 300-500 men.[75] Yet it seemed that the loss of Fort Olivo failed to dishearten the defenders; rather, it only hardened

---

70   Oman, *Peninsular War*, Vol.IV, p.505.
71   Contreras, *Relation of the Siege of Tarragona*, p.13.
72   Quigley, *Antes morir que rendirse*, p.69.
73   Rovira i Gómez, *Tarragona a la Guerra del Francès*, p.66.
74   Suchet, *Memoirs of the War in Spain*, Vol.II, p.58, reports taking 130,000 cartridges, 47 guns, 50,000 sandbags, and vast quantities of powder and provisions.
75   Precise casualty figures for the engagement at Fort Olivo are difficult to gauge, given both sides' penchant for exaggeration. Belmas, *Journaux des siéges*, Vol.III, p.502, estimates that the French lost 525 and the Spanish 1,200 killed or wounded and 970 captured.

their resolve to protect Tarragona. The brave men of the Iliberia and Almería regiments were bent on avenging their defeat, and asked to lead a sortie to recapture the fort. Campoverde agreed, believing that the French would be vulnerable to an assault from the postern side of the fort. After laying down a heavy and quite effective bombardment against Fort Olivo that morning, 3,000 Spaniards under *Coronel* Edmundo O'Ronan sallied out of Tarragona. But the Spanish had underestimated the efficiency and professionalism of Suchet's veteran troops. The French had set about fortifying Fort Olivo to their own use immediately after taking it – stairs were carved in the breach and gangplanks thrown over the ditches to facilitate the movement of reinforcements. Command of the fort and the 1,100 men placed there was given to Ficatier. The sortie was met with heavy fire from the fort and from the flank by nearby troops. Unable to break through the barricaded rear gate, the sortie force retreated back to the city. The loss of Fort Olivo was the turning point in the Siege of Tarragona, for what had thus far been a stalemate now swung in favour of the French. Spanish losses were steadily mounting, and the garrison resorted to using the Tarragona cathedral as an overflow hospital for the wounded.[76]

The noose was tightening around Tarragona, but there were still ample resources and opportunities to stop Suchet. Earlier, Colonel Green had proposed a plan for part of the garrison to be transported out of the city into the Catalonian countryside to raise a new army, heavily made up of *somatenes*.[77] Campoverde took this into consideration and convened a council on 30 May with the members of the Catalonian Supreme Junta and generals. There he proposed that he would form a new army by re-joining the divisions of Eroles and Sarsfield and recruiting from the countryside to attack Suchet from behind and threaten his lines of communication, which was accepted as the plan of action. With Caro being sent to Valencia to raise more reinforcements, Campoverde decided that command of the city would be given to *Mariscal de Campo* Juan Senen de Contreras, who had just arrived from Cádiz and been in Tarragona for less than a day. Contreras objected vehemently, citing his complete lack of familiarity with Tarragona and its inhabitants as a newcomer, but it was to no avail. Though competent, Contreras had none of the rapport that other commanders such as Caro had with the populace and the garrison, which downgraded the quality of Tarragona's leadership at a critical time. To further complicate matters, Campoverde split command of the city's defence by appointing the capable Sarsfield commander of the port fortifications extending from Fort Francoli to the lower city. The creation of a semi-independent command within Tarragona inevitably caused friction with Contreras, and it is to his credit that the issue did not escalate any further than it did.[78] Worse, Campoverde decided to take with him 3,000 carbines and an abundance of medical supplies, further depriving Tarragona of critical resources. With pressure on the city mounting, many officers found it convenient to declare themselves sick and depart the city; such pusillanimity at times left captains in charge of whole regiments![79]

76   Manuel Maria Fuentes i Gasó, et al., *Memòria del segte i ocupació de Tarragona: La Guerra del Francès en els fons documentals de l'Arxiu Històric Arxidiocesà de Tarragona (1808-1814)* (Tarragona: L'Arxiu Històric Arxidiocesà de Tarragona, 2012), p.123.
77   Quigley, *Antes morir que rendirse*, p.71.
78   Andrés Eguaguirre, Sucesos Verdaderos Del Sitio y Plaza de Tarragona (Valencia: Imprenta Patriótica del Pueblo Soberano a cargo de Vicente Ferro, 1813), pp.9-10.
79   Rovira i Gómez, *Tarragona a la Guerra del Francès*, p.67.

On 1 June, Campoverde left the city with his staff and several prominent citizens on HMS *Cambrian* with the promise that he would return in a week with a powerful army with which to raise the siege. In many ways this was a sound decision; Campoverde, as supreme commander in Catalonia, would be better off in the field to disrupt French operations than shut up in a besieged city. Thus far, the Catalonia Junta at Montserrat had failed to muster a large force of *somatenes*, and they would certainly benefit from Campoverde's presence. Of the wealthy citizens who had left the city, Contreras ordered their assets to be confiscated, reeling in 300,000 francs to be put to use in the defence. Codrington and Doyle had been hard at work calling in old friends and making new ones in Valencia, to much success. A conference with Carlos O'Donnell and his brother, the indomitable Enrique O'Donnell, who, ignoring the advice of his doctors and still bleeding from his wounds, travelled over 100 miles by carriage on bumpy roads just to attend and contribute what he could, went very well. The O'Donnells agreed to provide an additional division of 4,000 men under *Mariscal de Campo* José Miranda, while Enrique would lead the rest of the Valencian army to the Ebro and threaten Suchet's supply depots.[80]

Meanwhile, Rogniat and Valée declared that everything was ready to begin the siege against the lower city. With Fort Olivo in their possession, the French opened the first parallel on the night of 1 June, just under 280 yards from the Orleans Bastion, the centre-piece of the main crownwork protecting the lower city.[81] Several thousand workers and trench guards laboured in the night to complete the first elements of a massive system of siege lines, aiming to finish the protective works before daylight marked them as targets for the Spanish artillery. Three batteries were positioned along the first parallel – battery No. 11 had eight 16-pounders to target the fortification connecting Fort Francoli with the rest of the city, battery No. 12, made up of four mortars, bombarded the Orleans bastion and Fuerte Real with their arcing shots, as did the three howitzers of the leftmost battery No. 13.[82] A communication trench was dug to the bridge over the Francoli, but after deeming that bridge to be too exposed, a second bridge was constructed behind the first. An additional bridge was constructed farther upstream to facilitate communication between the supply depots of the right bank and the siege lines of the left. The left end of the parallel was anchored on a redoubt and protected by Fort Olivo, and the right end, close to the Francoli River, was covered by the batteries on the right bank. On the night of 3 June, a sap from the right end of the parallel was dug downward along the riverbank to get closer to Fort Francoli. As the parallels crept closer to the city, they would come in range of the enfilade fire of Fort Francoli's guns; thus, it was necessary to capture this position. The next two days saw continued progress as the French opened the second parallel, and pushed to within 65 yards of Fort Francoli. An incessant bombardment lasting from 3:30 a.m. to 7:30 p.m. practically reduced Fort Francoli to rubble and knocked out six of the fort's seven guns, but the young Swiss *Coronel* Antonio de Roten and his garrison – two battalions of the Regimiento

---

80   Quigley, *Antes morir que rendirse*, p.90.
81   Contreras, *Relation of the Siege of Tarragona*, p.18. French sources often refer to this bastion as the 'Bastion des Chanoines.'
82   Arteche y Moro, *Guerra de la Independencia*, Vol.X, p.264. Battery No. 11 was not fully ready until the night of 6 June.

de Almansa plus artillerymen – held on with determination, repulsing an attack on the night of 6 June.

The French batteries resumed their fire on Fort Francoli on 7 June, and 12 hours of relentless bombardment left the fort breached on the left side, dysfunctional, and wholly untenable. At 7:00 p.m., Contreras ordered de Roten to evacuate the shattered remnants of his garrison.[83] All the guns and their crews were out of the action, as were 104 of the 250 infantrymen. Some three hours later, Saint Cyr Nugues directed three French assault columns of 100 men each from the 1er and 5e Légère to storm the fort from different directions to overwhelm the defenders.[84] Much to their surprise they found the fort deserted; Roten had conducted his withdrawal in complete secrecy. Eager for glory, the French light infantrymen attempted a push towards the city, but were stopped by the guns of the Prince lunette. Under heavy canister fire, the French took to fortifying Fort Francoli in case the Spanish sortied to retake it. The French spent the next two days extending the second parallel to Fort Francoli, where a battery of six 24-pounders (No. 14) was positioned to target the harbour. This forced the British squadron to move to the eastern harbour below the upper city, further isolating the lower city.[85] On the night of 8 June, 300 Spanish grenadiers sortied out and caught the trench guards by surprise, killing several and stealing some supplies before falling back. Despite the steady losses of their outer works, the lower city defenders maintained an active defence under Sarsfield's energetic leadership. They did not stop their fire on the besiegers, continuing to inflict losses and often driving daytime progress to a crawl, while the night saw raids and sally parties. Another sortie was launched on 11 June, when Sarsfield led out 300 men at midnight. They battled the trench guards for about two hours, then fell back after inflicting some damage to the siege works. A few minor French raids and assaults were repelled in turn, but the bombardment never ceased, and the garrison was anxious for aid. Doyle wrote to Henry Wellesley, that:

> The extraordinary speed and gallantry with which the enemy advances can only be resisted by conduct such as that of this garrison. Be clear that a field has never been so contested. Each meter gained is paid with a high price, and in proportion to the increase in danger, the determination of the Spaniards seems to be increasing. I cannot, in any way, do justice to their noble conduct and in the same way, to the cheerful disposition with which they endure incessant labors. His attentive duty can hardly be credited under heavy and relentless enemy fire. It is extremely unbelievable. I trust and certainly hope that our efforts to help this important point will not be unsuccessful. Surely all the promises of General Charles O'Donnell will bear fruit as will the tireless efforts of Captains Codrington, Adams, and Bullen whose assistance has been incalculable.[86]

---

83   Contreras, *Relation of the Siege of Tarragona*, p.19.
84   Quigley, *Antes morir que rendirse*, p.95. Codrington and Doyle returned to Tarragona that day. Codrington recounts that the grenades onboard the ship were immediately taken to fight a French attack, implying that Roten and his men contested the fort for some time.
85   Arteche y Moro, *Guerra de la Independencia*, Vol.X, p.266.
86   Quigley, *Antes morir que rendirse*, p.119.

Meanwhile, Campoverde had reached Igualada on 3 June, where he found Sarsfield with 3,000 men. He packed that general off to Tarragona to serve under Contreras (hence, Sarsfield's presence in Tarragona as related above) and assumed command of the field force, summoning Eroles and rallying all nearby detachments. In two weeks Campoverde mustered a force of 5,280 infantry and 1,183 cavalry, but he still believed that this was not enough to engage Suchet and was desperate for reinforcements from Valencia, so much so that he offered to give Carlos O'Donnell supreme command if he would come to Catalonia with his troops.[87] O'Donnell declined this offer, but met with Doyle, Codrington, and Caro to discuss how Miranda's promised division could be used best. Caro, representing Campoverde, wished for Miranda's division to join the Campoverde's field force to assist in relieving the city, while Doyle, concerned for Tarragona after the fall of Fort Francoli and distrustful of Campoverde, proposed that Miranda be sent to the beleaguered city and take part in a massive breakout attempt. After some discussion, Doyle had his way and it was decided to send Miranda's division to Tarragona. On 11 June, Miranda's 4,000-strong division was packed into a few ships of Codrington's squadron at Peñiscola.[88] However, while en route, Miranda told Codrington that he had secret orders that his division was under no circumstances to be landed in Tarragona – instead, it was to join Campoverde's field force in stark contrast to the agreed-upon plan. A party between the ranking commanders was soured not only by the poor wine, but the revelation that Miranda had no such 'secret orders' that mandated him to join Campoverde, as a matter of fact, O'Donnell's orders explicitly told him to disembark in Tarragona.[89] Miranda was simply refusing to do so on his own initiative and doing what he thought was best for the Spanish cause, and nothing more could be done on the matter.[90] Thus, much to the disappointment of the garrison, the arrival of Miranda's division at Tarragona on 13 June was temporary, for it continued on to join Campoverde's army; their presence had done nothing except to give false hope to the garrison and promptly lower it. That night, the energetic Sarsfield launched another sortie against Fort Francoli, never giving Suchet a moment of rest. Likewise, the Anglo-Allied fleet continued their operations, often sending in gunboats armed with carronades to bombard the French lines. Thus far, the French had the balance of successes in the siege. The Spanish defenders had maintained a heavy fire on the French, but despite inflicting terrible casualties, they had overall been unable to stymie the progress of the besiegers, who crept closer every day. By 15 June, the French had advanced three separate saps by zigzag to the Orleans bastion, the Del Rey demi-lune guarding its left face, and the Prince lunette. Worse for the Spanish, five new batteries had been built along the length of the second parallel embracing the city walls, within 120 yards of them:[91]

- Battery 15: four 8-pounders
- Battery 16: three 16-pounders, two 6-inch mortars

87   Oman, *Peninsular War*, Vol.IV, p.506.
88   Quigley, *Antes morir que rendirse*, p.101. HMS *Blake* transported 800 soldiers, for a total of 1,300 men aboard a 55-metre long ship!
89   Quigley, *Antes morir que rendirse*, p.106.
90   Quigley, *Antes morir que rendirse*, p.106.
91   Suchet, *Memoirs of the War in Spain*, Vol.II, p.72.

- Battery 17: six 24-pounders
- Battery 18: three 16-pounders
- Battery 19: three 24-pounders

The siege had reached its most critical moments. Despite steady French gains, the Spanish defenders had made them pay for every yard in blood and showed no sign of giving up. Graindor, who was often on trench duty, recounted 'we never went to the trenches without leaving some killed or wounded from each company.'[92] Thus far Suchet had suffered around 2,000 casualties, and had yet to even reach the inner city.[93] Both sides drew in reinforcements: Suchet called in Abbé's brigade and the 115e Ligne to the siege lines, while Contreras received an odd battalion here and there. Contreras knew that it would only be a matter of time before the French took the city by force, and sent desperate appeals for Campoverde to launch an offensive against Suchet.[94] But the situation was desperate for the French too. The siege thus far had been an extremely costly war of attrition which was fast draining Suchet's small army. Between the garrison and Campoverde's army, Suchet was actually outnumbered, and he needed to finish the siege before the Spanish could coordinate a powerful attack. For both sides, it was a race against time.

On 16 June, 54 French cannon opened a devastating bombardment on the lower city. The Spanish were ready and had packed their ramparts with infantry and sandbags. In desperation, the defenders waged a close-range duel with the batteries, hurling grenades at the saps and redoubling their musketry, sustaining such a ferocious defence that they managed to reduce the effectiveness of the French guns by killing or wounding many of the gunners. The fortress artillery also managed to severely damage the second parallel. For their efforts, the French only managed to create a small breach in the Orleans bastion and set fire to two Spanish magazines. Amidst the heavy fighting, Doyle was hit in the shoulder by a sharpshooter and taken aboard the *Blake*, but the active military agent continued his duties in defending the city. The civilians in the city were suffering especially heavily. Hundreds of the poorer women and children lived in tent cities, unwilling to leave either because their relatives were fighting in the garrison or because they were unable to pay the hefty fee for a ticket out of the city by ship.[95] Now their homes came under fire from the hail of shot and shell, but, despite the daily terror wrought by the siege, the defenders, both on the ramparts and within the city, held strong. Codrington, directing his gunboats in counter-battery fire, recounted how 'I saw a poor man dressed in rags running towards a store full of women and children, which had been hit by an enemy shell. He tried to lessen the effect with sand while taking people out. The shell apparently exploded in his face, but did not touch him, although the shrapnel passed close to our heads.'[96] The ever-increasing wounded and some of the luckier civilians were ferried out of the city on the British ships.

---

92   Graindor, *Mémoires de la Guerre d'Espagne 1808-1814*, p.56.
93   Suchet, *Memoirs of the War in Spain*, Vol.II, p.77.
94   Oman, *Peninsular War*, Vol.IV, p.517.
95   Quigley, *Antes morir que rendirse*, p.129. Captain Adam of HMS *Invincible* was so infuriated by the divisive cost of passage that he began to take civilians on board his vessel for free.
96   Quigley, *Antes morir que rendirse*, p.129.

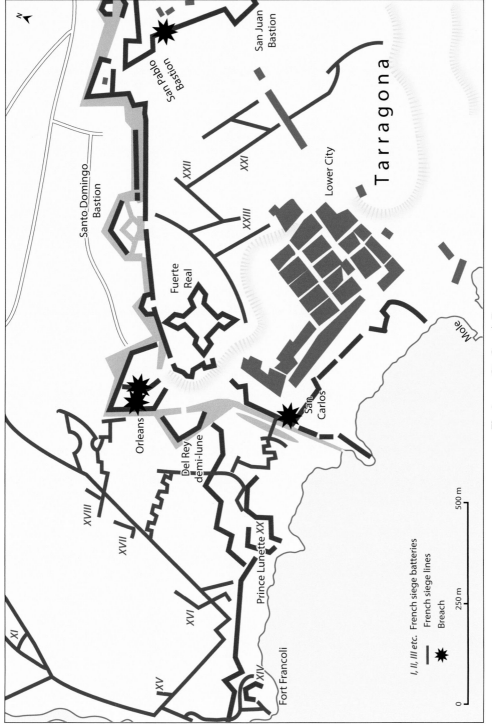

The Lower City Breach Zone.

Despite the ineffectiveness of the sanguinary daytime artillery duel, Suchet ordered a night-time assault on the Prince lunette. Two assault columns of the 1er Légère under *Chef de Bataillon* Javersac of Austerlitz fame led the attack, while a reserve of 350 men of the 116e Ligne waited to exploit any success.[97] As the attackers rapidly scaled the ditch and cut down the palisades, they were met with a deadly fusillade and a storm of grenades which killed Javersac, but the other column managed to get around the flank of the enemy and drove out the defenders. The French attempted to push on, but were caught in a crossfire and driven back by the 2° de Saboya and Almería, which Contreras had deployed to counter the attack. Licking their wounds, the French were quick to establish a lodgement in the Prince lunette to protect its occupants from the fire of the San Carlos bastion and use it as a viable launching point for assaults. Despite the best efforts of the Spanish, the French repaired the damage to their siege lines within a day and created Battery No. 20 on the captured Prince lunette, from where four 24-pounders could breach the right face of the San Pedro bastion. Meanwhile, the sap against the Orleans bastion was expanded to the covered way to prepare a storming of the breach. Similarly, the sap against the Del Rey demi-lune was pushed to the glacis, from where a third parallel was dug to the Prince lunette. By their own reports, the French were losing at least 60 men a day to the close-range fire of the defenders, yet their push was unrelenting.[98] Knowing that the walls of the lower city would be stormed any day, Contreras committed 6,000 of his 8,000-man garrison there, including his best troops. But Contreras himself was rarely found in the lower city, and command of that sector was given to the capable Sarsfield, who conducted the defence with great energy.

Now reinforced by Miranda's division, Campoverde marched on Montblanc with 11,000 men, from where he sent detachments to harass French foraging parties and convoys. However, he was kept in check by Abbé's field force and failed to draw attention away from the siege. On 18 June, Codrington wrote:

> The aid on which the garrison has the most right to place its trust is that of the Campo Verde army, which will join tomorrow on the heights of Alforja and Riudecols, between Reus and Falset, with its Right extended towards Montroig. The cavalry consists of 1,000 horsemen in very good order, commanded by General Caro, the Catalan division of around 4,500 men, commanded by the Baron de Eroles and the division of Valencia, increased by a battalion to constitute the same number, commanded by General Miranda. All this under the command of the Marquis of Campo Verde. Some of the troops are new and the Marquis may not trust them in the open, but they can go a long way in cutting off supplies from Tortosa by destroying all of General Suchet's detachments.[99]

Yet Campoverde sat miles away, having hardly moved his army. He had promised to return in a week with an army and threaten Suchet's rear – it had been two weeks and there was

97   Quigley, *Antes morir que rendirse*, p.130. Zehnpfennig asserts that Suchet launched three assault columns to attack the Prince lunette and take the San Carlos bastion from the rear by way of the beach, but that only the attack on the Prince lunette succeeded.

98   Suchet, *Memoirs of the War in Spain*, Vol.II, p.79.

99   Quigley, *Antes morir que rendirse*, p.133.

still no sign of his appearance. Despite reports that Suchet's lines were weak around the Barcelona road, for 150 Spanish cavalrymen managed to ride out of Tarragona on 15 June by this route with scant opposition and establish communications with the field force, Campoverde stuck to his time-consuming policy of sending out detachments to harass Suchet's supply lines.[100] On 16 June a Spanish detachment attempted to threaten Mora, but were swiftly defeated by some cuirassiers and infantry; on 20 June Baron Eroles moved with 5,000 men to the Mora-Falset region to prey on French convoys. Suchet was forced to weaken Harispe's blocking force to replenish his heavy losses at the main siege lines before the lower city. Despite some local success in harassing French detachments, Campoverde's strategy ultimately failed to force Suchet's hand and draw him away from Tarragona, for the French had stockpiled enough supplies at Reus, and Suchet saw through the Spaniard's intentions.[101] Higher-value targets, such as the French artillery park and hospital at Reus, were not attacked, and it became clear that Campoverde was plainly unwilling to risk a pitched battle. Contreras attempted to reason with Campoverde, sending calculations that if the garrison and field army attacked simultaneously and 'if we do our duty, Suchet's army is lost...', but his pleas for help were answered with only reassurances, plus a request for Sarsfield to join Campoverde.[102]

While Campoverde dithered, Tarragona continued to suffer. Doyle reported on 18 June that the Orleans, San Jose, and San Carlos bastions were so badly damaged that they could be stormed at any moment. However, the French preferred to extend their entrenchments, so the Spanish were able to conduct repairs with what few materials were left. The cannon in the lower city bastions had been nearly all taken out, so Sarsfield had resorted to using sharpshooters as the primary means of resistance. Likewise, he had the houses of the lower city fortified and the streets barricaded – Tarragona would go the full distance in carrying on the legacy of Zaragoza. The French intensified their bombardment on 21 June. One of the first Spanish counterbattery shots struck the magazine of Battery No. 20 in the Prince lunette and caused an explosion, but the battery was quickly rendered serviceable again in merely a few hours. By 4:00 p.m. that day, the French siege guns, firing at pistol-shot range, had opened five massive breaches all along the walls of the lower city, particularly in the Orleans and San Carlos bastions, as well as in Fuerte Real, and silenced the few remaining Spanish cannons. Suchet lost no time in assembling an assault force to storm and seize the lower city, hoping to take immediate advantage of the breaches before the defenders could refortify them. That evening, the Spanish sentries watched with great trepidation as French assault columns marched from their encampments and into the forward trenches. Palombini, on trench duty that day, was tasked with leading some 1,000 men drawn from the elite companies of the French regiments. The composition of the attack force was as follows:

- 1st Column (*Colonel* Bouvier): 300 men of the 116e, 117e, and 121e Ligne.
- 2nd Column (*Capitaine* Thiebaut): 50 sappers and grenadiers of the 115e Ligne.

---

100 Codrington, *Memoir of the Life of Admiral Sir Edward Codrington*, Vol.I, p.220.
101 Suchet, *Memoirs of the War in Spain*, Vol.II, p.87.
102 See Contreras, *Relation of the Siege of Tarragona*, pp.91-94, for Campoverde's notes. Letter of 16 June, from Contreras to Campoverde; from Eguaguirre, *Sucesos Verdaderos*, pp.46-48.

- 3rd Column (*Chef de Bataillon* Fondzelski): 300 men of the 1er and 5e Légère and the 42e Ligne.
- 4th Column (*Capitaine* Baccarini): 50 grenadiers of the 115e Ligne.
- 5th Column: (*Colonel* Bourgeois): 300 carabiniers of the 1er Légère.

Montmarie commanded a reserve of the 5e Légère and the 116e Ligne on the left, to watch for counterattacks from the upper town and to support the main attack. *Colonel* Robert was given orders to support the attack on the right by advancing along the shore with the elite companies of the 5e Légère and the 42e, 115e, and 121e Ligne.[103] Suchet unleashed his assault columns at 7:00 p.m. that evening against the battered Orleans and San Carlos bastions, and the curtain wall between them. A column made a feint out of Fort Olivo, and Harispe directed some howitzers to bombard the upper city to distract the garrison for a few precious minutes. *Colonel* Bouvier's column seized the Orleans bastion by clambering over the rubble of the breach and overthrew its defenders with such *élan* that the Spanish had not even had enough time to detonate the two mines in the breach which would have shattered the assault. The defenders rallied at the redan of the inner wall just behind the bastion, but were hard pressed and forced into the city. Thiebaut's small detachment cleared the Del Rey demi-lune before joining Bouvier's column. They pressed on into the city, only to find that the breach made in the Fuerte Real was not practicable; this hardly deterred the French and they simply assaulted the fort with scaling ladders.

Chef de Bataillon Fondzelski's and *Capitaine* Baccarini's columns attacked the San Carlos bastion, but faced tougher resistance than Bouvier had, and Fondzelski's column crowded the breach, unable to advance.[104] Only the arrival of *Colonel* Bourgeois' column provided Fondzelski's column with the impetus to charge up the breach and seize the bastion. The two columns pushed into the city in pursuit of the fleeing defenders, and split up as Bourgeois swung north to attack the Fuerte Real from the south while Bouvier's men fought for the fort walls in the north. Fuerte Real's garrison put up a determined resistance, but was simply overwhelmed by the onslaught. Fondzelski made for the harbour of the lower city, where he found the Spanish troops rallying to organize a defence. Fondzelski's men took cover in houses, forcing the Spanish into an ugly house-to-house brawl for the city. The French held on, and it was not long before the arrival of *Colonel* Robert with his reserve tipped the battle in favour of the French elites, who butchered the defenders as they routed; the Spanish finding their escape routes cut off and desperately seeking a way to the upper city. Undoubtedly many civilians were also killed in the chaotic fight and as some French plundered the city.

The Spanish command had been incapacitated by a tragic farce which, even more ironically, occurred during the French assault. Contreras had received the order from Campoverde for Sarsfield to join his army that morning, and sent down a passport to Sarsfield as well as orders for *Brigadier* Velasco to replace him. Despite the fact that Suchet was visibly massing his troops for an assault, Sarsfield left at 3:00 p.m., telling no one except for *Colonel* José Carlos, to whom he transferred command, despite Carlos'

---

103 *Colonel* Robert's force likely totalled some 500 men. Suchet, *Memoirs of the War in Spain*, Vol.II, p.80, places his main attack force at 1,500 men.
104 Suchet, *Memoirs of the War in Spain*, Vol.II, p.82.

objections, upon which Sarsfield did no more than to inform Contreras that Carlos thought himself unsuited for command.[105] Thus, when the French attacked, Contreras was under the assumption that Sarsfield had not left yet and still held command of the lower city. Velasco hurried down to take command of troops whose dispositions he hardly knew, only to be swept up in the street fighting. Without an effective command system to direct reserves and provide solid leadership at the moment of crisis, it is no surprise that the French were able to overwhelm the lower city garrison. The defence of the lower city collapsed within 20 minutes, and the Spanish fled for the upper city. Some 300 who were cut off managed to reach the port to be rescued by the British ships. From the ramparts above St John's Gate, Contreras watched the flashes of musketry and shadows slashing at each other down in the lower city in horror, realizing that his men were being overrun as groups of them fled through the gate into the upper city. The French were in close pursuit of the fleeing Spanish to try and capture the gate while it was still open. Anticipating this, Contreras ordered the gate to be closed on friend and foe alike, then yelled for the Spanish still trapped on the other side to press against the wall and re-form, separating themselves from the French.[106] With the way cleared, the defenders on the ramparts opened fire with canister shot to hold back the French as the Spanish retreated through the reopened gates. Some French grenadiers rushed the gate as it closed in their face and attempted to batter it down with the butts of their muskets, but were quickly shot down. A few had managed to sneak in with the Spanish, only to be discovered and killed.[107]

Contreras reported that the Spanish lost no more than 500 men in the fall of the lower city, while Suchet admits to 120 killed and 362 wounded.[108] The French also captured a quantity of artillery, which they would soon turn on the remaining defenders of Tarragona. The greatest loss for the Spanish was the shattering of morale. Now confined to the upper city, many defenders felt that the end was near. Many more were frustrated at Campoverde's lack of action.

Immediately after the lower city had been secured, Palombini reorganized the scattered French troops, while *Colonel* Henri led 800 workers in fortifying the lower city to make preparations for a siege against the upper city.[109] A sunken lane formed the foundation for the first parallel within the city, and the nearby houses were turned into strongholds. French engineers spent the next few days surveying Contreras' last line of defence, while captured Spanish guns were hauled into batteries. The wall guarding the inner city was old and weak, and the engineers determined that the best point of attack would be between the San Juan and San Pablo bastions, the two northernmost bastions of the inner city wall.

105 Oman, *Peninsular War*, Vol.IV, pp.512-513.
106 Contreras, *Relation of the Siege of Tarragona*, p.23.
107 Suchet, *Memoirs of the War in Spain*, Vol.II, p.84.
108 Oman, *Peninsular War*, Vol.IV, p.514.
109 Vacani, *Storia delle campagne*, Vol.III, p.182.

The City is Lost

Tarragona now entered its most desperate hour. Heavy casualties and a determined defence had failed to halt Suchet's ambitions, and now the French held the lower city. It was common knowledge that the medieval wall of the upper city stood little chance against the French siege guns, and that it would only be a matter of time before the entire city fell. Driven away from the lower city, Codrington's squadron was now restricted to Milagro Point, a barely suitable harbour where landings were made impossible in even slightly rough waves.[110] Such a location was hardly tenable for the merchant ships, which left for other ports. Yet the British squadron remained, despite coming under bombardment, doing their best to offload supplies and evacuate the wounded and civilians, while continuing to provide fire support. From 11:00 a.m. to 1:00 p.m. on 22 June, the ships fired on the French works in the inner city and the garrison launched a small sortie. Suchet constructed a battery comprised of a howitzer and two 24-pounders to target the embarkation point, but this caused more noise than any damage. Still, for the allies, it was becoming an uphill battle.

With the defence of Tarragona looking increasingly hopeless, Contreras decided that the preservation of his sizable garrison took precedence over holding the city. Thus, he made up his mind to abandon Tarragona. It was impossible to move his garrison by sea as the Spanish no longer had possession of the main harbour.[111] As such, Contreras decided that the garrison would sally out when the French breached the upper city in conjunction with an attack by Campoverde. Green, who met with Contreras to discuss the plan, wrote to Lord Liverpool:

> I understand that General Contreras proposes to carry out an escape plan with the garrison… when the enemy opens a breach. At the same time the Marquis of Campo Verde with his army… which with the Valencians has 10,000 men, will attack from the outside. It is expected that both united forces, which together would add 18 to 19 thousand men, can surround the French if they occupy Tarragona. A decision on this important event is expected in two days…[112]

Campoverde finally realized this as well, and, knocked out of his slumberous inaction, ordered his force to march to Tarragona. It departed Montblanc on 23 June, drawing up camp at Vila-rodona, just 15 miles north of Tarragona.[113] The next day it marched in two divisional columns – Miranda's Valencian division would attack the Italians, while Sarsfield's Catalan division, accompanied by Campoverde himself, would take another route and emerge on Miranda's left flank. Suchet was given early notice of their advance when his cavalry outposts skirmished with Campoverde's cavalry, and organized a total of 8,000 men of Harispe's division, part of Frère's division, and all of the cavalry above Fort Olivo to defend the French siege lines. Habert's division, Peyri's division, Abbé's brigade, and the rest of Frère's division were entrusted with carrying on the siege.[114]

---

110 Oman, *Peninsular War*, Vol.IV, p.515.
111 Contreras' report, from Appendix 18, Suchet, *Memoirs of the War in Spain*, Vol.II, p.422.
112 Quigley, *Antes morir que rendirse*, p.151.
113 Oman, *Peninsular War*, Vol.IV, p.516.
114 Oman, *Peninsular War*, Vol.IV, p.516.

The bustle of activity and sudden troop movements in the French camp was not lost on the beleaguered defenders of Tarragona. That Suchet had formed his troops for battle could only mean that the long-awaited relief army had arrived. The defenders leapt into action at this hope, and Contreras organized a force to sally out and attack the French rear to support Campoverde. They waited eagerly, and continued to wait as the long minutes passed into tiring hours. Yet there was nothing, not even the distant fire of skirmishers heralding the arrival of battle.

Upon finding Suchet's force, Miranda had been intimidated by it, and informed Campoverde that he would not advance any further. Campoverde likewise lost his nerve and stopped the advance. Believing that he faced no chance against Suchet, he ordered his entire force to retreat without even bringing up Sarsfield to support Miranda. It was small consolation for the defenders of Tarragona that at least the disgraceful retreat had been hidden by the hills. Campoverde's reasoning finds justification in that by no means was victory certain; in fact Suchet had faced longer odds before and triumphed. III Corps enjoyed a fearsome reputation that certainly played on Campoverde's decision-making. Yet it was undeniable cowardice on Campoverde's part to simply abandon Tarragona to its fate. Suchet had faced an army of 11,000 to his front and up to 4,000 sallying from Tarragona with just 8,000 of his own, and averted a confrontation that could have gone either way.

Campoverde still had the nerve to ask Contreras to send out Velasco with the Iliberia and Almería regiments, believing that he needed more men to attack Suchet.[115] By this point Campoverde was scraping the bottom of the barrel. Few *somantes* rallied to his army, for they had lost all respect for him. News of a British expeditionary force compelled Campoverde to send Eroles to find it and add it to his force. What truly disgraced Campoverde's behaviour was his attempted character-assassination of Contreras by sending letters to generals in the garrison instructing them to overthrow Contreras if he showed any sign of surrendering. The generals showed these letters to Contreras, who, though demoralized, still agreed to send out the troops Campoverde requested.[116] Their departure was only stopped by poor weather which made embarkation from the Milagro impossible.

A small sliver of hope came for Contreras and the defenders of Tarragona with the arrival of five transports from Cádiz led by HMS *Regulus* on 26 June. At long last, Cádiz had answered the city's pleas for help. After much persuasion from the Cádiz Regency, Lieutenant General Thomas Graham had given the go-ahead for the relief convoy, without waiting for approval from Lord Wellington, no easy decision, for Cádiz was also under siege at the time and needed every man it could get. The convoy held a few reinforcements from Valencia and Murcia who were immediately disembarked into the city, but the convoy's real prize was a British expeditionary force of 1,178 men under Colonel John Byne Skerrett.[117] There was one caveat however; as much as Graham and the Cádiz Regency wished for the

---

115 Oman, *Peninsular War*, Vol.IV, p.517.

116 Oman, *Peninsular War*, Vol.IV, p.518.

117 Oman, *Peninsular War*, Vol.IV, p.519. Skerrett's force consisted of the 2/9th and 2/47th Foot, a detachment of the 3/95th Rifles, and half a company of the Royal Artillery (100). Skerrett also had orders from Graham to use his riflemen to give training to the Catalans and form light infantry companies armed with rifles. The Cádiz Regency also sent orders for Contreras to bolster his ranks by recruiting from deserters, a practice which had been going for some time already!

presence of Skerrett's force to energize resistance efforts, Graham was conservative with the lives of British soldiers, writing to Skerrett in his orders that:

> Before disembarking your detachment, you will affirm to the governor that you must have free and open communication with His Majesty's ships at all times, and in case the need arises to surrender the square that you will have the freedom to withdraw the troops from your command to the ships before the capitulation. He will keep the squadron leader in the Mediterranean [Codrington] well informed about the situation.[118]

The result was that Skerrett's small force was operating on orders to act carefully and not disembark if Tarragona was deemed hopeless or if the recovery of the British troops would be difficult. The waters in the Milagro Point were so rough that landing was impossible at times; a sailor volunteered to swim the crashing waves to deliver letters for Contreras, which dictated the conditions under which Skerrett's force would operate and asked a number of detailed questions Skerrett had. Doyle, Codrington, and several other British officers already on the scene answered Skerrett's questions, conveying their realistic opinion that the city could not be held and the recovery of any disembarked British troops would be difficult due to the conditions around the Milagro point and the constant French bombardment.[119]

Skerrett, accompanied by engineer Lieutenant Harry D. Jones, and Captain A.M. Hunt of the Royal Artillery who were to offer observations in their field of expertise, was only able to come ashore at 10:00 p.m. when the tide had subsided, to meet with Contreras and see the situation for himself. The next morning, they were joined by Codrington, Doyle, and a few other British captains. Contreras conveyed his honest opinion that Tarragona would fall any day, but laid out his plan for the garrison to mount a breakout attempt to join Campoverde. This would occur on the seemingly less screened eastern wall of the city, as the main French attack was to take place from the west from the inner city.

The British officers spent the afternoon inspecting the defences of the upper city and concluded that, as Contreras had said, the upper city was barely defensible. Lieutenant Jones spoke for all the British officers in writing:

> As the foot of the escarpment is quite exposed to the enemy's fire, and not composed of solid masonry, a breach could be made six hours after the enemy opened fire. As, moreover, the embankment will not admit the making of any trench behind the breach, and the situation of the houses is also of no benefit, the garrison has little chance of preventing the assault. On the other hand, I have observed that only the entrances of one or two streets have been blocked, and that seems to be the only internal defence, therefore, it is reasonable to suppose that the town would be in possession of the enemy twelve hours after he had made a practicable breach. The parapets are in a very miserable state. The artillery is not even under cover, and the merlons are very thin.[120]

---

118 Quigley, *Antes morir que rendirse*, p.158.
119 See Quigley, *Antes morir que rendirse*, p.160-164, for Skerrett's questions and the answers he received.
120 Quigley, *Antes morir que rendirse*, p.167.

By this point, Contreras' priority was not even the defence of Tarragona, it was the preservation of his garrison. The poor condition of Milagro point was the final nail in the coffin: it would be impossible for the British to escape if the waters became rough, as they so often were. After some discussion, and notwithstanding that Skerrett personally wished to disembark into the city to aid in its defence, the British officers concluded it would be unwise to send their force into the city without the guarantee of its preservation.[121] Contreras similarly agreed with the verdict, though he wished for Skerrett to join the planned sortie in some way. By the time the British officers prepared to return to their ships, it was already quite dark, and the waves of the Milagro point were at their worst. Codrington and the others were forced to jump blindly off ledge onto the boat, only guided by the voice of the helmsman, and, as if to reinforce the point that the evacuation of several hundred British troops would be nigh impossible, the group came under fire from a French cannon.[122]

The next day saw the arrival of Eroles, bearing new orders from Campoverde. After meeting with Eroles, Contreras proclaimed to his garrison:

> Today the Baron of Eroles has been here, who has given his word to return tomorrow with the purpose of having the honour of leading you, and with your strength expel the enemies of the city and lead you on a general sortie to assist the army. When the enemy attacks, the army must fearlessly repel him. Courage soldiers! Have firm determination to resist at all costs and thus all dangers will cease…[123]

Yet behind the veneer of coordination were suspicions and petty rivalries. Campoverde's orders essentially meant for Eroles to usurp Contreras' authority. In a separate note to the British, Campoverde revealed that Eroles was to take much of the garrison immediately to join Campoverde, irrespective of whether Contreras refused as he likely would:

> Mariscal Barón de Eroles will go to Tarragona and will bring 4000 men from his garrison who will meet with this army to later attack the enemy with the purpose of forcing him to raise the siege. If General Contreras refuses to surrender this force, the baron is fully authorized to remove the entire garrison and leave the city due to the situation to which Contreras has been reduced…[124]

Once the garrison had sallied out and joined the main army, Campoverde intended to turn it against Macdonald in Ampurdan with the assistance of Skerret's force. Skerrett accepted this plan as an alternative means of contributing to the fight, and even decided to accompany Eroles back to Campoverde's headquarters at El Vendrell to discuss how to best use the British expeditionary force, if landing it in Tarragona was out of the question. Skerrett would be in for a rude shock however. Upon arrival, he immediately noticed that the high command of the 1º Ejército was operating on an atmosphere of confusion, insubordination, and internal rivalries. Indeed, during the meeting a dispute broke out between the Spanish

---

121 Quigley, *Antes morir que rendirse*, p.166.
122 Codrington, *Memoir of the Life of Admiral Sir Edward Codrington*, Vol.I, p.248.
123 Quigley, *Antes morir que rendirse*, p.173.
124 Quigley, *Antes morir que rendirse*, p.173.

generals.[125] Nor was Campoverde confident in attacking Suchet's siege lines as he had been ordered to do by the Catalan Junta, because he had little faith in his inexperienced army and Contreras had a streak for refusing to obey Campoverde's orders. Even Sarsfield was sceptical of the plan, and opined that Skerrett's force would only be destroyed if they tried to support Campoverde's attack. As such, the British were left with little direction as to how to use their force. The whole encounter left a bitter taste amongst the British officers. Green noted that:

> From the conversation arose the conviction of the dangerous imbecility and almost disorder of the Marquis of Campo Verde and the even more alarming confusion and insubordination that seemed to reign among the generals, so much so, that it was very difficult to decide in what way to use the British force with any effect. Finally, it was decided to undertake a sortie from Tarragona with 4000 men with the objective of joining the army of the Marquis of Campo Verde and that the British would then act according to the circumstances.[126]

In the end, the British were left to sit back on their ships with their powerful force and see how the situation played out. Back in Tarragona, the confusion was even greater. To enact his proposed sortie, Campoverde had ordered that the garrison would break out at 4:00 p.m. on 24 June at a signal via optical telegraph. The soldiers of the garrison were assembled in the covered way, and waited with excitement, for they knew the French screening the east side of the city were weak. *Brigadier* Andrés Eguaguirre wrote, 'The chiefs, officers and soldiers knew with evidence that the French did not have on that side forces capable of containing the furious impetus that would be done to them.' But there they waited at the ready for a signal that would never be sent, for interminable hours, until 7:00 p.m., when the garrison walked back dejectedly into the city, for Campoverde had failed them once again.[127]

Suchet was hard-pressed for time too. He was aware of the presence of Skerrett's expeditionary force, not to mention Campoverde's looming army, and wanted to conclude the siege before either party took action against him. The second parallel against the wall of the upper city was completed on 25 June under heavy fire, and four separate breaching batteries were formed, but it proved to be difficult and time-consuming to haul a grand total of 22 heavy guns into place.

Contreras drew up his final plans of departure: At 8:00 p.m. on the night of 29 June, the garrison was to leave the city by the Rosario gate in three columns. *Coronel* Roten would lead the advance guard of 1,500 men, *Mariscal de Campo* Juan de Courten the centre column of 2,000, and *Brigadier* Eguagierre directed the rear column of 2,900, of which 400 grenadiers would form the rearguard. 1,000 men would remain on the walls to fire on the French as a distraction, supported by another rearguard of 1,000. A secondary line

---

125 Contreras, *Relation of the Siege of Tarragona*, p.46. Such was the state of confusion in the headquarters that at one point Campoverde had sent Contreras orders that *Coronel* O'Ronan was to embark with 3,000 of the garrison on the 28th or the 29th. Contreras assented, but nothing more was heard of from Campoverde on the matter!

126 Quigley, *Antes morir que rendirse*, p.178.

127 Eguaguirre, Sucesos Verdaderos, p.16.

of defence had been constructed by fortifying and loopholing the houses on the Rambla, a wide street which spanned the width of the upper city. In theory the over-eager French would suddenly stumble into an open street devoid of cover and be met with a hail of fire from the fortified houses. Contreras never expected these defences to repel the French; such measures were only meant to buy time for the defenders on the walls to join the rest of the escaping garrison. The artillery was to be spiked at the last minute, while the wounded, who could not be carried on the dangerous retreat, would be taken under the care of Doyle and loaded onto the British ships.[128] As for the citizens of Tarragona who would be left behind, Contreras could only hope that they would be spared the horrors of a sack.

Suchet's hurried efforts succeeded in getting the breaching batteries ready on the night of 27 June, despite losing 60 men to close-range fire that night alone, and the guns opened fire at 4:00 a.m. the morning of the 28th. The old city walls crumbled under the barrage of cannonballs, and by noon, the bombardment had created a sizable hole in the curtain wall between the San Juan and San Pablo bastions. In addition, a hit on the magazine of the Cervantes bastion caused an explosion which rendered that bastion useless. Without proper bomb-shelters or even barracks, the Spanish garrison in the upper city could do little but stand about in the street or shelter in houses and endure the bombardment.

As the French bombardment raged on, Contreras distributed a printed proclamation to the citizenry and garrison which detailed the plan for Eroles to lead the garrison out the next day in conjunction with an attack by Campoverde. This proved to be a horrendously foolish error. Throughout the siege, both sides had been employing deserters, prisoners, and spies as a valuable source of information – the Spanish even suspected the artillery commander of the upper city wall to be a spy – and it was almost expected that one way or another, the news would leak out to Suchet. One Spanish officer reasoned that 'That paper or proclamation did not take two hours to reach the hands of General Suchet'.[129] Despite making no mention of it in his memoirs, Suchet did get his hands on a copy of the pamphlet, and it prompted him to kick the siege into overdrive and storm the upper city before Contreras could put his plan into fruition.[130]

Suchet mustered his attack columns for the assault while his guns continued to fire. Command of the first wave, some 1,500 elite infantrymen who readied themselves in the forward parallels, was given to Habert. Engineer *Capitaines* Valessie, Maillard, and Pinot would head the attack with their sappers, followed by 16 elite companies drawn from the 1er and 5e Légère, the 14e, 42e, 114e, 115e, 116e, 117e, and 121e Ligne, and the 1er Vistule, which were divided into three columns, each led by an officer of the Italian division – *Colonelli* Ordioni and St Paul and *Capo di Battaglioni* Felici.[131] The Italian troops themselves would follow in the second wave, led by Ficatier, who held 1,200 men of the 1er and 5e Légère and the 4°, 5°, and 6° di Linea in the houses of the lower city to support Habert's attack as needed. A reserve unit of five battalions under Montmarie took position outside the walls of the lower town, tasked with advancing along the northern wall of the upper city, seizing the Rosario bastion, and entering the city through the gate of the same name.

---

128 Arteche y Moro, *Guerra de la Independencia*, Vol.X, p.305.
129 Quigley, *Antes morir que rendirse*, p.181.
130 Quigley, *Antes morir que rendirse*, p.194.
131 Suchet, *Memoirs of the War in Spain*, Vol.II, p.93.

According to Suchet, Montmarie's force originally had orders to support Habert's main attack, but the French received information from a deserter about the formidable second line of defence along the Rambla.[132] In response to this update, Suchet altered Montmarie's assignment to stay out of fire until Habert's men opened the Rosario gate from the inside of the city, and then strike at the Rambla line from behind.[133] The rest of the attackers were given orders to split left and right to roll up the defenders on the walls. In total, the French attack force numbered around 7,300 men.[134] Though the attack had been planned to take place at night, Suchet's preference in order to offer his troops the cover of darkness, it was decided that such a massive assault would take place earlier to allow for better coordination between the different columns. Amongst the French elite troops shuffling to their posts, there was an air of nervous anticipation of the uncertain. Graindor and his friends made their final farewells to each other, 'we said to each other this was perhaps the last moment of my life, we knew that a large garrison was defending this place'.[135] But there was altogether an even more dangerous aura which filled the trenches of the assault companies – exasperation and anger. The French, Italian, and Polish troops were exhausted and frustrated by the stubborn resistance against them and the miserable war of attrition. There was a pent-up fury that waited to be unleashed – one decorated Italian grenadier, *Sergente* Bianchini of the 6° di Linea, who had distinguished himself in the storming of Fort Olivo, when asked by Suchet what further rewards he desired, responded only that he wanted to lead the assault into the upper city.[136] It was such men whom the garrison of Tarragona faced in this final act of the siege.

As soon as a massive 30-foot breach had been opened between the San Juan and San Pablo around 5:00 p.m. the guns fell silent before firing the cannonade to signal the assault, Habert waved his men forwards, and a mad dash across 130 yards of coverless ground to the breach began. However, there was hardly an initial hail of lead to contest the dead space. Contreras' pamphlets that morning had also been an attempt to raise morale by hiding the fact that a breaching of the walls was imminent. As such, many of the garrison were under a false sense of security, and Suchet's assault caught them off guard and wholly unprepared.[137] There were but 200 cazadores present on the wall to contest the French onslaught, for despite the breach being the obvious focal point of the assault, most of the garrison was scattered about the city or holding the Rambla street. But what defenders were at the walls unleashed a devastating storm of lead that momentarily pinned the attackers at the breach between the San Juan and San Pablo bastions, where the Spanish artillerymen rapidly depressed their guns to fire at the highly vulnerable targets. The deadly crossfire even felled the formidable Bianchini.. 'We push each other, we climb the breach rapidly, the killed and wounded still obstruct the passage', recounted Graindor. 'Our company, we are still at the base of the breach [where]

---

132 Suchet, *Memoirs of the War in Spain*, Vol.II, p.94.

133 Arteche y Moro, *Guerra de la Independencia*, Vol.X, p.311.

134 Quigley, *Antes morir que rendirse*, p.182.

135 Graindor, *Mémoires de la Guerre d'Espagne 1808-1814*, p.58.

136 Graindor, *Mémoires de la Guerre d'Espagne 1808-1814*, p.58.

137 Quigley, *Antes morir que rendirse*, p.182. In his account of events, Contreras depicts a stubborn and heroic resistance at the breach and the Rambla, in which he was in the thick of. His account could not be farther from the truth, for Suchet's attack caught the garrison off guard, and Contreras had placed his main line of defence at the Rambla, not the breach.

we cannot hold out, two intersecting bastions fire on us with grapeshot, in less than two minutes twenty voltigeurs of our company are killed or wounded, we push each other, we climb to escape this bad position.'[138]

But the ferocity of the Spanish fire was not enough, and the French gathered enough impetus to clamber over their fallen comrades and storm through the breach. The French caught hardly a moment of rest, for they were now met by heavy fire from the main Spanish defensive line at the Rambla, manned by the Regimiento de Almansa. Yet this obstacle too, was overwhelmed as the French braved the musketry to rush the houses, bash down the doors with axes and musket butts, and put the defenders to the sword.

While Ficatier's reserves followed Habert's columns into the breach, Montmarie launched his attack against the Rosario bastion. The French hacked down the palisades of the covered way and fell into the ditch, where they came under fire from the Spanish defenders. It was only by the use of a climbing rope dangling from the side of the bastion which the Spanish had neglected to reel in that a few voltigeurs were able to gain a foothold in the bastion and steadily drive off the defenders.[139] The Rosario bastion was supposed to be closed off from the rest of the city, but the sector commander, *Coronel* Canaleta, had inexplicably left the gate open, allowing the Montmarie's men to pour in and attack the Rambla line from behind, trapping its defenders.[140] Rogniat turned his reserves southward along the city wall to sweep the defenders and fought their way to the southern wall to cut off escape routes to the shore. Everywhere the disorganized Spanish units fled, abandoning their weapons and equipment in their haste to escape. There was little quarter – many fleeing soldiers and civilians had to leap from the ramparts to escape the bayonets, breaking limbs in the process.[141]

In the chaos of the siege, Courten, who had been tasked with leading the centre column of the proposed sortie, carried out the plan in desperation. As the French rushed in from the west, a disorderly mass of 3-4,000 soldiers plus a horde of civilians dashed out of the eastern gate to escape the city. They ran along the Barcelona road, only to come under fire from Harispe's entrenched men and a concealed battery. Courten then turned his men towards the beach, in the hopes of being evacuated by the British ships, but were promptly charged by *Colonel* Jacques-Adrien Delort's 24e Dragons. It was no contest as the demoralized Spanish scattered or ran back to the city, many managing to swim out to the British ships, which upon seeing their plight, dashed in cannons blazing to save as many as they could. Some 600, many of whom were wounded, were rescued in this fashion.[142] But many more were sabred and slaughtered by the French cavalry, who only took Courten and the survivors prisoner when their bloodlust had been sated. As Harispe's infantry were rounding up the surrendering Spanish, at around 7:30 p.m., 30-odd cavalrymen of the Tarragona garrison approached the scene of confusion and charged, attempting to break through the French infantry. None escaped.

Back in the city, Contreras personally led a battalion of the Regimiento de Saboya forward with sword in hand, throwing this last reserve into the fray to give the disordered defenders

---

138 Graindor, *Mémoires de la Guerre d'Espagne 1808-1814*, p.58.
139 Suchet, *Memoirs of the War in Spain*, Vol.II, p.98.
140 Eguaguirre, Sucesos Verdaderos, p.26.
141 Maffre-Baugé, *Superbe et Généraux Jean Maffre*, p.90.
142 Codrington, *Memoir of the Life of Admiral Sir Edward Codrington*, Vol.I, p.230.

Civilians escaping the sack of Tarragona, by F. Campana, From Adolfo Blanch, *Cataluña: Historia de la Guerra de la Independencia* (Barcelona: Imprenta y Librería Politécnica de Tomás Gorchs, 1861), Vol. II. (Public Domain)

José González's final stand at the Tarragona Cathedral, by Horcholle, From Louis Adolphe Thiers, *Histoire du Consulat et de l'Empire* (Paris: Lheureux, 1865), digitized by the British Library

a rally point and perhaps even break out of the city. Contreras was bayoneted in the abdomen and captured, and the counterattack collapsed without his leadership, for his men thought their commander to be dead and threw down their weapons to flee or surrender.[143] With the fall of the Rambla and Contreras' capture, organized resistance in Tarragona collapsed to small bands of men fighting tooth-and-nail in the streets and houses. Campoverde's brother, *Coronel* José González made his famed last stand at the stairs of the Tarragona cathedral, where he and his 300 men fought to the bitter end. Many other groups met similar fates as the French stormed house after house.[144]

The confused and desperate last-ditch resistance by the defenders unleashed on the part of the French an ages-old praxis, the sacking of a city. From Troy, Tyre, and Baghdad, to Rome and Magdeburg, Tarragona joined a long list of cities to suffer from this cruel practice. Lazare Carnot denounced the sacking of besieged cities, no matter what condition they surrendered in, and it was certainly not always the norm. According to Professor Philip Dwyer:

> The sacking of towns, during which soldiers committed murder and rape in what is often described as an uncontrolled "frenzy", was part and parcel of eighteenth-century warfare...it was based on a "law of war", an unwritten understanding that the soldiery would be rewarded for their hardships, and often the lack of pay, endured during a siege by being given permission to loot the town, unless it capitulated before the final assault.[145]

The tradition of war dictated that the garrison of a fortress should surrender with full honours when its walls were breached. Tarragona had failed to do so, and for that the city would pay a heavy price. Suchet's men were frustrated at a siege that had cost them over 5,000 casualties, and were hell-bent on exacting a heavy vengeance on Tarragona. Likewise, another informal 'rule of war' dictated that any civilians caught with weapons could be executed – a practice carried out zealously when the city fell.

The brutal house-to-house fighting led to many civilians being shot indiscriminately, and as the fighting subsided, the French, Italian, and Polish soldiers turned to pillaging the city as punishment for its resistance, inflicting *la furia francese* upon its hapless inhabitants. The sack of Tarragona was far worse than the more widely known British sack of Badajoz. Eguaguirre estimated that in the final storming alone, 2,500 Spanish soldiers and 3,130 civilians were killed, including 200 women and 130 children, in the violence, rape, and looting which followed as French and allied soldiers ran amok in the burning streets.[146] Graindor describes 'a frightening spectacle...in the streets, in the houses, everything is strewn with the dead and wounded.'[147] Spanish accounts describe a scene out of hell. One eyewitness

---

143 Contreras, *Relation of the Siege of Tarragona*, p.34-35.
144 Eguaguirre, *Sucesos Verdaderos*, p.31, asserts that few survivors from the Rambla were able to make it to the cathedral and thus, there was no organized resistance at its steps.
145 Philip G. Dwyer, '"It Still Makes Me Shudder": Memories of Massacres and Atrocities during the Revolutionary and Napoleonic Wars', *War in History*, 16/4 (2009), pp.381–405, quoting p.385
146 Prada, *Tarragona*, p.209.
147 Graindor, *Mémoires de la Guerre d'Espagne 1808-1814*, p.58.

later wrote, 'some were thrown out of the windows and roofs, others dragged by feet; others killed with the bayonet and sabre blows, and others burned with the torch'[148] Many civilians committed suicide or threw themselves from the ramparts in the hopes of escaping rather than suffer at the hands of the French. The French meted out special cruelty against the religious figures they so hated, conducting summary executions of a number of Franciscan friars. Like in most sieges of the era, many officers felt it below their rank and honour to partake in the brutalities and occupied themselves with rescuing a few fortunate civilians, but all attempts at restoring order were in vain until the next morning. The 900 wounded and civilians who sought refuge in the cathedral were spared, as the French stepped over the bodies of González's men to pillage the treasures of the church.[149]

One can only imagine the thoughts going through the minds of Doyle, Green, Skerrett, and Eroles as they watched the city they had strove so hard to defend burn from the decks of their ships. Neither Lérida nor Tortosa had surrendered after their walls were breached, but both were spared such violence (though Lérida did endure a targeted bombardment of its civilian population and a fair amount of pillaging), so why Tarragona? As Dwyer noted, the prolonged and determined resistance of the garrison and populace of Tarragona had exhausted and infuriated Suchet's army. Though crimes against civilians by soldiers were punishable in various ways by the French Penal Code of 1796, it speaks volumes that the normally iron-handed Suchet took no subsequent action to reprimand his soldiers.[150] It is highly unlikely that Suchet to allowed the sack to occur 'accidentally' and out of his control. Suchet's implicit permission for his troops to sack Tarragona was a display of calculated violence to dissuade other cities from resisting.

Order was restored the next morning by Habert, who was appointed temporary commandant of Tarragona. Thus ended the 55-day siege, which had claimed thousands of lives on both sides. That day, the Spanish officers who had been captured on the beach were marched through the smouldering city, where they bore witness to burned and wrecked homes, the wounded and dying bleeding out on the streets, and charred corpses. The entire city reeked of the stench of burning flesh, for the French forced civilians to pile up the corpses and burn them in pyres to prevent the plague from spreading. Taken to the barracks, they were met by Habert, who drew out of his pocket a piece of paper – Contreras' declaration of the Spanish sortie plan – and informed the officers that it had taken not two hours to get into the hands of Suchet.[151] Suchet met with the wounded Contreras and blamed him for the unnecessary bloodshed by prolonging resistance, and failing to capitulate when the city had been breached. Contreras retorted that his garrison had a fair chance at repulsing the French, and that he would be a coward if he had surrendered in the presence of a relief army.[152]

---

148 Anon, *Asalto Y Saqueo De Tarragona En 1811: Es Copia De Un Manuscrito Que Se Conserva En La Biblioteca De Uno De Los Conventos De Religiosos Menores De Cataluña* (Tarragona: F. Arís, 1911), pp.12-13.

149 Several Spanish accounts of describe the cathedral as the scene of a massacre, however, both Graindor and a Spanish officer named JT who had been captured in the final storming, more impartial sources, corroborate each other that it was a place of sanctuary. See Quigley, *Antes morir que rendirse*, p.193; Graindor, *Mémoires de la Guerre d'Espagne 1808-1814*, p.58.

150 Dwyer, "'It Still Makes Me Shudder'", p.386; Suchet, *Memoirs of the War in Spain*, Vol.II, p.100.

151 Quigley, *Antes morir que rendirse*, p.194.

152 Contreras, *Relation of the Siege of Tarragona*, p.38.

Suchet's brother-in-law and aide-de-camp, *Captaine* Anthoine de Saint-Joseph, was given the honour of bearing the news of the bloody victory to Paris.

Out of the 22,000 men Suchet besieged Tarragona with, 924 had been killed in action, and 3,369 wounded for a total of 4,293, and of the wounded, Suchet estimates that '... scarcely half could be restored to the service or survive their wounds, so dreadfully were they mutilated.'[153] This count does not include the sick, which brings French casualty totals closer to 6,000, around 25-30 percent of the besieging force. Casualties for the Spanish are difficult to estimate, and vary by the historian. An official report states that in the entire siege, the Spanish suffered 10,900 people killed (including 1,900 who died of wounds and 750 who died on the way to captivity), 8,650 wounded, and 8,200 captured, in addition to damages totalling 88.5 million reales.[154] Oman estimates that Spanish military casualties alone in the siege amounted to 15,000, including 8,000 captured.[155] Though III Corps had paid a heavy price for Tarragona, a significant portion of the 1° Ejército had been bottled up and captured with the city, just as Suchet had hoped. Considering the amount of resources and men the Spanish had poured into the defence of Tarragona, the implications of the city's fall were enormous. The last stable harbour in Catalonia by which the 1° Ejército could maintain contact with the British and Valencia was gone.

The cause for the Spanish defeat at Tarragona can largely be placed at the feet of the Campoverde and the 1° Ejército commanders, who could have done far more to hamper Suchet's siege operations. Whether that would have prevented the eventual fall of Tarragona is uncertain, but there is no shame in having done one's utmost. Suchet was certainly extremely lucky in the siege. By all accounts the defenders of Tarragona had put up a magnificent defence that inflicted heavy casualties on the French. Had Campoverde been more aggressive, Suchet would have found his siege efforts greatly disrupted.

News that Tarragona had fallen reached the 1° Ejército when bedraggled and breathless *Brigadier* Velasco, one of the few to escape the final storming, stumbled into headquarters. That was the end of Campoverde's army. Desertion began to run rampant among the demoralized recruits, and with Suchet now poised to turn on him, Campoverde retreated from Vendrils to Cervera. Miranda requested to return to Valencia with his division, seeing that his original mission of relieving Tarragona was impossible. This sparked a furious debate amidst the 1° Ejército command. Some objected to Miranda leaving, while others despaired that Catalonia was lost and sought to evacuate the entirety of the 1° Ejército.[156] Campoverde was a defeated and broken man, and passed all authority onto his subordinates, who argued as to what to do next. At a council of war on 1 July, the ranking generals of the 1° Ejército voted that the situation in Catalonia was beyond salvation, and that they should evacuate both Miranda's division and the 1° Ejército so that it could carry on the fight elsewhere. But the 1° Ejército commanders were taking the major factor of transportation for granted. When Codrington was informed of the proceedings, he agreed to take Miranda's division back to Valencia, but refused to take the remnants of the 1° Ejército due to both a lack of transportation and concern at the implications of abandoning Catalonia.

153 Suchet, *Memoirs of the War in Spain*, Vol.II, p.108.
154 Anon, *Asalto Y Saqueo De Tarragona En 1811*, p.25.
155 Oman, *Peninsular War*, Vol.IV, p.525.
156 Oman, *Peninsular War*, Vol.IV, p.529.

On 9 July, Miranda's division was embarked while his cavalry, some 900 troopers under *Coronel* Gasca, decided to conduct a bold overland journey through French-held Aragon. In a feat that can only be described as remarkable, Gasca and his men traversed 740 miles in six weeks through enemy territory and managed to re-join Carlos O'Donnell in Valencia.

With Miranda gone, Campoverde retired to Vich, where, on the evening of 10 July, he was greeted by Luis Roberto de Lacy y Gautier. Lacy had been sent from Cádiz to replace Campoverde as *Capitán General* of Catalonia in light of the latter's failure to relieve Tarragona. As Lacy was an outsider, his appointment was met with opposition from some of the 1° Ejército generals, who preferred to have Eroles lead them, but orders were orders and they reluctantly fell in line under his authority. While Campoverde fled the province, Lacy withdrew what was left of the 1° Ejército – some 2-3,000 miserable men, into the Catalonian mountains to Solonsa, where he began to slowly rebuild his battered army.

The Montserrat Operation

As he had in the aftermath of Lérida and Tortosa, Suchet utilized the momentum of his victory to secure more strategic objectives while his enemies were still stunned. With the plan being to invade Valencia after securing Catalonia, Suchet had every desire to ensure that Miranda's division be destroyed in Catalonia, or at the very least not make it back to Valencia to defend its home when Suchet launched his invasion. The divisions of Frère and Harispe, along with Abbé's brigade and Boussart's cavalry, were dispatched in pursuit of the 1° Ejército on the night of the 29th. Despite fire from the British fleet, the French reached the Spanish depot at Sitges, which was left exposed and unguarded in the wake of Campoverde's retreat. There the French bagged a number of stragglers, 800 wounded from the Tarragona garrison, and several supply ships. The capture of this port meant that Skerrett, who was just offshore with his men, would not be able to disembark, so Skerrett cancelled his plans to join the 1° Ejército and sailed back to Cádiz with absolutely nothing to show for his efforts.[157] Leaving Frère at Villafranca and Harispe at Sitges to prevent Miranda's division from embarking, Suchet traveled to Barcelona with a cavalry escort and Abbé's brigade. There Suchet met with the city's governor, Maurice Mathieu, to discuss the strategic situation. While Suchet had been covering himself with glory, the Armée de Catalogne was still engaged in its gruelling efforts to wrest Figueras from the Spanish, who were defending the city with the same determined spirit of Masséna at Genoa.[158] Furthermore, such was the guerrilla situation in Catalonia that French soldiers could hardly ever left their fortress-cities unless they were in force. Upon returning to Tarragona, Suchet dispatched Habert with his 4e Division to Tortosa to both prepare to invade Valencia and fortify the French outposts at the mouth of the Ebro. Musnier was to occupy Tarragona and Villafranca and put the area under French control. Suchet then travelled back to Barcelona on 9 July with

---

157   Sarramon, *Contribución a la historia*, Vol.I, p.56.

158   The Spanish proved to be substantially kinder than Massena in 1800; having resorted to eating rats themselves and unable to feed their French and Italian prisoners, the Figueras garrison released them all, whereas Massena had let his Austrian prisoners starve to death.

the intention of renewing operations against the 1° Ejército, but it was too late: for Miranda's division had managed to escape thanks to a diversionary action by Eroles.[159]

However, Miranda's escape was a glass half-full or half-empty situation. While Miranda would now be available to defend Valencia, his departure weakened the already vulnerable 1° Ejército.[160] Suchet now prepared to strike at the Catalonian base in the Montserrat mountain, which needed to be taken in order to secure the Barcelona-Lérida road. At the moment, 1,500 *miquelets* under Eroles occupied the mountain base, from where they could swoop down onto French convoys and patrols. In the three years the French had occupied Barcelona, they had never had the strength to attempt to take Montserrat, but now with the 1° Ejército broken in the aftermath of the Siege of Tarragona, there would be no better time to secure Barcelona's lines of communications. But before Suchet attempted to seize Montserrat, there were important personal matters to attend to. On 20 July Suchet arrived at Reus to find waiting for him an officer bearing orders from Paris and a letter from Berthier, signed by Napoleon himself:

> Wishing to give a proof to our satisfaction and confidence to the commander-in-chief Suchet, for the various services he has rendered us on repeated occasions, and in the taking of Lérida, Mequinenza, Tortosa, and Tarragona; We have decreed and decree as follows:
>
> Art. 1. The general of division Suchet is appointed marshal of the empire.
> Art. 2. Our minister of war is charged with the execution of the present decree.[161]

At last, Suchet's efforts in Spain had been rewarded with the long-awaited promotion from *général de division* to the coveted status of *Maréchal d'Empire*. Suchet did not have long to gloat over his personal accomplishments, for in true Napoleon fashion, the Emperor also noted in the despatch that Suchet should begin to prepare for the invasion of Valencia. As such, Suchet needed to quickly wrap up operations in Catalonia. On 22 July, columns led by Montmarie, Harispe, Frère, and Maurice Mathieu converged towards Montserrat.[162] On the 24th, Suchet held a council of war at El Bruc and laid out his plan of assault. Standing at an elevation of over 4,000 feet, the picturesque Montserrat mountain alone was a formidable foe for the 10,000 French lined up to storm its rocky slopes. Eroles and his men were well entrenched, and had established two batteries totalling 10 guns to cover the main mountain pass running from north of Montserrat up to the Abbey of Montserrat, which stood on a narrow plateau 3,000 feet up. But for all the intimidation factor the mountain position offered, it was a position with many weaknesses, most notably in the sheer number of men needed to hold a mountain of that size and cover the

---

159 Suchet, *Memoirs of the War in Spain*, Vol.II, p.114.
160 Ramón Pírez y Pavía, José Luis Arcón Domínguez (ed.), *Apuntaciones sobre el Ejército de Valencia en 1811* (Valencia: Ediciones Simtac, 2010), p.64. Upon returning to Valencia, Miranda's division was reduced to nearly half its strength after 1,700 men simply deserted – they were later convinced to re-join only after a full pardon was granted.
161 Napoleon to Suchet, 8 July, from Suchet, *Memoirs of the War in Spain*, Vol.II, p.116.
162 The Catalan Junta had fled to Solsona on 3 July.

numerous trails.[163] Montmarie's brigade was posted at Collbató to block the rear road leading to the Abbey, Frère and Harispe held the roads to Igualada and Manera, while Maurice Mathieu held El Bruc, to act as a reserve for Abbé's brigade of five battalions, which was to conduct the main assault up the main mountain road.

The next morning, Abbé led his brigade of the 1er Légère, 114e Ligne, and three cannon up the road to the Abbey of Montserrat, closely followed by Maurice Mathieu and some of his troops. The French made good progress and encountered little opposition until they reached the Ermita de Santa Cecilia, where the first Spanish battery was sited. Keeping the rest of his troops out of range of the Spanish guns, Abbé deployed his skirmishers to pick off the gunners, which they did with deadly efficiency; some of the voltigeurs even managed to climb up onto higher ground and fire down onto the Spanish battery from its right flank. With the Spanish guns suppressed, Abbé then sent forwards two grenadier companies to storm the battery. As the Spanish gunners and their supporting infantry fell back to the second battery, the grenadiers followed in hot pursuit so as to prevent the second battery from firing without hitting their own men.[164] Abbé next committed a battalion of the 1er Légère into the battle. The French frontal attack combined with the enfilade fire of the voltigeurs weaving their way around the rocky slopes above was enough to force even the second Spanish defensive line. The Spanish gunners died defending their guns. The way to the Abbey was clear, and Abbé reorganized his column to continue the advance. But just as he did so, he was alerted to a great commotion up and around the path in the Abbey. Thinking that Montmarie had attacked the Spanish rear from Collbató, Abbé urged his column forward at the double. But when the exhausted French reached the Abbey, they found that the rest of the Spanish defenders had all but routed. As it turned out, some of the French skirmishers clambering on the slopes in support of the main attack on the battery had taken it upon themselves to press on, and their initiative was well-rewarded by the discovery of several side-roads which allowed them to amass 300 of their number to the rear of the Abbey. Their sudden attack caught Eroles' reserve by total surprise, and Spanish morale was broken when they learned that the two defensive lines on the main road had been taken. The whole of the Catalan force fled in panic down the eastern slopes, a few tumbling to their deaths but most escaping the French bayonets safely. When all was said and done, the capture of Montserrat had cost the French 200 men and the Spanish 400. Suchet stationed two regiments to hold the mountain, and departed with the rest of his force. Leaving the bulk of his army in Lower Catalonia, Suchet rode to Zaragoza to oversee preparations for the invasion of Valencia. All that remained to be done was to await the return of the units on prisoner escort duty and clear Aragon of the guerrillas.

The Guerrilla War

In an effort to once more centralize administrative control over Spain, Napoleon decided to send French treasury officials to regulate the provincial governments of his generals. While

---

163   Oman, *Peninsular War*, Vol.IV, p.533.
164   Suchet, *Memoirs of the War in Spain*, Vol.II, p.122.

Suchet's Second Military Government was functioning quite well, Napoleon was displeased with Aragonese tax collectors who were falling short of their quotas and French military officials who were skimming funds. To that end, Berthier dispatched Baron Lacuée, who was to be the intendant of Aragon. Not only would financial matters fall under Lacuée's authority, but also judicial and administrative matters. The existing military officials were to be placed under his charge as well, while Bondurand, Suchet's chief administrator, was demoted to simply being an advisor to Lacuée.[165] Naturally, many were unhappy with this change in leadership.

Fortunately for Suchet, Lacuée was not entirely a bumbling bureaucrat and was sensitive to the needs of the army. At the time of Lacuée's arrival in Zaragoza in May of 1811, Suchet and his army were in the process of besieging Tarragona. Both men realized that restructuring the Aragonese government at this time could endanger the field army's supply system, and so Lacuée held off on replacing Suchet's Aragonese officials until the end of the siege.

However, upon the completion of the Siege of Tarragona, Lacuée found his situation to be quite difficult. Napoleon had failed to estimate the amount of personnel the new civilian administration would need – it was far more than the half-dozen French treasury officials Lacuée had brought with him to supervise the native bureaucracy. To make matters worse, Lacuée was almost instantly on poor terms with Suchet, who despised the fact that an outsider was usurping his regime. Suchet made a scapegoat out of Lacuée for every misfortune, blaming his administration for poor harvests, guerrilla activities, and any internal affair that Suchet found to his displeasure.[166]

In the early months of the Tarragona operation, there was little guerrilla activity in Aragon. With some 22,000 troops committed to the defence of Aragon, Suchet was rightly confident that his base of operations would remain secure during his offensive. *Général de Brigade* Henriod, Governor of Lérida, led a successful expedition against the Belianes *partida*, destroying it and bringing back the head of its leader as a macabre trophy.[167] Further north, 14 Aragonese gendarmes stationed at Jaca conceived a plot to betray the citadel to the guerrillas, but they were discovered, and in any case there were hardly any guerrillas around to take advantage of such opportunity. In Lower Aragon, Chlopicki faced down the guerrilla bands of Mariano Larrodé (El Pesoduro) and José Tris (El Malcarado). Chlopicki pressed his troops hard in forced marches across rough mountain terrain in chasing guerrillas, with most of his casualties coming from desertions. Chlopicki was then sent towards the Navarre border to assist Reille. He found success when he, Reille, and *Général de Division* Marie-François Auguste de Caffarelli du Falga of the Armée du Nord conducted a joint operation that temporarily dispersed Mina's guerrillas.

At the other end of the province, the guerrillas targeted convoys leaving the French supply depot at Mora. A convoy of less than 200 French and Polish troops from the 115e Ligne and 1er Vistule were ambushed by a unit of 5-600 men under *Coronel* Villamil.[168]

---

165 Alexander, *Rod of Iron*, p.104.
166 Alexander, *Rod of Iron*, p.105.
167 Alexander, *Rod of Iron*, p.95.
168 Józef Mroziński, 'An account by Captain Mrozinski of the 1st Vistula Legion', <https://www.jpnorth.
    co.uk/publications/articles-napoleonic-and-french-revolution/captain-mrozinski/>, accessed 2

Caught out in the open, the escort troops lost their entire convoy and took 70 casualties before they were able to reach the sanctuary of a hermitage, where they were surrounded. The trapped French and Poles attempted to cajole the five Aragonese fusiliers with them to run the guerrilla cordon and summon the Mora garrison, for it was they who would be shot as collaborators if the group was forced to surrender, but the Aragonese refused, saying that they would prefer to die later than sooner. The French and Poles then turned on the three Spanish hostages with them, who they forced to swear on the altar that they would make for Mora.[169] But when these dubious messengers were let loose, all three fled for their homes or were captured by the guerrillas. The next day, the Spanish requested multiple times for the escort to surrender, and, when turned down, closed in on the hermitage to lay wood and hay to try and burn the French out. It seemed as if all hope was lost, and the group even considered sortieing out in the night – an ill-fated plan given the presence of some 50 Spanish cavalry on the Mora road. But they needed not resort to such desperate measures. That evening, the Spanish were driven off by the arrival of *Colonel* Dupeyroux with the 115e Ligne. As it turned out, the garrison at Falcet had heard the firing, and sent out a spy to investigate. Word of the attack soon reached Mora, and it was good fortune that, just at that time, the 115e Ligne was on hand, passing through Mora to get to Reus and reinforce Suchet's besieging force.

On 9 May HMS *Invincible* led a small flotilla of two frigates and 10 xebecs to attack the French outpost at Sant Carles de la Rapita, near where the Ebro flowed into the sea. The fire-power of the flotilla was supported on land by a sizable force of Valencians. After landing five cannon for the Valencians to use and several hours of heated duelling with the fortress guns, the British ships sailed away as darkness fell. Though the British had left, the Valencians were closing in on the fort, and *Capitaine* Pinot, the French garrison commander, decided to retreat to Amposta. They reached the town undetected by way of the marshes. From Tortosa, a column of 800 infantry and 50 cavalry under *Chef de Bataillon* Bugeaud was dispatched to defend Amposta and retake La Rapita. They arrived that night and surprised part of the Valencian force which had taken up position in the town. At dawn Bugeaud's column and Pinot's men charged the remaining Valencians and defeated them, capturing the five guns in the process.[170] Though the fort at Sant Carles de la Rapita had been retaken, Suchet opted to abandon the post in favour of focusing on Tarragona, rather than committing resources to repairing the damage on the fort and garrisoning it.

Villacampa and Obispo had been able to do little during the siege of Tarragona due to the strong French garrisons of the right bank. Even as Suchet siphoned off troops to reinforce his siege force, he was careful enough to still keep just enough troops to contest the guerrillas. As a result, Villacampa had to proceed with caution, and when he advanced against Teruel in July he found the battalion of the 114e Ligne under *Chef de Bataillon* Lefebvre forming the Teruel garrison to be more than a match him. All Obispo could do was forage for grain. Around that time, Durán advanced into Calatayud with 2,400 men to try and unite with Villacampa and Obispo. On 23 July he clashed indecisively with a Neapolitan patrol, and on the 25th arrived before Calatayud. The city's Neapolitan and Polish garrison sallied out and

January 2022.
169 Mroziński, 'An account by Captain Mrozinski of the 1st Vistula Legion'.
170 Suchet, *Memoirs of the War in Spain*, Vol.II, p.31.

managed to force Durán to retreat, but the inexperienced Neapolitans suffered heavy losses in their wild attack before falling back to the Merced convent, where they hunkered down.[171] While the guerrillas milled about in helpless inactivity, probing French lines for a weakness, Suchet crushed Tarragona and turned the attention of his powerful force back to Aragon.

All across Aragon Suchet's columns were set in motion: Compère advanced with 2,000 men west to drive off Durán; Peyri moved with *Général de Brigade* Éloi Charles Balathier de Bragelonne's brigade to the Valencian border, clearing guerrillas and collecting taxes along the way; and Harispe chased Villacampa and Obispo back to Valencia. Campillo, one of Villacampa's subordinates, was beaten at Longarés on 22 August by elements of the Cariñena garrison, his line broken by a charge of 50 cuirassiers.[172] Suchet ordered the 228 Spanish captured from that engagement to have the phrase '*traitres a la patrie*' branded on them.[173] Further south, the Valencian army skirmished with Habert before Tortosa, and got the worst end of it.

On the left bank the French were also met with triumph. The fall of Tarragona and the complete loss of confidence in Campoverde's 1° Ejército triggered a mass exodus of Catalan deserters into Aragon, estimated at some 2,500 by mid-July.[174] These men posed little military threat and only sought to escape the hardships of war, though they found little solace in Aragon. They sold their guns for food, only to be arrested by local authorities who turned their very weapons back onto them! Some of the more organized bands raided towns and were hunted by the gendarme garrisons. Chlopicki's brigade moved away from Navarre to the Gallego river north of Zaragoza to try and mop up this rabble, but a large portion of the Catalans were able to go into hiding, join a guerrilla group, or return to Catalonia. Many more died from exhaustion and starvation. The result of this was that Chlopicki's absence on the Navarre border gave Mina enough time to recover after being beaten by Reille at Lerín.

Further east, the Cadet *partida*, which had risen in the wake of the destruction of the Belianes *partida*, had a target painted on its back almost instantly by Henriod, the destroyer of its predecessor. The Governor of Lérida pursued it mercilessly, until the *partida* had eroded to just Cadet himself and a few followers. When these exhausted guerrillas retreated into the town of Urgel, they were set upon by the inhabitants and Cadet was killed. Of course, the French were overjoyed to hear another anecdote of Spanish collaboration, and, in true Henriod fashion, the Governor of Lérida, acting as if he were some medieval warlord, had Cadet's corpse decapitated and impaled the head above the Lérida gate as a warning to the consequences of defying French rule. Pesoduro, one of Mina's subordinates, likewise suffered failure after failure when his ambush of a 50-man patrol on 23 July near Sadava was repulsed. His own men were in turn ambushed on 26 July by the gendarmes of the Exea garrison, who killed 50 guerrillas and executed 20 more in the aftermath.

There remained just one final counterinsurgency operation before Suchet's next campaign. Honorine, and Suchet's newborn daughter Louise, were set to return to Spain. Their arrival and security were of the utmost importance for Suchet, who kept the details of their journey

171 Alexander, *Rod of Iron*, p.98.
172 Sarramon, *Contribución a la historia*, Vol.I, p.101.
173 Alexander, *Rod of Iron*, p.97.
174 Alexander, *Rod of Iron*, p.98.

secret from nearly all. Intercepted Spanish messages revealed that the guerrilla leader Sarasa planned to intercept and kidnap Suchet's family, for Sarasa's own wife and children had been placed in prison.[175] Concerned, Suchet travelled to Jaca, to oversee the safe arrival of his family on 10 August. Naturally, Honorine's return back into Aragon was met with days upon days of feasts and celebrations, and such was the enthusiasm of the celebrations in Jaca that Roquemorel reduced the city's war contributions.

In Don Alexander's words, 'The conduct of this [Tarragona] campaign represented the most successful execution of the conventional counterinsurgent balancing act during the Peninsular War.'[176] The reasons for the successful French defence of Aragon were simple: there were enough troops of good quality available to fill the needed garrisons and form mobile columns. The taking of Lérida and Tortosa also deprived the guerrillas of safe bases to operate from and resupply, while giving the French powerful bases from which to conduct counter-guerrilla operations. By this point, the French occupation of Aragon was at its highest point yet. The guerrillas had been repulsed at nearly every turn, and local hostility to the French had turned to antipathy at worst and overt support at best. Von Brandt recalls:

> I was in Saragossa on 2 July when I heard news of the fall of Tarragona. This news was met with much rejoicing at Saragossa, not only by the French but also by quite a few of the Spanish. They organised a series of bullfights, but these, and the bulls, were a real fiasco. I also helped organise a theatrical production in a badly lit and dirty room.[177]

As a whole, the lightning success of Suchet's Catalonian campaign was one which rightfully propelled him into the annals of French history as among the best generals of the First French Empire. In a single year he had conquered four major fortresses and subjugated an entire province while solidifying control over another. During the sieges of Lérida and Tarragona, the Spanish had managed to put together a relief force, yet both had failed. At the heart of the failed Spanish relief operations was the tactical superiority of III Corps. Margalef saw a single regiment of cuirassiers rout an entire Spanish division, while at Tarragona, the 1º Ejército delayed itself in relieving the city in its futile effort to find more troops to match French quality with quantity. Suchet's own abilities cannot be discounted, and it was through his logistical and operational prowess that his troops could simultaneously conduct successful field operations and occupy Aragon.[178]

Then there was also the issue of Spanish over-reliance on fortresses. The heroic defences of Zaragoza and Girona were rarities in the history of sieges, yet they became so symbolic that they seeped their way into Spanish military doctrine. Zaragoza had shown what could be accomplished by a determined resistance, now every fortress city and its population was expected to fight to the last and deal tremendous damage to the French. Only Tarragona came somewhat close to that level of defence. In general, the more troops the Spanish

---

175 Fuertes, *La ocupación francesa de Zaragoza*, p.120-121.
176 Alexander, *Rod of Iron*, p.95.
177 Brandt, *In the Legions of Napoleon*, p.165.
178 A more thorough analysis is included in Volume 2.

packed into fortresses, the more were lost, unless a successful relief operation was mounted from outside.

Thanks to the operational and organizational talents of Suchet, the determination of his subordinates, and the tactical mastery of the troops, the Armée d'Aragon had come a long way since the demoralizing defeat at Alcañiz. By this point Suchet and his men were masters of siege warfare; no fortress could withstand their methodical and ferocious assaults, while in the field the disciplined infantry and hard-striking cavalry of the Armée d'Aragon reigned supreme. Aragon had been secured and Lower Catalonia conquered; the stage was set for Suchet's next campaign. The coming years would challenge Suchet as never before, for the guerrillas he had suppressed would strike back with a redoubled vengeance that would push Suchet's counter-guerrilla methods to the brink, and foes new and old would emerge to challenge the newest *Maréchal d'Empire* as he marched to his next objective: Valencia.

Appendix I

III Corps at the Battle of Alcañiz

Général en Chef: *Général de Division* Louis-Gabriel Suchet
Chef de l'Etat-Major: *Général de Brigade* Jean-Isidore Harispe
Artillery: *Général de Brigade* François Louis Dedon-Duclos

Suchet's Escort
64e Ligne detachments and 40e Ligne Voltigeur Company (one battalion, plus one company, 450)

1st Division: *Général de Division* Laval
1st Brigade: *Général de Brigade* Montmarie
    14e Ligne (two battalions, 1,080)
    3e Vistule (two battalions, 964)
Divisional Artillery
    18/3e Régiment d'Artillerie à Pied (one company, four 4-pounders, 51 men on 1 April)
    4/Bataillon du Train d'Artillerie de la Garde (one company, 63 men on 1 April)

2nd Division: *Général de Division* Musnier
1st Brigade: *Général de Brigade* Fabre
    114e Ligne (three battalions, 1,627)
    1er Vistule (two battalions, 1,039)
2nd Brigade: *Général de Brigade* Buget
    115e Ligne (three battalions, 1,732)
    121e Ligne (one battalion, 400)
Divisional Artillery
    22/3e Régiment d'Artillerie à Pied (one company, four 4-pounders, 57 men on 1 April)
    2/12e Bataillon Principal du Train (one company, 56 men on 1 April)

Cavalry: *Général de Brigade* Wathier
    4e Hussards (three squadrons, 326)
    1er Cie, 1/1er Lanciers de la Vistule (one company, 83)
    13e Cuirassiers (two squadrons, 200)
    7/5e Régiment d'Artillerie à Cheval (one company, four 8-pounders, 33 men on 1 April)
    5/Bataillon du Train d'Artillerie de la Garde (one company, 74 men on 1 April)

Sources:

Nafziger Order of Battle Collection, 809ESAG: French and Spanish Orders of Battle at Alcaniz, Army of Aragon 23 May 1809; Nafziger Order of Battle Collection, 809DSXA: Artillery, French Army of Spain, 1 April 1809; Santiago, *Alcañiz, María, y Belchite 1809*, p.75; Lipscombe, *Peninsular War Atlas*, p.127.

Appendix II

2° Ejército de la Derecha at the Battle of Alcañiz

Comandante en Jefe: *Capitán General* Joaquín Blake y Joyes
Mayor General de Infantería: *Brigadier* José Obispo
Artillery: *Brigadier* Martín García y Loygorri

Division of *Teniente General* Areizaga
Column of *Coronel* Carbón (Voluntarios de Daroca)
    Voluntarios de Daroca (one battalion, 489)
    Tiradores de Doyle (one battalion, 297)
    Voluntarios de Aragón (one battalion , 214)
    Tiradores de Cartagena (one company, 64)
Column of *Coronel* Cucalón (Reserva de Aragón)
    Batallón de Reserva de Aragón (one battalion, 1,161)
    Tiradores de Murcia (one battalion, 660)

Division of *Teniente General* Marqués de Lazán
Advance Guard: *Coronel* Hernández de Tejada (Fernando VII)
    Voluntarios de Valencia (one battalion, 354)
    Regimiento de Ferdinand VII (one battalion, 273)
    Combined Grenadiers (Regiments of América and 5° de Suizo Traxler) (four companies, 466)
With Artillery Park
    Regimiento de América (one battalion, 557)

Division of *Mariscal de Campo* Roca
Column of *Coronel* Andriani (2° Regimiento de Saboya)
    2° Regimiento de Saboya (one battalion, 319)
    Regimiento de América (one battalion, 557)
Column of *Teniente Coronel* Pírez (1° Regimiento de Valencia)
    1° Regimiento de Valencia (three battalions, 1,713)
Column of *Coronel* Menchaca (Cazadores de Valencia)
    Cazadores de Valencia (one battalion, 673)
    Voluntarios de Zaragoza (one battalion, 588)

Cavalry: *Brigadier* Ibarrola (Húsares Españoles)
  Regimiento de Santiago (two squadrons, 214)
  Húsares Españoles (two squadrons, 168)
  Regimiento de Olivenza (one squadron, 95)

Artillery and Support: *Brigadier* Loygorri
  Horse Artillery (one company, six guns, 99 men)
  Foot Artillery (two companies, 13 guns, 159 men)
  Sappers (one company, 50)
  Armed Civilians (one battalion, 161)

Not present at battle
  Tercio de Miquelets de Tortosa (one battalion, 829)
  3/Voluntarios de Zaragoza (one battalion, 494)

Sources:
Nafziger Order of Battle Collection, 809ESAG: French and Spanish Orders of Battle at Alcaniz, Army of Aragon 23 May 1809; Santiago, *Alcañiz, María, y Belchite 1809*, p.74; Lipscombe, *Peninsular War Atlas*, p.127.

Appendix III

III Corps in the María Campaign

Général en Chef: *Général de Division* Louis-Gabriel Suchet
Chef de l'Etat-Major: *Général de Brigade* Jean-Isidore Harispe
Artillery: *Colonel* Sylvain-Charles Valée

1st Division, Detachment
1st Brigade: *Général de Brigade* Habert
    14e Ligne (two battalions, 680)
    2e Vistule (two battalions, 800)
Divisional Artillery
    18/3e Régiment d'Artillerie à Pied (one company, four 4-pounders, 51 men on 1 April)
    4/Bataillon du Train d'Artillerie de la Garde (63 men on 1 April)

2nd Division: *Général de Division* Musnier
1st Brigade: *Général de Brigade* Fabre
    114e Ligne (three battalions, 1,500)
    1er Vistule (two battalions, 1,000)
2nd Brigade: *Général de Brigade* Buget
    115e Ligne (three battalions, 1,700)
Divisional Artillery
    22/3e Régiment d'Artillerie à Pied (one company, four 4-pounders, 57 men on 1 April)
    2/12e Bataillon Principal du Train (one company, 56 men on 1 April)

3rd Division, Detachment
1st Brigade: *Général de Brigade* Robert
    116e Ligne (two battalions, 1,100)
    117e Ligne (two battalions, 1,500)

Cavalry: *Général de Brigade* Wathier
    4e Hussards (three squadrons, 326)
    1er Cie., 1/1er Lanciers de la Vistule (one company, ~83)
    13e Cuirassiers (four squadrons, 480)
    7/5e Régiment d'Artillerie à Cheval (one company, four 8-pounders, 33 men on 1 April)
    5/Bataillon du Train d'Artillerie de la Garde (one company, 74 men on 1 April)

Reserve
    5e Légère (one battalion, 490)
    64e Ligne and 40e Ligne Voltigeurs   (one battalion and one company, 450)

Not Present at Maria
At Monte Torrero: *Général de Division* Laval
    44e Ligne (two battalions, 1,000)
    3e Vistule (two battalions, 964)
    20/1er Régiment d'Artillerie à Pied, (one company, six guns, 73 men on 1 April)
    4/12e Bataillon Principal du Train, (one company, 47)
Camino de Canal
    121e Ligne (?)
    7/3e Régiment d'Artillerie à Pied (half-company, two 4-pounders, 22 men)
Zaragoza Garrison: *Colonel* Haxo
    121e Ligne (one battalion, ~400)
    21/3e Régiment d'Artillerie à Pied (half-company, two 4-pounders, 62 men)

Sources:
Nafziger Order of Battle Collection, 809DSXA: Artillery, French Army of Spain, 1 April 1809; Santiago, *Alcañiz, María, y Belchite 1809*, p.77; Lipscombe, *Peninsular War Atlas*, p.129.

Appendix IV

2° Ejército de la Derecha in the María Campaign

Comandante en Jefe: *Capitán General* Joaquín Blake y Joyes
Mayor General de Infantería: *Brigadier* José Obispo
Artillery: *Brigadier* Martín García y Loygorri

Advance Guard: *Coronel* Creagh de Lacy
    Regimiento de Almería (two battalions, 989)
    2° Cazadores de Valencia (one battalion, 1,027)

1st Division: *Teniente General* Marqués de Lazán
    2° Regimiento de Valencia (three battalions, 1,710)
    Regimiento de América (two battalions, 790)
    1° Voluntarios de Zaragoza (one battalion, 588)
    3° Cazadores de Valencia (one battalion, 400)

3rd Division: *Mariscal de Campo* Roca
    1° Regimiento de Saboya (three battalions, 2,480)
    Regimiento de Granada (one battalion, 796)
    Provincial de Ávila (one battalion, 830)
    Tiradores de Cariñena (one battalion, 692)
    Tercio de Tortosa (one battalion, 829)

Cavalry: *Brigadier* Donohù
    Regimiento de Olivenza (four squadrons, ~590)
    Regimiento de Santiago (one squadron, ~105)

Artillery and Support
    Foot Artillery (two companies, 17 guns, 200 men)
    Sappers (three companies, 307)

Not Present at Battle
2nd Division: *Teniente General* Areizaga
    Combined Grenadiers (Regiments of América and 5° Suizo Traxler) (one battalion, 454)
    Regimiento de Fernando VII (one battalion, 273)

1/Voluntarios de Aragón (one battalion, 1,161)
2/Voluntarios de Aragón (one battalion, 214)
Cazadores de Valencia (one battalion, 355)
Cazadores de Palafox (one battalion, 1,200)
Tiradores de Murcia (one battalion, 660)
Tiradores de Cartagena (one company, 64)
Tiradores de Doyle (one battalion, 297)

Cavalry
Húsares Españoles (two squadrons, 168)
Regimiento de Santiago (one squadron, ~105)
Partida de Guijarro (one squadron ~100)

Horse Artillery (one company, 8 guns, 120)
Gastadores de Aragón (one company, 103)

Sources:
Nafziger Order of Battle Collection, 809FSBK: Spanish Army, 2nd Army of the Right, 15 June 1809; Santiago, *Alcañiz, María, y Belchite 1809*, p.76; Lipscombe, *The Peninsular War Atlas*, p.129.

Appendix V

III Corps During the Siege of Lérida April/May 1810

Général en Chef: *Général de Division* Louis-Gabriel Suchet
Chef de l'Etat-Major: *Général de Brigade* Jean-Isidore Harispe
Artillery: *Général de Brigade* Sylvain-Charles Valée
Engineers: *Général de Brigade* Joseph Rogniat

Division	Brigade	Unit	Composition	Strength at Lérida	Strength in Aragon	Location
1st Division *Général de Division* Laval	**1st Brigade** *Général de Brigade* Montmarie	14e Ligne	Four battalions	–	2,101	Zaragoza
		3e Vistule	One battalion	–	1,229	Right Bank
	2nd Brigade: *Général de Brigade* Chlopicki	44e Ligne	Two battalions	–	1,416	Calamocha
		2e Vistule	Two battalions	–	1,568	Calamocha
2nd Division: *Général de Division* Musnier	**1st Brigade:** *Général de Brigade* Pâris	115e Ligne	Four battalions	1,804	387	Huesca and Zaragoza
		1er Vistule	Two battalions	1,508	–	
	2nd Brigade: *Général de Brigade* Vergez	114e Ligne	Two battalions	563	675	Monzón
		121e Ligne	Four battalions	1,649	514	Monzón
		3e Vistule	One battalion	608	–	

Division	Brigade	Unit	Composition	Strength at Lérida	Strength in Aragon	Location
3rd Division: *Général de Brigade* Habert	**1st Brigade:** *Général de Brigade* Habert	5e Légère	Two battalions	960	–	
		116e Ligne	Three battalions	960	539	Balaguer
		117e Ligne	Four battalions	1,799	347	Balaguer
Reserve Brigade: *Général de Brigade* Buget		114e Ligne	Two battalions	1,216	–	
Cavalry: *Général de Brigade* Boussart		4e Hussards	Four squadrons	328	321	Various Locations
		13e Cuirassiers	Four Squadrons	452	373	Various Locations
		1er Cie., 1/1er Lanciers de la Vistule	One company	80	–	
Artillery, Engineers, and Support	**Artillery**	20/1er Régiment d'Artillerie à Pied	One company	–	85	Various Locations
		18/, 21/, 5/3e Régiment d'Artillerie à Pied	Three companies	140	48 (25ᵉ Compagnie)	Various Locations
		7/5e Régiment d'Artillerie à Cheval	One company	73	–	–
		4-6/3e, 5/6e, 1-4/12e Bataillons Principal du Train	Eight companies	423	172 (5/3e, 2 and 4/12e)	Various Locations
	Siege Train	4/, 14/3e Régiment d'Artillerie à Pied	Two companies	80	–	
		2e Artisan Compagnie d'Artillerie	One company	18	–	
		1-6/1er, 1-3/3e Bataillons Principal du Train	Nine companies	843	–	

Division	Brigade	Unit	Composition	Strength at Lérida	Strength in Aragon	Location
	Engineering Troops	2/1er Bataillon de Pontonniers	One company	62	–	
		4/2e Bataillon de Mineurs	One company	65	–	
		2/, 4/5e Bataillon de Sapeurs	Two companies	196	18	
Aragon Garrison Troops		Alcañiz Garrison	–	–	152	Alcañiz
		Monzón Garrison	–	–	167	Monzón
		Jaca Garrison	–	–	1,349	Jaca
		Benasque Garrison	–	–	200	Benasque
		2e Légion des Gendarmes	Six squadrons	–	1,198	Left Bank

French Siege Batteries at the Siege of Lérida

1. Four 8-inch mortars
2. Four 16-pounders
3. Four 24-pounders, two 16-pounders
4. Two 16-pounders, two 12-pounders, two 6-inch howitzers
5. Two 12-inch mortars, two 6-inch mortars
6. Two 8-inch howitzers
7. Four 6-inch howitzers
8. One 6-inch howitzer, one 8-pounder

Sources:
Nafziger Order of Battle Collection, 810ESAQ: French III Corps, April 1810; Nafziger Order of Battle Collection, 810FSAV: French Forces, Siege of Lerida, May 1810; Nafziger Order of Battle Collection, 810DSXA: Artillery of French Army of Spain, 1 April 1810; Belmas, *Journaux des siéges*, Vol III, pp.129-131 ; Alexander, *Rod of Iron*, p.75; Lipscombe, *Peninsular War Atlas*, p.159.

Appendix VI

Spanish Forces in the Lérida Campaign

Lérida Garrison Surrendered on 14 May, 1810

(Does not include the two battalions of city militia and 346 civilian artillerymen, who were released)
Commander: *Mariscal de Campo* Jayme Garcia Conde
Governor: *Mariscal de Campo* José González
General Officers and Staff (17)
Infantry
    2/Voluntarios de Huesca (one battalion, 1,485)
    1/Legiónes Cataluña (one battalion, 949)
    1/2° de Santa Fe (one battalion, 893)
    1/Tiradores de Murcia (one battalion, 796)
    2/Regimiento de Traxler 5° de Suizos (one battalion, 1,466)
    1/Regimiento de Fernando VII (one battalion, 844)
    Miquelets (one battalion, 324)[1]
Cavalry
    Regimiento de Olivenza (one squadron, 134)
Artillery and Support
    1ª Compañía del 1° Regimiento de Artillería de Línea (1 company, 132)
    7ª Compañía del 1° Regimiento de Artillería Ligero á Caballo (1 company, 126)
    Sappers (123)

O'Donnell's Relief Army

Capitán General Enrique O'Donnell
Reserve Division: *Mariscal de Campo* Miguel Ibarolla
Brigade of *Brigadier* Garcia Navarro
    1/, 2/Regimiento de Aragón (two battalions)

---

1   Includes four officers from the Tiradores de Doyle, who were presumably attached to the Miquelet battalion.

1/Regimiento de Valencia (one battalion)
1/Voluntarios de Daroca (one battalion)
Brigade of *Brigadier* Despuig
1/, 2/Guardias Valonas (two battalions)
1/Regimiento de Santa Fe (one battalion)
1/Fieles Zaragozanos (one battalion)
Artillery (three guns)

4th Division: *Coronel* Ramón Pírez (brigading unknown)
Regimiento de Kayser 3° de Suizos (two battalions)
Regimiento de América (unknown strength)
Legión Cataluña (unknown strength)
Castilla de Vieja (unknown strength)
Castilla de Nueva (unknown strength)

Cavalry
Coraceros Españoles (half-squadron)
Maestranza de Valencia (half-squadron)
Húsares de Valencia (one squadron)
Húsares de Granada (one squadron)

Total: 9,000 men

Sources:
Navarro's testimony on the battle, from Suchet, *Memoirs of the War in* Spain, Vol.I, p.351; Lipscombe, *The Peninsular War Atlas*, p.159; Belmas, *Journaux des siéges*, Vol III, p.162 ; Arteche y Moro, *Guerra de la Independencia*, Vol VIII, p.504.

Appendix VII

French Forces at Mequinenza, June 1810

2nd Division: *Général de Division* Musnier
1st Brigade: *Général de Brigade* Pâris
    1er Vistule (one battalion, 731)
2nd Brigade: *Général de Brigade* Vergez
    114e Ligne (three battalions 1,678)
    121e Ligne (three battalions 1,765)
3rd Brigade: *Général de Brigade* Montmarie
    14e Ligne (two battalions, 846)
Artillery: *Général de Brigade* Valée
    20/1er Régiment d'Artillerie à Pied (one company, 68)
    18/3e Régiment d'Artillerie à Pied (one company, 64)

Engineers: *Général de Brigade* Rogniat
    4/2e Bataillon de Mineurs, (detachments, 31)
    4/, 6/4e Bataillon de Sapeurs (two companies, 147)
    2/5e Bataillon de Sapeurs (one company, 108)
    4e Compagnie Bataillon du train du Génie (one company, 87)

Sources:
Nafziger Order of Battle Collection, 810FSAW: French Siege Forces, Mequinenza, June 1810;
Belmas, *Journaux des siéges*, Vol III, pp.194-195.

Appendix VIII

French Siege Forces at Tortosa, December 1810

Général en Chef: *Général de Division* Louis-Gabriel Suchet
Chef de l'Etat-Major: *Colonel* Saint-Cyr Nugues
Artillery: *Général de Brigade* Sylvain-Charles Valée
Engineers: *Général de Brigade* Joseph Rogniat

1st Division: *Général de Division* Harispe
1st Brigade: *Général de Brigade* Chlopicki
    44e Ligne (two battalions, 1,542)
    2e Vistule (two battalions, 1,687)

2nd Division: *Général de Division* Musnier (at Ulldecona)
1st Brigade: *Général de Brigade* Páris
    115e Ligne (two battalions, 1,360)
    1er Vistule (one battalion, 490)
2nd Brigade: *Général de Brigade* Vergez
    114e Ligne (two battalions, 928)

3rd Division: *Général de Brigade* Habert
1st Brigade: *Général de Brigade* Abbé
    5e Légère (two battalions, 979)
    116e Ligne (two battalions, 1,388)
2nd Brigade: *Général de Brigade* Bronikowski
    117e Ligne (two battalions, 1,864)

Artillery: *Général de Brigade* Valée
    3/, 20/1er Régiment d'Artillerie à Pied (two companies, 117)
    14/, 18/, 21/, 22/3e Régiment d'Artillerie à Pied (four companies, 220)
    7/5e Régiment d'Artillerie à Pied (one company, 35)
    1-6/1er, 1-6/3e, 1-4/12e, Bataillons Principal du Train (15 companies, 1,163)

Engineering Troops: *Général de Brigade* Rogniat
    2/1er Bataillon de Pontonniers (one company, 95)
    4/2e Bataillon de Mineurs (one company, 68)

4/, 6/4e Bataillon de Sapeurs (two companies, 202)
2/, 4/5e Bataillon de Sapeurs (two companies, 177)
4e Compagnie Bataillon du train du Génie (one company, 88)

Siege Batteries at the Siege of Tortosa

1. Four 24-pounders
2. Two 24-pounders, two 16-pounders, two 6-inch howitzers
3. Four 10-inch mortars
4. Two 12-inch mortars, two 6-inch howitzers
5. Four 24-pounders
6. Four 16-pounders
7. Two 8-inch howitzers
8. Four 8-inch mortars
9. Three 24-pounders, two 6-inch howitzers
10. Six 12-pounders, two 6-inch mortars
11. Two 10-inch mortars
12. (breaching battery) Four 24-pounders

Sources:
Nafziger Order of Battle Collection, 810LSAZ: French Siege Forces, Tortosa, December 1810; Lipscombe, *Peninsular War Atlas*, p.159; Jacques Vital Belmas, *Journaux des sièges*, Vol III, pp.446-448.

Appendix IX

Tortosa Garrison in January of 1811

Governor of Tortosa: *Brigadier* Miguel de Lili Idiáquez, Conde de Alacha
Second in Command: *Brigadier* Isidoro de Uriarte

Regimiento de Soria (one battalion, 897)
Cazadores de Orihuela (three battalions, 1,577)
1° de Legión Cataluña (four battalions, 2,215)
2° de Legión Cataluña (four battalions, 1,504)
Voluntarios de Aragón (one battalion, 610)
Dragones del Rey (one squadron, 22)
Voluntarios de Palafox (one battalion, 461)
Artillery (354)
Naval Artillery (898)
In hospital (952)

Sources:
Nafziger Order of Battle Collection, 811ASBE: Spanish Garrison of Tortose & 4th Division, 1st Spanish Army, 2 January 1811.

Appendix X

Armée d'Aragon in May 1811

Général en Chef: *Général de Division* Louis-Gabriel Suchet
Chef de l'Etat-Major: *Colonel* Saint-Cyr Nugues
Artillery: *Général de Brigade* Sylvain-Charles Valée
Engineers: *Général de Brigade* Joseph Rogniat

Division	Brigade	Unit	Composition	Strength	Detachments	Location
1st Division: *Général de Division* Harispe	**1st Brigade:** *Général de Brigade* Salme	7e Ligne	Four battalions	1,413	557	Lerida
		16e Ligne	Three battalions	966	469	Tortosa
	2nd Brigade: *Général de Brigade* Palombini	2° Leggera	Two battalions	1,170	–	–
		4° di Linea	Two battalions	947	–	–
	3rd Brigade: *Colonnello* Balathier	5° di Linea	Two battalions	981	–	–
		6° di Linea	Two battalions	904	–	–
2nd Division: *Général de Brigade* Habert*	**1st Brigade:** *Général de Brigade* Montmarie	5e Légère	Two battalions	1,139	101	Zaragoza
		116e Ligne	Three battalions	1,807	–	–
3rd Division: *Général de Division* Frère	**1st Brigade:** *Général de Brigade* Laurency	1er Légère	Three battalions	1,661	–	–
		1er Vistule	Two battalions	880	–	–

Division	Brigade	Unit	Composition	Strength	Detachments	Location
	2nd Brigade: *Général de Brigade* Callier	14e Ligne	Two battalions	1,106	–	–
		42e Ligne	Four battalions	1,520	534	Lerida
Cavalry: *Général de Brigade* Boussart		4e Hussards	Two squadrons	202	–	–
		13e Cuirassiers	Three squadrons	505	–	–
		24e Dragons	Three squadrons	476	–	–
		Dragoni Napoleone	Two squadrons	258	–	–
Artillery, Engineers, and Support	**Artillery**	20/1er Régiment d'Artillerie à Pied	One company	49	–	–
		14/, 18/, 21/, 22/3e Régiment d'Artillerie à Pied	Four companies	234	–	–
		14/6e Régiment d'Artillerie à Pied	One company	46	–	–
		11/7e Régiment d'Artillerie à Pied	One company	74	–	–
		7/2e Régiment d'Artillerie à Cheval	One company	93	–	–
		9/1° Reggimento Artiglieria a piedi	One company	67	–	–
		1/1° Reggimento Artiglieria a cavallo	One company	65	–	–
		2e Artisan Compagnie d'Artillerie	One company	38	–	–

Division	Brigade	Unit	Composition	Strength	Detachments	Location
		1er, 3e, 4e, 9e, 12e, Bataillons Principal et Provisoire du Train	16 companies	1,297	–	–
		3/1° Battaglione del Treno	One company	93	–	–
	Engineering Troops	4/2e Bataillon de Mineurs	One company	65	–	–
		7/2e Bataillon de Sapeurs	One company	87	–	–
		4/, 6/4e Bataillon de Sapeurs	Two companies	191	–	–
		2/,4/5e Bataillon de Sapeurs	Two companies	184	–	–
		5ª Compagnia Battaglione Zappatori	1 company	84	–	–
		4e Compagnie Bataillon du train du Génie	1 company	97	–	–
		2/1er Bataillon de Pontonniers	One company	94	–	–
		2e Ouvriers	One company	38		
	Support	Ambulance	–	167	–	–
		Equipage militaire	–	402	–	–
Aragon Garrison *Général de Division* Musnier	**1st Brigade:** *Colonel* Dupeyroux	115e Ligne	Four battalions	–	2,457	Morella
	2nd Brigade: *Général de Brigade* Chlopicki	14e Ligne	One battalion	–	564	Cinvocillas
		2e Vistule	Two battalions	–	1,975	Cincovillas
		4e Hussards	One squadron	–	200	Cincovillas

Division	Brigade	Unit	Composition	Strength	Detachments	Location
	3rd Brigade: *Général de Brigade* Pâris	44e Ligne	Two battalions	–	1,634	Molina
		3e Vistule	Two battalions	–	2,025	Molina
		4e Hussards	One squadron	–	300	Molina
	4th Brigade: *Général de Brigade* Abbé	114e Ligne	Four battalions	–	2,132	Teruel
		121e Ligne	Four battalions	–	2,095	Teruel
		13e Cuirassiers	One squadron	–	300	Teruel
Neapolitan Division: Général de Division Compère		1º Leggera	One battalion	–	~1,750**	Calatayud, Zaragoza
		1º di Linea (Re)	One battalion			
		2º di Linea (Regina)	One battalion			
		1º Cacciatori a Cavallo	One squadron			
		2º Cacciatori a Cavallo	One squadron			
Garrisons		2e Légion des Gendarmes	Six squadrons (including 10e Escadron rebuilding)	–	1,208	Left Bank
		Jaca	?	–	456	Jaca Area
		Benasque	?	–	196	Benasque Area
		Zaragoza	?	–	45	Zaragoza

* Habert promoted to *Général de Division* on 25 June.
** Divisional total; no individual unit strengths available.

Batteries at the Siege of Tarragona

1. Two 24-pounders
2. Two 12-inch mortars
3. Two 24-pounders
4. Two 10-inch mortars
5. Three 8-inch mortars
6. Four 24-pounders

7. Three 16-pounders
8. Two 6-inch howitzers
9. Six 24-pounders
10. Four 12-inch mortars
11. Eight 16-pounders
12. Two 10-inch mortars, two 8-inch mortars
13. Three 6-inch howitzers, two 12-inch mortars
14. Six 24-pounders
15. Four 8-inch howitzers
16. Seven 24-pounders, three 16-pounders, two 6-inch mortars
17. Six 24-pounders
18. Three 16-pounders
19. Three 24-pounders
20. Four 24-pounders
21. Eight 24-pounders
22. Six 24-pounders
23. Four 12-inch mortars
24. Four 8-inch howitzers

Sources:
Nafziger Order of Battle Collection, 811ESAL: French & Spanish Forces in the Siege of Tarragona, 24 May – 28 June, 1811; Nafziger Order of Battle Collection, 811ESBD: French Forces a Tarragona, 4 May 1811; Lipscombe, *Peninsular War Atlas*, p.229; Alexander, *Rod of Iron*, p.96; Belmas, *Journaux des siéges*, Vol III, pp.554-559.

Appendix XI

Tarragona Garrison

Comandante en Jefe: *Capitán General* Luis González y Torres de Navarro Castro, Marqués de Campoverde

Garrison Commander: *Mariscal de Campo* Juan Senen de Contreras

Note that the strength of the Tarragona Garrison was always fluctuating and different sources provide different unit strengths, and even units.

Regular Garrison
>   Legión Cataluña (five battalions, 1,936)
>   Regimiento de Tarragona (one battalion, 125)
>   Regimiento de Castilla La Nueva (one battalion, unknown strength)
>   Voluntarios de Palma (one battalion, unknown strength)
>   Artillery (793)
>   Sappers and Engineers (166)

Courten's Division
>   Regimiento de América (two battalions, 351)
>   Regimiento de Almansa (two battalions, 613)
>   Regimiento de Almeria (two battalions, 464)
>   Regimiento de Granada (three battalions, 365)
>   3° Regimiento de Suizos Kayser (one battalion, unknown strength)

10 May Reinforcements
>   Regimiento de Santa Fe (two battalions, 343)
>   2° Regimiento de Saboya (two battalions, 655)
>   Regimiento de Gerona (one battalion, 241)

29 May Reinforcements
>   Regimiento de Iliberia (three battalions, 368)
>   Cazadores de Valencia (one battalion, 664)

Others
>   Regimiento de Zaragoza (one battalion, 280)
>   Grenadiers (164)
>   1° Regimiento de Saboya (one battalion, 502)
>   Húsares de Cataluña (one squadron, 166)
>   Detachments and random officers (70)

Sources:

Nafziger Order of Battle Collection, 811ESAL: French & Spanish Forces in the Siege of Tarragona, 24 May – 28 June, 1811; Lipscombe, *Peninsular War Atlas*, p.229.

Rovira i Gómez, Salvador-J., Tarragona a la Guerra del Francès, (Universitat Rovira i Virgili, 2019, Google books), p.63.

Bibliography

Archival Sources

Biblioteca Virtual de Defensa
    Archivo Cartográfico de Estudios Geográficos del Centro Geográfico del Ejército, C.51-N.29: Memoria acerca del estado actual de este Primer ejército formada de orden del Señor General en Jefe del mismo y dirigida al Excelentísimo Señor Don Juan Murray Teniente General del ejército británico.
    Archivo Cartográfico de Estudios Geográficos del Centro Geográfico del Ejército, C.59-N.15: Memoria sucinta de la posición que podría tomar parte de 3er exercito relativamente a la que ocupan los enemigos de Castalla y demás pueblos de la sierra de Alcoy.
    Archivo Cartográfico de Estudios Geográficos del Centro Geográfico del Ejército, C.66-N.49: Partes de la acción de Alcañiz en 1809.
Portal de Archivos Españoles (PARES)
    Diversos-Colecciones, 78, N.62: Diario del sitio de la plaza de Tortosa durante el mes de Agosto.
    Diversos-Colecciones, 78, N.67: Defensa de Lérida por los Españoles contra los franceses en mayo de 1810.
    Diversos-Colecciones, 82, N.45: Partes sobre las operaciones realizadas en la linea de Valencia en los ataques del día 26 de diciembre de 1811.
    Diversos-Colecciones, 104, N.47: Operaciones y movimientos del 2º y 3º Ejército de Valencia correspondientes al año de 1813.
    Diversos-Colecciones, 126, N.66: Diarios histórico militares de las operaciones de la división mallorquina en Valencia, Cataluña y Aragón entre marzo y septiembre de 1813.
    Diversos-Colecciones, 127, N.20: Oficio del General Villacampa dando parte a Nicolás Mahy del ataque de sus tropas a la linea sobre Valencia en 26 de Diciembre de 1811.
    Diversos-Colecciones, 127, N.24: Manuel Carbón, Jefe de la Vanguardia de las tropas que formaban la linea sobre Valencia, da parte al General Mahy de sus operaciones en 26 de Diciembre de 1811.
    Diversos-Colecciones, 195, N.68: Reseña de los alborotos en Lérida, muerte del general Reding y de las primeras operaciones realizadas por Blake en 1809.
El Archivo Histórico Nacional
    Estado, 46, J: Nombramiento del general Suchet como comisario regio en Aragón.
    Estado, 3099: Represión del bandidaje y de las guerrillas en Aragón.
    Estado, 13, F: Proclama a los soldados napoleónicos para que deserten.
    CONSEJOS, 12868, EXP. 2: La Junta de Aragón solicita dinero y armas.
Memòria Digital de Catalunya
    La Gloriosa reconquista de las plazas de Lérida, Monzón y Mequinenza por el primer ejército nacional.

Resumen histórico de la insurrección de Cataluña desde el año 1808 hasta diciembre de 1813, que sirve de prospecto á la obra calcográfica ó colección de estampas que representan los principales sucesos acaecidos en dicha época.

Al Sr. Gobernador de la plaza de Alicante … consiguiente a la capitulación de Valencia consentida por el general Blake.

Biblioteca Nacional Hispánica/Biblioteca Digital de España

0000079729: Manifiesto de las acciones del Mariscal de Campo D. Francisco Espoz y Mina … en el Alto Aragón ó país comprendido en la izquierda del Ebro.

David Rumsey Map Collection

Items 12140.006 through 12140.019

Nafziger Order of Battle Collection

Items between 809ESAM and 814DSAB

Printed Primary Sources

Anon, *Almanach impérial* (Paris: Tetsu, 1806).

Anon, *Asalto Y Saqueo De Tarragona En 1811: Es Copia De Un Manuscrito Que Se Conserva En La Biblioteca De Uno De Los Conventos De Religiosos Menores De Cataluña* (Tarragona: F. Arís, 1911).

Bonaparte, Joseph, *Mémoires et correspondance politique et militaire du Roi Joseph.* 2e éd. (Paris: Perrotin, Libraire-Éditeur, 1854).

Bonaparte, Napoleon, Joseph Bonaparte, *The confidential correspondence of Napoleon Bonaparte with his brother Joseph, sometime king of Spain: selected and translated, with explanatory notes, from the "Mémoires du roi Joseph"* (London: J. Murray, 1855).

Bonaparte, Napoléon, *Correspondence de Napoléon 1er* (Paris: Imprimerie Impériale, 1866-1867).

Brandt, Heinrich von, *In the Legions of Napoleon: The Memoirs of a Polish Officer in Spain and Russia 1808-1813* (Barnsley: Frontline Books, 2017).

Bugeaud, Thomas R., *Memoirs of Marshal Bugeaud From His Private Correspondence and Original Documents 1784-1849* (London: Hurst and Blackett, 1884).

Codrington, Edward, *Memoir of the Life of Admiral Sir Edward Codrington* (London: Longmans, Green, and Co., 1873).

Contreras, Juan Senen de, *Relation of the Siege of Tarragona and the Storming and Capture of That City by the French in June, 1811* (London: J. Booth, 1813).

Desbouefs, Marc, *Souvenirs du capitaine Desboeufs : les étapes d'un soldat de l'Empire (1800-1815)* (Paris: Alphonse Picard et Fils, 1901).

De Neef, Jonas, *Devils, Daggers, and Death: Eyewitness accounts of French officers and soldiers during the Peninsular War(1807-1814)* (Lulu, 2022).

Eguaguirre, Andrés, *Sucesos Verdaderos Del Sitio y Plaza de Tarragona* (Valencia: Imprenta Patriótica del Pueblo Soberano a cargo de Vicente Ferro, 1813).

Espoz y Mina, Francisco, *Memorias del general Don Francisco Espoz y Mina: escritas por él mismo* (Madrid: M. Rivadeneyra, 1851).

Gonneville, Aymar-Olivier Le Harivel de, *Recollections of Colonel de Gonneville* (London: Hurst and Blackett, 1875).

Graindor, Jacques-Abraham, *Mémoires de la Guerre d'Espagne 1808-1814* (France: Points d'ancrage, 2002).

Gurney, W.B., *The Trial of Lieutenant General Sir John Murray, Bart. By a General Court Martial, Held at Winchester* (London: T. Egerton, 1815).

Gurwood, John (ed.), *The Dispatches of Field Marshal the Duke of Wellington, K. G. During His Various Campaigns in India, Denmark, Portugal, Spain, the Low Countries, and France* (London: Parker, Furnivall, and Parker, 1845).

Halen, Juan Van, *Narrative of Don Juan Van Halen's Imprisonment in the Dungeons of the Inquisition at Madrid...* (New York: J&J Harper, 1828).

Jolyet, Jean-Baptiste, 'Épisodes des guerres de Catalogne (1808-1812)', *Revue des études napoléoniennes*, Vol. XVI (1919), pp.182-214.

Lacépède, Comte de, *État général de la Légion d'honneur, depuis son origine* (Paris: Chez Testu et Ce, 1814).

Maffre-Baugé, Emmanuel, *Superbe et Généraux Jean Maffre* (Paris: Fayard, 1982).

Maltzen, Maurice de, et al., *Correspondance inédite du baron Maurice de Maltzen: officier du génie à l'armée d'Espagne 1809-1810* (Brain-le-Comte: C. Lelong, 1880).

Maria Fuentes i Gasó, Manuel, et al., *Memòria del segte i ocupació de Tarragona: La Guerra del Francès en els fons documentals de l'Arxiu Històric Arxidiocesà de Tarragona (1808-1814)* (Tarragona: L'Arxiu Històric Arxidiocesà de Tarragona, 2012).

Morin, Jean-Baptiste, 'Souvenirs du Colonel Morin sur son séjour en Espagne (1812-1813)', <https://www.napoleon.org/histoire-des-2-empires/articles/souvenirs-du-colonel-morin-sur-son-sejour-en-espagne-1812-1813-annotes-par-le-colonel-paul-willing>.

Mroziński, Józef, 'An account by Captain Mrozinski of the 1st Vistula Legion', <https://www.jpnorth.co.uk/publications/articles-napoleonic-and-french-revolution/captain-mrozinski/>.

Pírez y Pavía, Ramón, José Luis Arcón Domínguez (eds), *Apuntaciones sobre el Ejército de Valencia en 1811* (Valencia: Ediciones Simtac, 2010).

Rogniat, Joseph, *Relation des Sièges de Saragosse et de Tortose* (Paris: Chez Magimel, Libraire Pour l'Arte Militaire: 1814).

Santisteban, Rafael, *Manifesto del Brigadier Don Rafael Santisteban* (Alicante: Nicolas Carratalá é Hijos, 1812).

Schepeler, Andreas Daniel Berthold von, *Histoire de la révolution d'Espagne et de Portugal, ainsi que de la guerre qui en résulta* (Liège: J. Desoer, 1829-1831)

Suchet, Louis-Gabriel, *Memoirs of the War in Spain From 1808 to 1814* (London: Henry Colburn, 1829).

Vacani, Camillo, *Storia delle campagne e degli assedj degl'Italiani in Ispagna dal MDCCCVIII al MDCCCXIII* (Milan: P. Pagnoni, 1845).

Ward, S.G.P., 'The Diary of Lieutenant Robert Woollcombe, R.A., 1812-1813', *Journal of the Society for Army Historical Research*, 52/211, pp.161-180.

Wellington, 2nd Duke of (ed.), *Supplementary Despatches, Correspondence, and Memoranda of Field Marshal Arthur, Duke of Wellington* (London: John Murray, 1860).

Whittingham, Samuel Ford, *A memoir of the services of Lieutenant-General Sir Samuel Ford Whittingham* (London: Longmans, Green, and Co., 1868).

Secondary Sources

Anon. *Annales de la Société Entomologique de France* (Paris: La Société 1845).

Anon. *Visite de Leurs Majestés Impériales de Russie à Dunkerque, Reims et Compiègne* (Paris: Imprimerie National, 1901).

Aldeguer, Rafael Zurita, *Suchet en España: Guerra y sociedad en las tierras del sur valenciano (1812-1814)* (Madrid: Ministerio de Defensa, 2015).

Alexander, Don W., *Rod of Iron: French Counterinsurgency Policy in Aragon During the Peninsular War* (Wilmington: Scholarly Resources Inc., 1985).

Arcón Dominguez, José Luis, 'La Batalla de Castalla 21 de julio de 1812', *Desperta Ferro*, Special Ed. No. 2.

Arcón Domínguez, José Luis, *Sagunto, La Batalla por Valencia* (Valencia: Simtac Ediciones, 2002-2022).

Arteche y Moro, José Gómez de, *Guerra de la Independencia: historia militar de España de 1808 a 1814* (Madrid: Imprenta y litografía del Depósito de la Guerra, 1886-1902).

Belmas, Jacques Vital, et al. *Précis des campagnes et des siéges d'Espagne et de Portugal de 1807 à 1814* (Paris: A. Leneveu, 1839).

Belmas, Jacques Vital, *Journaux des siéges faits ou soutenus par les Français dans la péninsule, de 1807 à 1814* (Paris: Chez Firmin Didot frères et cie, 1837).

Benavides, Nicolás, José Yague, *El Capitán General don Joaquín Blake y Joyes* (Madrid: Servicio Geográfico Militar, 1957).

Bertaux, Maurice Jules. *Historique du 114e régiment d'infanterie* (Niort: Imprimerie Th. Mercier, 1892).

Blanch, Adolfo, *Cataluña: Historia de la Guerra de la Independencia* (Barcelona: Imprenta y Librería Politécnica de Tomás Gorchs, 1861).

Boot, Max, *Invisible Armies* (New York: Liveright Publishing Corporation, 2013).

Broers, Michael, *Napoleon's Other War: Bandits, Rebels, and their Pursuers in the Age of Revolution*, (Oxford: Peter Lang Ltd, 2010).

Bukhari, Emir, *Napoleon's Marshals* (Oxford: Osprey, 1979).

Burnham, Robert, *Charging Against Wellington: The French Cavalry in the Peninsular War: 1808-1814* (Barnsley: Frontline Books, 2011).

Carrasco Álvarez, Antonio, 'La Guerra irregular en España, 1808-1812 : un análisis comparativo: las divisiones de guerrillas en Valencia', *Revista de historia militar*, 54:107 (2010) pp.73-106.

Carter, Brent C., *French Counterinsurgency Efforts (COIN) in Spain during the Napoleonic Era–A Modern Analysis Through the Lens of the Principles of COIN in US Joint Doctrine*, Air Command and Staff College (2014).

Chabret, Antonio, *Sagunto: su historia y sus monumentos* (Barcelona: Tipografía de los Sucesores de N. Ramírez y C., 1888).

Chandler, David (ed.), *Napoleon's Marshals* (London: Weidenfeld and Nicolson Ltd, 1987).

Dempsey, Guy C., *Napoleon's Mercenaries: Foreign Units in the French Army Under the Consulate and Empire, 1799 to 1814* (Barnsley: Frontline Books, 2016).

Detaille, Edouard (trans. Maureen Reinertsen), *L'Armée Française* (New York: Waxtel & Hauser, 1992).

Dunn-Pattinson, R.P., *Napoleon's Marshals* (London: Methuen & Co., 1909).

Dupré, Charles-Laurent, *Les Fastes du 14e Ligne* (Paris: Anselin, 1836).

Duriau, Etienne, *André-Joseph Boussart,-De Binche a Bagnère-de-Bigorre, itineraire d'un général d'empire* (Charleroi: IPH Editions, 2003).

Durand, Charles, *Historique Du 117e Régiment D'infanterie De Ligne* (Orléans: Imprimerie de Georges Jacob, 1875).

Dwyer, Philip G. '"It Still Makes Me Shudder": Memories of Massacres and Atrocities during the Revolutionary and Napoleonic Wars', *War in History*, 16/4 (2009), pp.381–405.

Elting, John R., *Swords Around a Throne* (New York: The Free Press, 1988).

Esdaile, Charles J., *Fighting Napoleon: Guerillas, Bandits, and Adventurers in Spain 1808-1814* (New Haven: Yale University Press, 2004).

Esdaile, Charles J., *Napoleon's Wars: An International History 1803-1815* (New York: Viking Penguin, 2008).

Esdaile, Charles J., et al., *Popular Resistance in the French Wars* (London: Palgrave Macmillan, 2005).

Esdaile, Charles J., *The Duke of Wellington and the Command of the Spanish Army 1812-14* (London: Macmillan, 1990).

Esdaile, Charles J., *The Spanish Army in the Peninsular War* (Manchester: Manchester University Press, 1988).

Espés, Carlos Franco de, 'La Administración Francesa en Aragon: El gobierno de mariscal Suchet, 1809-1813', *Revista de historia Jéronimo Zurita*. 91 (2016), pp.89-126.

Fernandez y Domingo, Daniel, *Anales ó Historia de Tortosa* (Barcelona: Establecimiento Tipográfico de Jaime Jepus: 1867).

Fuertes, Jaime Latas, *La ocupación francesa de Zaragoza (1809-1813)* (Zaragoza: Asociación Cultural "Los Sitios de Zaragoza", 2012).

Gates, David, *The Spanish Ulcer* (London: George Allen & Unwin, 1986).

Gennequin, Philippe, 'The Centurions vs the Hydra: French Counterinsurgency in the Peninsular War (1808-1812)', U.S. Army Command and General Staff College (2011) <https://apps.dtic.mil/dtic/tr/fulltext/u2/a547277.pdf>.

Huber, Thomas M., *Compound Warfare: That Fatal Knot* (Fort Leavenworth: U.S. Army Command and General Staff College Press, 2002).

Hugo, Abel, France militaire. *Histoire des armées françaises de terre et de mer de 1792 à 1837* (Paris: Delloye: 1838).

James, William, *The Naval History of Great Britain* (London: Macmillan and Co., 1902).

Lacépède, Comte de, *État général de la Légion d'honneur* (Paris: Chez Test et Cie, 1814).

Lázaro, José Vicente Arnedo, 'No Sin Hacen Tortillas Sin Romper Huevos: Villena y La Batalla de Castalla del 21 de Julio de 1812', *Revista Villena* (2013), pp.119-132.

Lepage, Jean-Denis G.G., *French Fortifications 1715-1815: An Illustrated History* (Jefferson: McFarland & Company, 2009).

Lepetit, Gildas, 'Soumettre les arrières de l'armée. L'action de la Gendarmerie impériale dans la pacification des provinces septentrionales de l'Espagne (1809-1814)', *Stratégique* (2009), pp.257-277.

Lemelin, David J., 'Marshal Suchet in Aragon', *Military Review* 78:3 (1998), pp.86-90.

Lipscombe, Nick, *The Peninsular War Atlas* (Oxford: Osprey Publishing, 2010).

Lipscombe, Nick, *Wellington's Eastern Front: The Campaign on the East Coast of Spain 1810-1814* (Barnsley: Pen and Sword Military 2016).

Martinien, Aristide, *Tableaux, par corps et par batailles, des officiers tués et blessés pendant les guerres de l'Empire (1805-1815)* (Paris: Henri Charles-Lavauzelle, 1899).

Martin, Emmanuel, *La gendarmerie française en Espagne et en Portugal (campagnes de 1807 à 1814)* (Paris: Léautey, 1898).

Morgan, John Leckey, 'The Army of Catalonia: Organization, Operation, and Logistics: 1807-1814', Loyola University of Chicago (1994) <https://ecommons.luc.edu/luc_diss/3478>.

Napier, William Francis Patrick, *History of the War in the Peninsula and in the South of France* (New York: D. & J. Sadlier & Co., 1873).

Oman, Charles, *A History of the Peninsular War* (Oxford: Clarendon Press, 1902-1930).

Picard, Louis Auguste, *La cavalerie dans les guerres de la révolution et de l'empire* (Saumur: Librairie Militaire, 1895).

Pivka, Otto von, *Brunswick Troops 1809-15* (London: Osprey, 1985).

Prada, Antonio Moliner, *Tarragona (mayo-junio 1811): Una ciudad sitiada durante la Guerra del Francés*, (Spain: Doce Calles, 2011).

Quigley, Adam G., *Antes morir que rendirse: Testimonios británicos en el asedio de Tarragona 1811* (2019, Kindle E-book).

Quigley, Adam G., *Tarragona 1813: El arduo camino hacia la liberación* (Tarragona: Fundació Privada Mútua Catalana, 2022).

Rebolledo i Bonjoch, Francesc, 'La Guerra del Francès al Pla D'Urgell', Quaderns de El Pregoner d'Urgell, 32 (2019), pp.45-64, at <https://raco.cat/index.php/QuadernsPregonerUrgell/article/view/356293>

Reynaud, Jean-Louis, *Contre-Guerilla en Espagne (1808-1814): Suchet pacifie l'Aragon* (Paris: Economica, 1992).

Rollet, Jean-Phillipe, 'Conqueror and Administrator: Civil and Military Actions of Marshall Louis-Gabriel Suchet in the Spanish Province of Aragon 1808-1813' (Master's Thesis, United States Marine Corps Command and Staff College 2008).

Rovira i Gómez, Salvador-J., *Tarragona a la Guerra del Francès* (Tarragona: Universitat Rovira i Virgili, 2019).

Salvadó i Joan Martínez, Roc, *200 anys de la Guerra del Francès a les terres de l'Ebre* (Benicarló: Onada Edicions, 2016).

Rousseau, François, *La Carrière Du Maréchal Suchet Duc D'Albuféra: Documents Inédits* (Paris: Firmin-Didot, 1898).

Santiago, Francisco Vela, *Castalla 1812 y 1813 Dos batallas por el domino del Levante español* (Madrid: Almena, 2014).

Santiago, Francisco Vela, *Alcañiz, María, y Belchite 1809* (Madrid: Almena, 2017).

Sarramon, Jean, *Contribución a la historia de La Guerra de la Independencia de la Península Ibérica contra Napoleón I* (Ministerio de Defensa: 2010).

Sauzey, Jean-Camille-Abel-Fleuri, *Les Allemands sous les aigles françaises: essai sur les troupes de la Confédération du Rhin, 1806-1814* (Paris: Librairie Militaire Chapelot, 1912).

Schwartz, Karl, *Leben des generals Carl von Clausewitz und der frau Marie von Clausewitz geb. gräfin von Brühl* (Berlin: F. Dümmler, 1878).

Smith, Digby, *The Greenhill Napoleonic Wars Data Book* (London: Greenhill Books, 1998).

Southey, Robert, *History of the Peninsular War* (London: John Murray, 1827).

Sutherland, Jonathan, and Canwell, Diane, *Wargame Scenarios: The Peninsular War, 1808–1814* (Barnsley: Pen & Sword Books, 2014).

Tone, John L., *The Fatal Knot* (Chapel Hill: University of North Carolina Press, 1994).

Trimble, William Copeland, *The Historical Record of the 27th Inniskilling Regiment* (London: William Clowes and Sons, 1876).

Vidal de la Blanche, Joseph, *L'évacuation de l'Espagne et l'invasion dans le Midi, juin 1813-avril 1814* (Paris: Berger-Levrault, 1914).

Witt, Kendall L., *Like a Slow, Gradual Fire: Spain's Irregular War in British Strategic Planning During the Peninsular War, 1808-1814* (Master's Thesis, The Citadel, 2019).

Yvert, Louis, *Historique du 13e Régiment de Cuirassiers* (Chartres: Imprimerie Garnier, 1893).

Digital Sources

Aguado, Javier Díaz, 'Accion de la Loma del Calvario, Muchamiel', *Guerra e Historia Publica* (2021), <https://www.guerra-historia-publica.es/assets/pdf/guerra-en-valencia/cartografia/estudios-militares/ACCION_DE_EL_CALVARIO_MUCHAMIEL_ALICANTE_25_DE_ABRIL_1812.pdf>.

Aguado, Javier Díaz, 'Primera Batalla de Castalla', *Guerra e Historia Publica* (2011), <https://www.guerra-historia-publica.es/assets/pdf/guerra-en-valencia/cartografia/estudios-militares/1a_BATALLA_DE_CASTALLA_21_de_Julio_de_1812.pdf>.

Anon. 'Santuario Virgen del Tremedal', *Orihuela del Tremedal*, <http://www.orihueladeltremedal.es/turismo/que-puedes-visitar/santuario-la-virgen-del-tremedal/>.

Camacho, Ricardo Pardo, 'La Guerra de la Independencia en la Provincia de Castellón: Dos Castellonenses', *Aular Militar* (2009), <https://www.aulamilitar.com/D08_14_1813.pdf?ID_SESION=IQYQAZLHRGFYQEOBEFVD>.

Contant, Dominique, Jonathan Cooper, Robert Ouvrard, 'Marshal Suchet and the Siege of Valencia', *The Napoleon Series* (2004), <https://www.napoleon-series.org/military-info/battles/1812/Peninsula/valencia/c_valencia1.html>.

Lasheras, Alberto, 'José Tris, "El Malcarau", ¿Héroe O Traidor?', *Desde Monegros* (2013), <https://www.desdemonegros.com/index.php?id=noticiadesarrollada2&idnoticia=2&seccion=p_nosotros&PHPSESSID=aor24q8vvkoa3gcrm62o61n2c2>.

Marco, Luis Antonio Pellicer, 'La Batalla de Alcañiz', *Asociación Cultural Los Sitios de Zaragoza*, <https://www.asociacionlossitios.com/colaboraciones.htm>.

Miró, Miquel, 'The Combat of the Ordal Cross: 13 September 1813', *The Napoleon Series*, <https://www.napoleon-series.org/military-info/virtual/c_ordal.html>.

Sánchez y Carcelén, Antoni, 'La Guerra del Francès a Lleida (1808-1814)', Hispania Nova, 8 (2008), <http://hispanianova.rediris.es/8/dossier/8d001.pdf>

'Martín De La Carrera', *Real Academica De La Historia*. Gobierno de España, <https://dbe.rah.es/biografias/46196/martin-de-la-carrera>

Index

From Reason to Revolution – Warfare 1721-1815

http://www.helion.co.uk/series/from-reason-to-revolution-1721-1815.php

The 'From Reason to Revolution' series covers the period of military history 1721–1815, an era in which fortress-based strategy and linear battles gave way to the nation-in-arms and the beginnings of total war.

This era saw the evolution and growth of light troops of all arms, and of increasingly flexible command systems to cope with the growing armies fielded by nations able to mobilise far greater proportions of their manpower than ever before. Many of these developments were fired by the great political upheavals of the era, with revolutions in America and France bringing about social change which in turn fed back into the military sphere as whole nations readied themselves for war. Only in the closing years of the period, as the reactionary powers began to regain the upper hand, did a military synthesis of the best of the old and the new become possible.

The series will examine the military and naval history of the period in a greater degree of detail than has hitherto been attempted, and has a very wide brief, with the intention of covering all aspects from the battles, campaigns, logistics, and tactics, to the personalities, armies, uniforms, and equipment.

Submissions

The publishers would be pleased to receive submissions for this series. Please contact series editor Andrew Bamford via email (andrewbamford@helion.co.uk), or in writing to Helion & Company Limited, Unit 8 Amherst Business Centre, Budbrooke Road, Warwick, CV34 5WE

Titles

No 1 *Lobositz to Leuthen: Horace St Paul and the Campaigns of the Austrian Army in the Seven Years War 1756-57* (Neil Cogswell)

No 2 *Glories to Useless Heroism: The Seven Years War in North America from the French journals of Comte Maurés de Malartic, 1755-1760* (William Raffle (ed.))

No 3 *Reminiscences 1808-1815 Under Wellington: The Peninsular and Waterloo Memoirs of William Hay* (Andrew Bamford (ed.))

No 4 *Far Distant Ships: The Royal Navy and the Blockade of Brest 1793-1815* (Quintin Barry)

No 5 *Godoy's Army: Spanish Regiments and Uniforms from the Estado Militar of 1800* (Charles Esdaile and Alan Perry)

No 6 *On Gladsmuir Shall the Battle Be! The Battle of Prestonpans 1745* (Arran Johnston)

No 7 *The French Army of the Orient 1798-1801: Napoleon's Beloved 'Egyptians'* (Yves Martin)

No 8 *The Autobiography, or Narrative of a Soldier: The Peninsular War Memoirs of William Brown of the 45th Foot* (Steve Brown (ed.))

No 9 *Recollections from the Ranks: Three Russian Soldiers' Autobiographies from the Napoleonic Wars* (Darrin Boland)

No 10 *By Fire and Bayonet: Grey's West Indies Campaign of 1794* (Steve Brown)

No 11 *Olmütz to Torgau: Horace St Paul and the Campaigns of the Austrian Army in the Seven Years War 1758-60* (Neil Cogswell)

No 12 *Murat's Army: The Army of the Kingdom of Naples 1806-1815* (Digby Smith)

No 13 *The Veteran or 40 Years' Service in the British Army: The Scurrilous Recollections of Paymaster John Harley 47th Foot – 1798-1838* (Gareth Glover (ed.))

No 14 *Narrative of the Eventful Life of Thomas Jackson: Militiaman and Coldstream Sergeant, 1803-15* (Eamonn O'Keeffe (ed.))

No.15 *For Orange and the States: The Army of the Dutch Republic 1713-1772 Part I: Infantry* (Marc Geerdinck-Schaftenaar)